Principal's Guide to Effective Family Involvement

Partnering for School Success

PUBLISHERS

Gaithersburg, Maryland
2002

All forms, checklists, guidelines, and policies and procedures are presented as examples and should certainly never be used as the basis for a legal document. They are intended as resources that can be selectively used and always adapted—with the advice of the facility attorney—to meet state, local, individual hospital, and specific department needs and requirements. "This publication is designed to provide accurate and authoritative information in regard to the Subject Matter covered. It is sold with the understanding that the publisher is not engaged in rendering legal, accounting, or other professional service. If legal advice or other expert assistance is required, the services of a competent professional person should be sought."
From a Declaration of Principles jointly adopted by a Committee of the American Bar Association and a Committee of Publishers and Associations

Library of Congress Cataloging-in-Publication Data

Principal's guide to effective family involvement: partnering for school success.
p. cm.
ISBN 0-7355-3622-8

1. Education—Parent participation—Handbooks, manuals, etc. 2. School principals—Handbooks, manuals, etc. 3. Home and school—Handbooks, manuals, etc. I. Aspen Publishers

LB1048.5 .P75 2002
371.02'012—dc21
2002027945

Editorial Services: Megg Mueller Schulte
Printing and Manufacturing: Terri Miner

The content of this book is from the following Aspen publications: M. Dietz, *School, Family and Community: Techniques and Models for Successful Collaborations*, D. Struck, *Involving Parents in Education: A Handbook for Elementary Schools*, Pro Principal, Principal to Principal, Home & School, Middle Years, Reading Connection, and *Recipes for Success*.

Copyright © 2002 by Aspen Publishers, Inc.

All rights reserved. No part of this publication may be reproduced; stored in or introduced into a retrieval system now known or to be invented; transmitted in any form or by any means (electronic, mechanical, recording, or otherwise); or used for advertising or promotional purposes, general distribution, creating new collective works, or for resale, without prior written permission of the copyright owner and publisher. An exception to this policy is the reproduction of forms, handouts, policies, or procedures contained herein solely for use within the site-of-purchase facility. Submit written permission requests to:
Aspen Publishers, Inc.,
Permissions Department,
200 Orchard Ridge Drive, Suite 200,
Gaithersburg, Maryland 20878.

Orders: (800) 638-8437
Customer Care: (800) 234-1660

About Aspen Publishers • Founded over 40 years ago, Aspen Publishers, Inc., New York, NY, serves the information needs of today's professional in the areas of law, business, education, and health care. Professionals rely on Aspen to provide timely analysis and practical information in the form of manuals, texts, journals, newsletters, electronic products, and on-line services—all skillfully authored by the country's leading authorities. With the acquisition of Loislaw, Aspen complements its unmatched proprietary content with affordable primary source material for legal research that is delivered on a subscription basis over the Internet. Loislaw offers more than 2,400 databases containing more than 11 million documents, including federal and state cases, statutes, administrative regulations, court rules, and other legal information. Visit Aspen's Internet site (http://www.aspenpublishers.com) for more information resources, directories, articles, and a searchable version of Aspen's full catalog, including the most recent publications.
Aspen Publishers, Inc. • The hallmark of quality in publishing
Member of the worldwide Wolters Kluwer group.

Library of Congress Catalog Card Number: 2002027945
ISBN: 0-7355-3622-8

Printed in the United States of America

1 2 3 4 5

Contents

For a detailed list of chapter contents, please see the first page of each chapter.

Introduction	....	*v*
Part 1: Principals		
Chapter 1–1	Welcome Family Involvement	1–1:i
Chapter 1–2	Strengthen Communication	1–2:i
Chapter 1–3	Recruit Family Volunteers	1–3:i
Chapter 1–4	Deal with Difficult Situations	1–4:i
Part 2: Teachers		
Chapter 2–1	Build Parent–Teacher Teams	2–1:i
Chapter 2–2	Work Together for Student Success	2–2:i
Chapter 2–3	Improve Parenting Skills	2–3:i
Index	....	*I:1*

Introduction

EFFECTIVE FAMILY INVOLVEMENT IS VITAL

From the federal government's "No Child Left Behind" Act to the neighborhood school, there's a growing awareness today that family involvement is essential to the success of education. As former U.S. Secretary of Education Richard Riley noted:

"Research shows that all families, whatever their income or education level, can take concrete steps that significantly help children learn. And yet families are often the missing link in American education."

As you know, children do better in school when their parents take an active interest in their education. Parents who make sure their children attend school, who care about their youngsters' performance, and who support school policy send the message to their children that education is important. These are the children who will do well in school and later in life.

In addition to improved academic performance, family involvement benefits schools in other ways. When parents see the positive side of your school, they'll tell others—and you'll see more community support for educational programs and extracurricular activities. Parents and other district residents who support your school can be powerful allies on issues that directly affect education, such as bond referendums.

But, as you know, getting busy parents actively involved in their children's education is often difficult. Here are some obstacles principals face:

- A whole generation hasn't seen the benefits of good parent involvement, says Principal Donna Marie Lossing Jones of Columbus, Ohio. "But we can't give up on parent involvement just because it's tough. We have to take this generation and lead it through the process—and help students see the benefits at the same time."
- Parents have distanced themselves from the education process. As a result, their priorities often get mixed up. "Just the other day, for example, a student was late to school because he had to get a haircut," says an Indiana principal. "And parents

miss conferences because of bowling, shopping, and things like that. We need to give them a sense of the importance of what we're doing!"
- Many parents want the best for their children—but aren't aware of how they can play an active role in their education. "Principals have to remember that parents often have never been told how they can become involved," says Assistant Principal Elaine Carlson of Sierra Vista, Arizona. "It's up to the schools to explain to parents what their role is and how they can be participants in their kids' school."

If you're like other principals, you're probably wondering what you can do to get parents to actively participate in their children's learning and your school programs. *Principal's Guide to Effective Family Involvement* will provide you with the necessary ideas and tools.

The first part explains what principals can do to increase family involvement. You'll learn how to:

- Evaluate existing family involvement initiatives.
- Create family friendly schools.
- Improve communication with all families.
- Recruit family volunteers.
- Handle discipline and other tough issues.

The second part is for teachers because their support is essential. It will help your teachers learn how to:

- Build parent–teacher teams.
- Conduct successful conferences.
- Foster at-home learning support.
- Meet parent needs.
- Partner on discipline.

Both parts contain profiles of successful programs, tips, forms, and handouts you can use immediately.

Part 1

Principals

Chapter 1–1	Welcome Family Involvement	1–1:i
Chapter 1–2	Strengthen Communication	1–2:i
Chapter 1–3	Recruit Family Volunteers	1–3:i
Chapter 1–4	Deal with Difficult Situations	1–4:i

Chapter **1–1**

Welcome Family Involvement

Evaluating Existing Programs	**1–1:1**
Program Assessment	1–1:1
Types of Assessment	1–1:1
Reasons for Lack of Involvement	1–1:3
Measures To Improve Participation	1–1:4
Conclusion	1–1:5
Creating Family-Friendly Schools	**1–1:7**
Create the Right Atmosphere	1–1:7
Welcome Parents into Your School	1–1:7
Invite Parents To Visit	1–1:8
Be Extra-Courteous If Visitors Sign In	1–1:8
Make Yourself Accessible to Parents	1–1:9
Spend Quality Time with Visitors	1–1:10
Beware of Language Barriers	1–1:10
If Parents Can't Come to You, Go to Them	1–1:11
Meet Parents on Their Turf	1–1:12
Reach Out to New Parents	1–1:13
Give Parents Their Own Room	1–1:13
Support Parents with Extra Services	1–1:14
Set Up Your Own Welcome Wagon	1–1:14
Take a Family Approach!	1–1:15
Keep Doors Open for Parents, Students	1–1:16
Special Events Bring Parents into the School	1–1:18
Family Nights Are a Family Affair	1–1:21
It's Tuesday: Drop in and Talk	1–1:22
Get More Parents Involved in Organizations	1–1:22

    Invite Parents To Take Part in Decision Making 1–1:24
    Not All Committees Have To Be Serious 1–1:27
    Build Parent Involvement with School Teams 1–1:28

Materials You Can Use **1–1:30**

    Survey on Parent Involvement 1–1:30
    Parent Involvement Survey 1–1:36
    Parent Interest Survey 1–1:37
    Learning Together—A Checklist for Schools 1–1:38
    Decision-Making Table 1–1:41
    Partners in Learning 1–1:44
    Parent/School Cooperative Checklist 1–1:46
    School Report Card 1–1:47
    Parent Satisfaction Survey 1–1:49
    15 Easy Ways To Increase Parent Involvement 1–1:50
    12 Easy Ways To Increase Parent Involvement Starting Today! 1–1:52
    How To Get Parents To Attend School Functions! 1–1:54
    Successful Parent Involvement Programs 1–1:56

Chapter **1–1**

Welcome Family Involvement

EVALUATING EXISTING PROGRAMS

PROGRAM ASSESSMENT

Before new parent and family programs are established, current programs should be reviewed and attempts should be made to determine why people do not participate in them. This process can be used to identify weaknesses in existing practices, to develop ideas for programs that would meet the needs of parents dissatisfied with current programs, and to prevent administrators from repeating mistakes that lead to lack of involvement.

Types of Assessment

Assessments should take place both internally and externally. In the internal assessment, principals or site administrators should complete a self-analysis of the number and types of opportunities offered for parent involvement. In the external assessment, parents and family members should be questioned about how they perceive the school's communications, involvement opportunities, cooperativeness, and overall atmosphere.

Internal Assessment

Some survey tools used by education researchers to assess the degree of parent involvement in schools may also be used as self-inventories to measure the individual school's responsiveness to parent needs.

The Survey on Parent Involvement is a portion of a survey developed by Michael Dietz, PhD, principal at Lake Shore Middle School in Mequon, Wisconsin. The survey was used to study parent involvement in the state's middle schools. Individual administrators can use the same form to evaluate a school's strengths and weaknesses simply by completing it and reviewing their responses. A second evaluation tool is a checklist developed by the Families in Education Program of the Wisconsin Department of Public Instruction (see Learning Together—A Checklist for Schools). This checklist can also be used to measure how actively administrators involve parents, families, and community members in schools. The list includes statements related to all six of Dr. Joyce Epstein's involvement categories (parenting and family skills, communication, learning at home, volunteering, governance and advocacy, and community outreach). For example, the statement, "We have a structured program to help parents assist their children with homework," is included under "Learning at Home." A principal checks the boxes next to those statements that apply and can then easily determine the areas in which the school must improve.

However, Dietz reminds administrators that, during the internal assessment, both program depth and program participation must be considered. A school may use 20 different outreach methods, he says, but if only a fraction of the target audience participates in those programs, the school neither truly involves parents and community residents nor realizes the benefits of successful programs.

Individual programs should be assessed, too, says Mercedes Fitzmaurice, senior research specialist at Research for Better Schools, in Philadelphia, Pennsylvania. A decision-making table developed by her agency helps school leaders evaluate programs on the basis of educational benefits to students, external benefits to students, benefits to parents and community residents, benefits to school staff and faculty, cost, and potential economic impact on the community at large. (See Decision-Making Table.) This table was developed primarily for small, rural schools with limited resources, to help them assess which programs would provide maximum benefit to students and the overall community. However, the same criteria can be applied to larger schools, many of which are in urban areas, where resources are limited and community return is important.

A unique feature of the table allows schools and districts to weight specific categories and questions according to local priorities. School leaders can assess programs on the basis of the needs of the school and community situations, rather than predetermined research criteria. Fitzmaurice recommends that small groups of school staff and community stakeholders work together to complete the table as a way to build consensus about the future of programs and proposals.

External Assessment

The purpose of outreach programs is to meet community needs and reflect residents' opinions on school issues. Consequently, identification of these needs and opinions is essential to the assessment process. One approach is to invite community stakeholders who are not part of the school community to complete the decision-making table. More pointed assessments may be needed, however, when programs involve a specific group of people, such as parents. Specific opinions should be gathered from a target audience by use of a telephone or direct mail survey.

All assessment procedures should be ongoing to monitor changes in community and parent needs and to ensure growth and success.

Reasons for Lack of Involvement

Key questions to be asked during the assessment phase are, "Why don't people become involved in school activities?" and "Do we, as school leaders, make everyone feel welcome?" Understanding the answers to these questions is essential to improving program participation rates. "You have to find [individuals'] involvement pressure points and address them," says Dietz.

Frequently, he says, people avoid schools because they do not feel comfortable there. Brown[1] notes Greenberg's finding[2] that many uninvolved parents feel unable to become involved in school activities because of their own negative experiences as students or because of differences between their cultural styles and/or socioeconomic levels and those of teachers. Other factors may also contribute to low participation rates.

Quality of Relationships with School Staff

Individuals relate to school personnel who listen and respond to their concerns. As a result, they are more likely to become involved in school activities. Swick[3] says findings by Comer and Haynes[4] suggest that when parents sense an inviting school climate, they are more supportive of teachers, and parent participation in school activities increases.

Several researchers have identified qualities that promote strong relationships between parents and teachers. Comer and Haynes say the teacher qualities that appeal most to parents are trust, warmth, closeness, positive self-image, effective classroom management, child-centeredness, positive discipline, nurturance, and effective teaching skills. Characteristics that influence relationships in general are warmth, openness, sensitivity, flexibility, reliability, and accessibility.

Likewise, Epstein[5] and Galinsky[6] found that the following teacher attributes are related to highly successful parent involvement: positive attitudes, active planning to involve parents, continuous teacher training, involvement in professional growth, and personal competence.

Internal assessments should examine these elements and identify all avenues for improvement.

Differences in Language and Culture

Schools and their neighborhoods are increasingly diverse, and it is imperative that administrators be attuned to cultural differences in all facets of education, including communication, partnerships, programs, and general administration. Recognizing and accommodating differences in these areas create a more inviting atmosphere for members of all cultures and often generate greater participation in school activities.

Attention to cultural differences also can pay dividends in attempts (1) to understand why parents do not participate and (2) to develop strategies to reverse that trend. Nicolau and Ramos,[7] for example, have found that Mexican-American parents see the school's role as instilling knowledge and the parents' role as providing for basic needs and teaching respect and proper behavior. They note that the two roles should not interfere with each other. After examining 42 projects to foster involvement, the researchers concluded that the following strategies can be used to improve a school's relationship with these parents: reception areas that include bilingual staff; telephone calls and written communication in Spanish, as well as English; and personal visits at a neutral site, such as a community center, rather than at school or in the home.[8]

Additional points to be conscious of when interacting with people of other cultures are the need to allow personal space and sufficient time for response to questions, the importance of eye contact, and the significance of touching.

Inappropriate Assignments and Feedback to Volunteers

Dietz says that administrators can benefit from applying the rule of "different strokes for different folks" to parents and community residents who volunteer to help with school projects. "It's a matter of applying principles of the *One-Minute Manager*[9] and giving people what they need."

If individuals are willing and able to take on responsibility, they should be given responsibility. If volunteers are not comfortable in the school environment, the teacher should begin with short-term, manageable tasks that require no background in education and minimal decision making. This approach addresses common fears of would-be volunteers—that they will be assigned projects for which they feel completely unqualified or, conversely, that they will be given monotonous tasks that do not capitalize on their talent and experience.

Measures To Improve Participation

Implementation of Policies To Promote Parent Participation

Schools that regularly invite parents to participate in activities and attend school functions should have in place a policy approved by the school board. This measure is especially important for schools that require or are considering a requirement that parents participate in a minimum number of school activities each year.

A family involvement policy document should begin with a statement of the school's desire for parent involvement. The policy should specify the degree of involvement expected and should give nuts-and-bolts information about how parents can become more active in school activities. Conversely, policies may also limit the extent to which parents may become involved. A policy may state that parents can participate on building committees and have input on site decisions, for example, but that they cannot vote on school governance issues, or vice versa.

In development of a family involvement policy, special attention should be paid to the policy's title. The goal is involvement regardless of the name of the policy, but it is important to show sensitivity to the fact that not all students live with their parents and that not all parents come in pairs. The policy should use language that openly invites all people who care for students to participate in school activities and should not cause a nonparent guardian to feel that he or she will not fit in or be welcome.

Three sample family-involvement policies are shown in Family–School Partnerships: Sample Policy. The first policy takes a top-down approach, stating obligations of the school board. The second policy addresses obligations of all parties involved, including school personnel and families. This policy also refers to parent volunteer requirements. The third policy, from San Diego, California, provides in list form what the school system is doing to promote family involvement. It continues in a second section, explaining what the previously mentioned points mean to administrators, staff, and families.

Self-Assessment of Leadership and Commitment

Self-assessment of administrative know-how is an important element in assessing and improving participation by parents. What qualities and skills do you, as a principal, bring to the partnership table? What are your personal strengths and weaknesses?

"The leadership element must be there in order for something to work," says Dietz. "The principal or administrator has [to] be willing and able to build a comfort zone for anyone he or she wants to involve in programs." Fitzmaurice says, "Mobilizing the community begins with committed leaders."

Commitment by staff, parents, and students is also essential. To reinforce responsibilities, school leaders may consider adopting a commitment pledge or contract that specifies each group's responsibilities. See Partners in Learning agreement for a sample contract. This student-parent-teacher-administrator agreement asks each party to read and sign, acknowledging that he or she understands what is required to improve student achievement levels. The agreement is an excellent way to define specific responsibilities so that situations do not occur in which one party thinks it is another's job to fulfill specific obligations, as sometimes happens between parents and teachers.

Development of Implementation Plans

For maximum success, programs must be started systematically, with well-defined roles for everyone involved. Comer and Haynes[10] found that each parent-related partnership program is and should be unique. They recommended that the program should encompass a needs assessment, goal statements, prioritization of activities, strategy development, implementation plans, and evaluation tools.[11]

Dietz agrees that administrators must have a multidimensional mental picture of the program before it is initiated. He uses the metaphor of an aircraft to illustrate the point. Administrators, he says, should first envision the program from 10,000 feet, where all elements—people and procedures—are visible. What is the overall flow of resources and information? What resources go into the program, and what is its outcome? Similar assessments should be made at lower levels—at 5,000 feet; 1,000 feet; and ground level. What does each component of the program look like? At ground level, what will be the responsibilities of specific individuals, and how will they be configured?

"This helps assess how well a program is planned and organized," he says.

Conclusion

School administrators should not "just start" a family and community involvement program or simply add more programs to their repertoire to say they are addressing the issue. Programs begun in such a haphazard way, at best, will likely yield only average results.

For maximum success, school leaders must put themselves and the involvement programs in question through a rigorous assessment process to determine what the community's needs are, how they can be best addressed, how current programs do and don't meet the needs, and how programs should be structured and evaluated. Understanding the reasons a program works or does not work is the best way to improve it. This approach is also the best way to increase program participation rates and, ultimately, student achievement levels. Schools benefit from written policies to formalize the commitment to involvement. Policies set both standards and expectations that motivate staff members to follow through with program plans.

References

1. P.C. Brown, Involving Parents in the Education of Their Children, *Educational Resources Information Center Digest,* ED308988 (Urbana, IL: ERIC Clearinghouse on Elementary and Early Childhood Education, 1989).
2. P. Greenberg, Parents as Partners in Young Children's Development and Education: A New American Fad? Why Does It Matter? *Young Children* 44 (1989): 4, 61–75.
3. K.J. Swick, Parent-Teacher Partnerships, *Educational Resource Information Center Digest,* ED351149 (Urbana, IL: ERIC Clearinghouse on Elementary and Early Childhood Education, 1992).
4. J. Comer and M. Haynes, Parent Involvement in Schools: An Ecological Approach, *Elementary School Journal* 91 (1991): 271–278.
5. J. Epstein, School/Family/Community Partnerships: Caring for the Children We Share, *Phi Delta Kappan* 76 (1995): 701–712.
6. E. Galinsky, Why Are Some Parent-Teacher Relationships Clouded with Difficulties? *Young Children* 45 (1990): 2–3, 38–39.
7. S. Nicolau and C.L. Ramos, *Together Is Better: Building Strong Relationships between Schools and Hispanic Parents* (New York: Hispanic Policy Development Project, 1990).
8. N.F. Chavkin and D.L. Gonzalez, Forging Partnerships between Mexican-American Parents and the Schools, *Educational Resource Information Center Digest,* ED388489 (Charleston, WV: ERIC Clearinghouse on Rural Education and Small Schools, 1995).
9. K. Blanchard and S. Johnson, *One-Minute Manager* (New York: William Morrow & Co., 1992).
10. Comer and Haynes, Parent Involvement in School.
11. Swick, Parent-Teacher Partnerships.

CREATING FAMILY-FRIENDLY SCHOOLS

CREATE THE RIGHT ATMOSPHERE

Parents' first impressions of your school are important. If they're negative, you'll be playing a game of catch up as you try to involve them in their children's education.

The first thing most parents notice is the condition of your school building and grounds. Are they up to snuff? Do you:

- Pick up all litter from lawns, sidewalks, playgrounds, and hallways?
- Make the front doorway and entry attractive to visitors?
- Display students' work, posters, or announcements on bulletin boards in the hallways?
- Make your central office a welcoming space? Do office staff keep it neat and presentable, with comfortable chairs in the waiting area?

Remember, though, that physical appearances are only part of the equation. A positive attitude by you and your teachers and support staff also plays an important role in making parents feel at home in your school.

Welcome Parents into Your School

Most visitors will enter your school near the front office, so it's essential that office staff understand that parents' comfort is a priority.

"The people in our main office go out of their way to make visitors comfortable," says Principal Francine Bullock of West Boylston, Massachusetts. "They've been instructed to greet all visitors and ask if they need directions."

If you're having a tough time convincing your staff that this effort is well spent, try Principal Patricia Ross' approach.

"I tell them to pretend that everyone who walks in our doors will be handed a slip of paper to decide whether staff members should get paid today," says Ross of Sierra Vista, Arizona. "That really gets them thinking about how important I believe welcoming parents is!

"I also tell my staff that we've all been places where policies, procedures, and paperwork take priority over people. We don't want our school to be like that because we want parents to see it as a place where the personal touch is still valued.

"For example, if a new parent comes to register a child, but doesn't have a birth certificate or immunization record, we politely make it clear we need that information," says Ross.

"We also want to avoid making the parent feel stupid for not bringing it along. Our attitude is: Yes, we need the information, but it's not the end of the world if we don't have it right now."

Ross says that someone from her office will take the parent on a tour of the school and introduce him or her to the nurse and counselor. Before the individual leaves, though, staff remind him or her that the documents are still required.

"I continually emphasize to office staff that people, especially parents, are our top priority," she says.

"I remind them to drop everything and serve the person. We need to remember that others aren't familiar with our school building. It's our job to make them comfortable. This way, their visit will be enjoyable, and they'll want to come back soon."

INVITE PARENTS TO VISIT

Many parents may not know that the welcome mat is always out at your school. To reach these parents, invitations often work.

"I want parents to feel free to walk in and talk with me and my teachers," says Principal Pat Burmaster of Chenoa, Illinois. "So I make a point of personally inviting them to come in and take a look at our school.

"For example, when I give a presentation to a community group, I extend a sincere invitation to everyone. I'd like to see more parents dropping by for a visit, and I tell them that over and over again."

BE EXTRA-COURTEOUS IF VISITORS SIGN IN

Because of security, many schools require visitors to sign in. If your school does this, be sure to make it nonthreatening to parents. "When parents visit our school, we ask them to report to the principal's office and sign a sheet," says Principal Gene Abel of Lakewood, New Jersey.

"We also give them identification badges to wear when they're in the building. Our school is in an urban area, and we have to use caution when any outside people are in the building. Because of these steps, though, we go overboard to be extra-friendly, so parents feel welcome visiting the school.

"I make sure someone greets parents and other visitors. If they don't know where to sign in or what the procedure is, we explain it."

Make Yourself Accessible to Parents

Today's parents are busy—which is perhaps the main reason they don't visit your school often. For two-career and single-parent families, time is a premium. To accommodate parents, let them know you're willing to work around their schedules. Here are a couple ways you can do this:

1. **Hold evening office hours.**
   A Washington principal has evening office hours once a month for an hour and a half.
   "Education is changing today, and so are parents' needs," he says. "We have to meet the needs of single-parent families and parents who both work nine-to-five.
   "For example, some parents recently asked me to discuss very specific test result information about their kids.
   "Since they work during the day, evening was the perfect time to give them the feedback they wanted."
2. **Offer prompt customer service.**
   Parents are just like customers in a store: They should be treated promptly and courteously. Good "customer service" will make them feel special and important. Bad customer service will turn them away in droves.
   "There's a department store in town, and I've noticed the length it goes to please customers," says the Washington principal. "For example, if it's late with a suit it promised, it will make a special delivery to your house and then give you a break on the price.
   "I try to do some of the same things to accommodate parents. For instance, I'll leave school during the day to visit them at their place of work. Or I'll visit them in their homes outside school hours."
   Another big part of good customer service is to know what your parent "customer" wants. The principal finds out with the help of a school report card he sends home to parents each year. (See School Report Card.)
   "I tabulate the results myself," he says. "As ugly as they sometimes are, I give each teacher representative a copy of the report. The reps then discuss the report cards with the teachers.
   "We use the reports to identify areas that a significant number of parents would like to see changed—and make them part of our goals for next year. This year, their chief concern was a buildingwide reading program, so that's our priority."

SPEND QUALITY TIME WITH VISITORS

As principal, you should be personally committed to making parents feel welcome at your school. If they don't feel comfortable, the chances are good that you won't see them again until there's a major problem—which is exactly the type of parent involvement you don't need!

"I try to make parents feel positive about their kids being in my school," says a Southwestern principal.

"For example, the mother of a student stopped by to ask how he was doing in a computer class.

"I told her, 'Let's take a walk upstairs, and I'll show you the computer room.' She was impressed with our equipment and with the fact that I was interested in her concerns."

The tour took only a few minutes, but the parent walked away feeling great because a principal cared!

BEWARE OF LANGUAGE BARRIERS

Many schools these days serve parent populations whose first language isn't English. If you want to get these parents involved in school, be sure to communicate with them in a language they understand!

"Our school is 70 percent Hispanic," says Principal Fred Ortman of Fontana, California. "We need to be welcoming to all our parents, many of whom speak only Spanish. So every communication we send home or anything about the school we submit to the media is in both English and Spanish.

"By making our communication user-friendly, we're doing our best not to exclude any families from our school."

I bet someone in your district or your school has the language proficiency to do this simple job.

If Parents Can't Come to You, Go to Them

If parents are reluctant to come to your building, try visiting them on their turf. This takes a time commitment on your part, but the rewards are obvious. Here are a few reasons to use home visits:

1. **To introduce yourself to new families in your school.**
   Before school starts in the fall, Principal Mick McCormack makes a list of incoming students whose homes he plans to visit.
   "The first few weeks of school, I went out every night from 6 to 8 to call on parents," he says. "I used a map of neighborhoods to plan the visits, and I must have gone to 100 new students' homes.
   "I introduced myself to the kids and parents at the door and asked if they had any questions. Then I let them know I wanted them to have a smooth transition to their new school. Our community is large, but the personal touch is still important.
   "The visits help eliminate the basic fears parents and kids have about entering a new school for the first time," adds McCormack.
   "I don't have statistics to prove it, but there have been fewer discipline problems with this group of kids than with any previous class. I feel that the visits also improved my relations with the home because when I phone parents, they remember my visits. And meeting new people in their homes is one of the most rewarding experiences in my 10 years as a principal."

2. **To be the bearer of good news.**
   A home visit can be an opportunity to surprise parents with goods news. Here's what Principal William Schofield of Gainesville, New York, does.
   To honor students chosen by their teachers as Super Achievers, Schofield makes personal visits to their homes. "I want to help kids develop self-esteem," says Schofield. "Before I took this job, I worked in the state prison system. I saw many problems there that I believe are caused by low self-esteem. I decided one way to increase kids' self-esteem is to visit them at home.
   "One night a week, I make my rounds. I start at 5 and finish about 8:30. My secretary calls a week ahead to arrange a time for the visits. I stay about 20 minutes, talk with parents, and brag about their kids.
   "Sometimes, parents tell their kids I'm coming. Often they don't, though, so it's a real surprise. Parents usually have their cameras or camcorders ready to record the event. During the visit, I give students a book to encourage a love of reading. Our PTA raises the money to buy the books.
   "I've made about 130 visits this year. Discipline referrals to my office have decreased by 60 percent compared to last year.
   "This is a lot of fun for me—a real boost—and I can see the kids' faces glowing in school the next day.
   "I ask teachers to nominate kids who are good school citizens to be Super Achievers. This opens the honor up to all students, not just the top academic kids."
   You don't even need a formal reason for home visits—bringing general, positive news can be just as effective with parents.
   "I try to think of positive reasons to drop by a student's home," says Principal Gene Durrett of Bakersfield, California. "I've stopped by the homes of kids who've been sick for several days to express my personal concern.

"I'll also stop by in the evening to congratulate a student who does well in a contest. Parents always react favorably because they appreciate my interest in their kids."

3. **To reacquaint yourself with the families of your students.**

Principal Dot Moran says that home visits give her a chance to see the home environment of her students and reintroduce herself to their families.

"I always talk about my family because I want them to know that I'm willing to share this information about myself. I also want to know more about their family life. Of course, I just don't ask people straight out. But if I see a family photo on the wall, I ask about the children or other people in it."

Meet Parents on Their Turf

If you can't get parents to come to the school, take the school to the parents. That message comes from Frank Villanueva, whose Webster Middle School is hosting a series of town meetings in the surrounding Stockton, California, community.

"It's hard to get the community to come to the school," says Villanueva, who is campus security monitor and parent liaison for the 1,400-student, grade 7-9 school. So the school is hosting town hall meetings at local community centers. At these "open forums," the principal speaks, along with representatives from the local community city and parks departments and the Stockton Parent Resource Center.

"We're trying to get something started" in the way of school-community communication," he says. "If parents can't make it here, we'll go there."

Including the parks and recreation leaders is an outgrowth of the local Community Alliance through Recreation and Education. "The basic concept is that we want to help the recreation department and community center be more than a place that hands out basketballs. We want to bring in parent issues."

The hope is that there will be a trickle-down effect. "We want students to come in with a good positive learning attitude. If we get solid homes, we get solid students," he says.

Parent Resource Center

Stockton already boasts a full-fledged, free-standing Parent Resource Center that serves the whole Stockton Unified School District. In operation for at least 20 years, the center is responsible for parent involvement training and education for the district, according to Jimmie Sasaki, parent involvement program specialist at the center.

Parent workshops are held on topics such as effective discipline, helping children manage anger, child achievement and parental expectations, as well as gangs and drug prevention, emotional intelligence, and helping parents become better partners in the educational process. Center personnel also train school personnel on parent involvement issues, Sasaki says.

The center holds some 20 workshops a year, each drawing about 20 parents. In addition, the center is open five days a week for drop-in visits by parents and offers books and videos on parenting and educational topics. The district has 40 schools serving about 36,000 students.

The district-funded center also provides outreach to schools. "All the topics we offer here, we'll bring to the school site and provide workshops," says Sasaki. The center hosts about 30 workshops at schools each year, and both child care and refreshments are offered, he says.

Reach Out to New Parents

In Superintendent Larry Giovacchini's community, parents of newborns get special congratulations. The school district gives them two outstanding resources that sets the stage for involvement in their children's education. Here's what parents can look forward to when the new baby arrives.

1. **A New Mom Packet.** "This contains information about our reading program, a brochure on disciplining young children and another brochure that answers questions typically asked by parents of newborns," says Giovacchini of Fishertown, Pennsylvania.

    "In addition, we tell parents about the services we provide that they may be eligible for.

    "The packet helps prepare them for a good working relationship with us in the future."

2. **A littlest Lions booklet.** "Some schools give parents footballs when they have a new baby," says Giovacchini. "But my thinking is that, if a school believes reading is important, it should give parents something related to it.

    "Our Littlest Lions booklet conveys this message perfectly. Our district mascot is a lion, and the booklet tells the story of a family of lions and their educational experiences."

    Giovacchini wrote the text and then handed it over to two staff members who edited, illustrated, and produced the booklet. "I write a message for each newborn's copy," he says. "For instance, it might go something like this, 'John, reading is the only true time machine. It can take you anywhere.' Parents love it, and they really appreciate the gesture."

Give Parents Their Own Room

Many parents feel the same way about visiting school as they do about a trip to the dentist: It has to be done, but it isn't going to be fun.

To encourage parent involvement, a Southern principal set aside unused space near the school's entrance for a Parent Lounge.

"In the past when parents visited the school, they sat around a cafeteria table," he says. "Now they have their own area."

"My PTA president arranged to have furniture, carpeting, pictures, and bookshelves donated for the lounge," he adds. "In the lounge itself, we arranged parenting literature on the tables and in bookshelves. It's good educational material, and parents are strongly encouraged to read it.

"The lounge isn't fancy, but it lets parents know they're welcome at the school. I definitely want them to feel this way—and giving them their own space helps."

Principal Patricia Ross says her school has also designated a room just for parents. "It has comfortable couches and chairs, and the coffee pot is always on. Parents not only sit and visit there, but they can also help teachers with some jobs.

"Teachers often leave little jobs in the room like cutting out pieces for bulletin boards or papers to be sorted," she says.

"If they choose, parents can do things while they're waiting to visit a classroom or talking with other parents."

To get parents to visit the school, you may have to help them with transportation. Student Support Coordinator Anne Cole of Roslindale, Massachusetts, says many minority parents her school serves have a difficult time getting to the parent center in her school.

"To solve the problem, a parent volunteer is spreading the word about our center in the minority community and has offered the use of a van to transport parents to it."

Support Parents with Extra Services

Let's face it. Families often have more immediate worries than how their children are doing in school. This is an issue you'll have to address before you can get some parents involved in your school.

If you really want these parents to feel welcome, you need to help them meet their personal needs. Here are four ways some schools are doing this.

1. **Offer basic health and social services.**

   A state grant made it possible for Principal Fred Ortman to begin Healthy Start in his school.

   The program has a nurse, child protective specialist, and a full-time community liaison aide who makes contacts and referrals for people who use the program.

   "In effect, we've set up a health clinic on campus that offers classes on nutrition and parenting," says Ortman.

   The clinic also has an examining room for medical services, where the nurse and a volunteer doctor perform routine medical procedures and tests.

   "We use a kitchen to teach nutrition programs in both English and Spanish. On a regular basis, a group of parents comes in to explain how to prepare nutritious meals.

SET UP YOUR OWN WELCOME WAGON

An Eastern principal tells me that her school has a Welcome Wagon for families new to the school district.

"A committee produced a brochure on the school that includes a calendar, enrollment figures, teachers' names, and some of the committees and organizations parents can get involved with," she says.

This principal asks committee members to personally deliver the brochure to new families. This gives families the opportunity to get immediate answers to any questions they have about the school system.

"This service is provided through a partnership of the county, school, and community."

Healthy Start also includes a food distribution program. "Participants pay $14 and receive $35 worth of groceries each month in return for two hours of volunteer service at the school. For example, a parent might volunteer to work in a classroom."

Principal Elaine Newton of Sierra Vista, Arizona, says her school received a federal grant to set up a family wellness center. "Our community has a large Hispanic population, so we used the grant money to hire two Hispanic women to reach out to mothers with children in the school system.

"The wellness center also offers parenting classes and schedules doctors and dentists to give presentations. The school provides free transportation and babysitting."

2. **Set up a clothing exchange.**

    "Several schools in our district are in affluent areas," says Newton. "Our wellness coordinators visit these schools to explain that some of our families could use extra help.

    "They talk about our program and ask for donations of used clothing. The clothes are cleaned and put in the clothing exchange room for parents to pick up."

    Many staff members at Newton's school donate their old clothes or those their children have outgrown. "We give away some really nice things, and the families appreciate the help. In fact, it means so much to them that they often return the clothing in good shape, so it can go back into the exchange room."

    Action: You could ask for donations from parents or even dry cleaners or clothing stores in your area.

3. **Help parents with emergency situations.**

    I bet there are families of students in your school that are going through tough times financially. "We've budgeted money for families that might need emergency help," says Newton.

    "For example, if a family is having money troubles and we know the electricity will be shut off, we help them out with cash.

    "Of course, the money goes directly to the utilities company or a landlord. Our wellness coordinators keep us posted whenever a family has an emergency need."

4. **Use your parent resource center to assist families.**

    Assistant Principal Carol Chanter of Casselberry, Florida, uses the Parent Resource Center in her school to help struggling families.

    "The center is where parents can find parenting materials on subjects they need information about.

    "It has videos, books, and brochures about services in the community that can help them. Parents can also check out materials and use them in their homes.

    "We've recently started tracking parents' use of the center to find out when it should be open and learn what subjects parents want more information on."

Take a Family Approach!

Principal Kay Larsen says her staff felt that their school needed to be restructured to make its families more welcome. And what better way to do this than to pattern the school after a family?

So they convinced their district superintendent and school board to adopt the Family Approach to education.

"Much of what we do is based on the British primary school system," Larsen explains. "My staff and I attended a weekend class to learn more about an innovative program used in Great Britain's elementary schools. As a result, we decided to incorporate many of its ideas.

"Our goal was simple: To create a safe, comfortable, and familiar school environment where students can concentrate on learning."

At Larsen's school, children are no longer assigned to grades. Instead, they're grouped in classes called families with kids of different ages. "For example, kindergartners are grouped with first-graders for a full day of school," says Larsen of Winfield, Kansas. "Second- and third-graders make up a family, as do fourth- and fifth-graders.

"Each family spends two years with the same teacher. This gives teachers a chance to develop trusting and long-lasting relationships with students and their parents. In addition, teachers no longer spend the first six weeks of school learning about their new students."

The family atmosphere also extends to the cafeteria, Larsen tells me. "We eat lunch family style, which encourages cooperation and good manners. My teachers agreed to give up their duty-free lunch to spend this time with the kids.

"One 'family' sets tables with silverware, plates, and centerpieces. Food is passed around the tables in bowls, and everybody waits until the rest of the table is served before he or she digs in.

"One teacher sits at each table, and families mingle. After lunch, the kids pitch in and help clear tables.

"Parents have told me how they've seen an improvement in their kids' table manners at home. In addition, they tell me that kids are helping clear the table, just like they do at school."

Another feature of Larsen's school is a 15-minute, all-school-led assembly at the end of each day. Its purpose is to allow selected students to share their achievements.

"Kids recite their poetry, show pictures they've drawn, and read stories," she says.

"This gives them the confidence, at an early age, to stand up before an audience and give a presentation—something we hope will become a life skill."

Keep Doors Open for Parents, Students

A Montana school has opened its doors twice: with a Family Education Center and an after-school homework club. The result? An increase in parent involvement and reduced student retention.

Principal Jan B. Riebhoff launched the Family Education Center two years ago to serve the five schools that make up the Belgrade, Montana, public schools. Riebhoff is principal of the system's intermediate school, which houses grades four through six.

"We needed for parents to have a place to come and get information," based on many parent requests for information on everything from attention deficit disorder to divorce to academics, Riebhoff says. First, she tried setting aside a section of her school's library, but that didn't work because the library is busy all day with children.

So, she took a room used for gifted classes in the morning, but empty in the afternoon, and set it up with:

- a television for viewing parenting videos;
- a computer;
- materials such as handouts and books; and
- children's furniture so parents could comfortably come in with their preschoolers.

The start-up money, totaling less than $10,000, came from Title I funds and federal and state safe and drug-free school programs. PTO fundraisers cover additional items that parents request.

More Parents Are Involved

By bringing more parents into the school, the center has wound up increasing parent involvement in the school. "As kids get older, parents don't think they have to be as involved. Really, the opposite is true," Riebhoff says. With this parenting center, parents with children of all ages get together and share ideas. "I've seen improved participation and more parents coming to parenting classes."

The family center is available to parents in the afternoons and evenings for drop-ins, workshops, parent support groups, and PTO meetings. Each month, free or low-cost workshops, offered by local professionals, are held on topics such as: how to be an authoritative parent; how to motivate your child to do chores and homework; how to encourage a discouraged child; how to create a win/win situation in conflict resolution; and understanding your child's reactions during and after divorce.

Homework Club

Meanwhile, an average of 20 to 25 students attend Belgrade's after-school homework club for one hour, Monday through Thursday. The club, named the BATT Club, for Boosting Academics Through Tutoring, provides tutoring for:

- children whose parents do not have time or are not home to help them with homework;
- students with failing grades;
- students at risk of failing; and
- students at social and/or emotional risk.

With a grant from the state board of crime control and school district funding totaling $12,000 to $15,000 a year, the program employs three teachers, providing a ratio of one teacher for every six to seven students. The funds also cover school supplies, computers, and calculators.

The grant allows for paid teachers, so there is consistency from week to week, and also from the classroom to the homework club as some regular classroom teachers do double duty. College student and parent volunteers supplement from time to time, Riebhoff says.

Student Responsibilities

At the BATT Club, students:

- sign in on their own log sheets when they arrive;
- take out their assignment books so the teacher knows what work they have to do;
- get started on their work;
- ask for help if they're struggling; and
- get one-to-one time with a tutor as needed.

About 10 kids are regulars, and others drop in on an as-needed basis. To stay in the program, good behavior is mandatory.

"We've had students who would have failed a grade pass because they got organized and on the right track" after attending the BATT Club, Riebhoff says. Of 500 students at the school, just one to two are retained each year. "I attribute most of that to this program," she says.

Teachers are very involved: They refer students to the program, come into the BATT Club to check on their students, and occasionally will stay and do some one-to-one tutoring.

The program began four years ago as an evening program (hence the name, BATT Club), but transportation proved a barrier. The following year, the school tried a two-day, two-hour schedule, but that didn't work either. The four-day, one-hour schedule has proven the most successful at bringing in both students and teachers. The club is held in the school library.

Lines of Communication

Students and parents are told about the BATT Club through the student handbook that goes home at the start of school, a flyer and permission sheet that are sent home, the parent open house, parent conferences, and the school's monthly newsletter and calendar.

Riebhoff advises principals interested in this kind of program to seek funding to get it off the ground. Investigate safe and drug-free school programs or any funding source for at-risk students. "It's hard to start a brand-new program and get funding from your school district without a proven program," she says. "But once it's successful, it's hard to close a program down."

Special Events Bring Parents into the School

A change of pace is often all you need to get parents involved in school functions. Many principals find that special events where parents and students participate boost parent involvement. Here are some events other schools are doing:

- **Family Night draws parent and community support to school.**

    Principal Brenda Dykes designates every third Thursday of the month as Family Night from 5 to 7 at her school.

    It's the perfect vehicle to bring parents and their children to school for an evening of positive educational activities.

    Since the program's inception, parent and community interest in her school has expanded by leaps and bounds. Here's how Family Night works.

    "We started on a small scale last fall," Dykes says. "I had asked our librarian and the staff member who runs the computer lab if they would keep their areas open one night a month for visitors. They were willing to take on this duty without pay.

    "This was our first Family Night, and it attracted about 60 parents and children. They enjoyed activities like working on computers and reading to each other in the library.

    "Each month, the popularity of the program grew. During December, we had 400 participants! When the rest of my staff saw the benefits of this one-to-one parent contact, we had to expand the program to include the entire school.

    "Teachers were chomping at the bit to open their classroom for activities—and they came up with some great ideas. For example, when we were preparing for our state assessment test, some teachers gave parents a mock test to show them how difficult the exam really is—and to emphasize its importance."

    As Family Night's popularity grew and its reputation spread, Dykes of Baytown, Texas, brought community groups and businesses into the program. "An Exxon refinery sent some of its employees to observe a Family Night," she says. "They came away impressed with the quality, uninterrupted family time it offers. The company now serves hot dogs, chips, and pop at Family Night. This has really boosted attendance because families can eat and then stay for the activities.

    "A hospital also does blood pressure screening for the elderly in the neighborhood, and the city has set up a booth to promote events like bicycle registration.

    "My role during Family Night is to prepare an agenda for each upcoming evening and mail it to parents," says Dykes. "I'm also on hand at the school during Family Nights to tell parents where they need to go for activities."

- **Monthly social for parents showcases student work.**

    "On the third Friday of each month we hold a parent social," says Principal Frank Denara of New Kensington, Pennsylvania. "It's very informal. Because we're a parochial school, the parents are invited to attend a liturgy.

    "After the liturgy, we invite parents to our commons area where there's a display of student work. We also invite parents to take a tour of the school.

    "Food and coffee are served, and I answer questions. I've found this is a good way to get new parents involved in school activities or encourage them to participate in the PTA. As many as 25 parents attend."

    Note: Many schools have regularly scheduled student recognition programs. These are perfect opportunities to hold a coffee before or after the event and invite parents to attend.

- **Breakfast calms parents' anxiety about visiting school.**

    One morning a month at Principal Yvonne Cobb's school, parents get the opportunity to eat breakfast with their son or daughter.

    "We serve breakfast from 7 to 8," says Cobb of Bethany, Oklahoma. "It's an extremely popular program. We've served as many as 200 parents. They enjoy it because coming to the school was a negative experience for many of them. But the more they're around the school, the more comfortable they are visiting it."

Because of the program's success, the cafeteria staff are sold on the idea—even though they have to start work earlier for the breakfasts. Parents pay for their own breakfast and have plenty of time to visit with teachers, eat, and get to work on time.

"We talked with the PTO about the program, and they liked the idea," says Cobb. "Letters were sent to the parents announcing the breakfasts. Once we started them, though, the message was passed by word-of-mouth."

- **Science Night lets parents and students work on a project together.**

    Science Night is a time for parents and their children to work together on a science project. A science teacher comes up with "fun" learning activities, designed to teach parents and kids about the laws of motion, gravity, and energy.

    "Our science coordinator plans the event," says Principal Chris Hetzel. "He received a mini-grant from a local foundation for about $3,000 to pay for the supplies for our latest night.

    "Parents were required to bring their child with them. Together, they produced a ballooned-powered vehicle that could cross water or land or shoot a rocket. The science teacher talked about Newton's laws. Then the parents and kids had two hours to build their vehicle.

    "They had all kinds of materials people had brought in to use for their vehicles. These included toilet paper tubes, old Styrofoam, and cardboard. The science coordinator purchased other items like balloons."

- **Literacy Night focuses on the importance of reading.**

    Literacy involves more than sitting down and reading a book. At Chris Hetzel's school, Literacy Night includes all forms of communication—books, plays, and videos.

    "Projects the kids have worked on all year are used," says Hetzel. "Kids can produce a book, mural, or poster, and each child has one written product to take home at the end of the evening."

    "We have plays, puppet shows, and videos the kids have made. Parents can walk around and see all the work their kids have done."

    "There's also a reading chair where someone is reading out loud all night long."

    "Kids can use computers to make covers for the books they wrote. An adult helps with our binding machine, so all the kids' books are bound."

- **Make and Take Night gives parents the chance to take a project home.**

    The title of this event really describes what happens at Principal Guinevere Durham's school. Parents and their children work on a project and, at the end of the night, have something to take home and use again.

    "We begin with the students singing three or four songs; then each parent/child group is given a project in a box or basket," says Durham.

    "These could be reading, spelling, or vocabulary games. Sometimes, we ask parents and children to make flash cards for adding and subtracting exercises."

    "Our teachers come up with appropriate games for different grade levels. The state provides special funding for parent involvement, so we decided to use it to buy supplies for our Make and Take projects."

- **Breadmaking workshop focuses on simple family activities.**

    Parents don't have to spend a bundle to do something fun with their family. In fact, sometimes the simpler the activity, the more quality time they have with each other.

"A local breadmaker puts a workshop on for us," says Teacher Debbie Hickman of Sierra Vista, Arizona. "She explains how a tradition like breadmaking can really be a family event.

"She has wonderful stories and legends to tell about making bread. She talks a lot about how her family loves to bake bread together and how it gives them something they can all take part in.

"Then she shares her recipes and secrets—and parents and kids are fired up to go home and make bread."

- **Chocolate Extravaganza is pure fun.**

  Everyone seems to enjoy knowing a little more about chocolate. A Chocolate Extravaganza at Hickman's school is an evening where parents and kids learn interesting facts about chocolate.

  Of course, sampling is a big part of the evening, and it always ends with some chocolate snacks!

  "We take the participants through the history of chocolate, describing its origins, where it's grown, processed, and then consumed," says Hickman.

  "It's always fun digging up little known facts about chocolate. For example, the Aztecs ground up bones and added them to their chocolate, and Montezuma drank chocolate from a gold goblet."

Family Nights Are a Family Affair

Want some great ideas for family nights at your school? Try these from Principal Bonnie Grigg at Northside Elementary School in Colorado:

- **Academic Fair:** Held each spring, this is a two-day fair usually centered around a theme. One year it was called "Past, Present, Future and All That Jazz" and tied in heavily with the music program. Students made instruments from the jazz era and staged performances for two nights. During the day the gym is open as a gallery for classes and the community to visit. Student work is displayed in various media, including writing, artwork, and computer stations.
- **Art in the Park:** The school collected old wooden chairs, and students painted them. Then parents and the community at large were invited to an auction. The take? About $800 to $1000.
- **Put Your Best Foot Forward:** Students brought in old shoes and decorated them. Local artists were asked to create "something about feet" and donate their work. Again, a communitywide auction was held, this time auctioning off the shoes and "foot" art.
- **Starry Starry Night:** The school set up large telescopes on a field and a star lab—a huge blow-up tent into which kids could crawl and view constellations—in the gym. Families rotated through stations, including an art station for drawing starry pictures and a library station for viewing books about astronomy.
- **Patriotic Night:** Held last fall after the September 11 tragedy, this event began with a high school teacher singing the National Anthem, a color guard ceremony, and an outdoor candlelight vigil. Local firemen passed a "boot," collecting almost

$400 for relief efforts. Stations included face painting of flags, stars, and stripes and other patriotic symbols. Kids made "Yankee doodle" hats, and families danced old dances such as the Virginia Reel.

Northside has one or two "big family productions" a year, Grigg says, and attendance is high. "We focus on tying it in with literature and academics in some way, so parents can see what we're doing."

It's Tuesday: Drop in and Talk

Principal Bob Mennonna figures he'd be working at home anyway, so why not work at school and invite parents to drop by? That's the philosophy behind his Tuesday Night In program, an evening of drop-in office hours he's held since 1993.

"It's real simple. Tuesday evening I have open office hours from 6:30 to 8. Parents can pop in anytime," says Mennonna, principal of Ashlawn Elementary School in Arlington, Virginia. Sometimes parents schedule an exact time; other times they just stop by, he says.

"It's a relaxed atmosphere. I get to know the parents," he adds. About four or five parents stop by each week. They'll talk about their own child, test scores, a project they'd like to help with or an idea they want to submit to the PTA. "Once in a while there's a complaint—too much homework or not enough homework, work that's too rigorous or work that's not rigorous enough. They feel they've been heard, and I put a note in the teacher's box."

To Mennonna, it seems like a natural idea. "I'd be doing paperwork at home anyway. I might as well do my work here and meet with parents at the same time."

Mennonna advertises his Tuesday Night In in the monthly PTA newsletter, at PTA meetings, and on a TV monitor in the school's hallway. Ashlawn has 380 children in preschool through grade 5.

Get More Parents Involved in Organizations

Effective PTA and PTO groups are wonderful vehicles for parent involvement in schools. The challenge is getting parents to join them and then motivating them to attend meetings. The following strategies can help you boost participation in parent organizations at your school:

- **Make parents want to become members.**
    Principal Kenny Clemons made the PTO so popular at his school that parents are asking to become members. Here's how he did it.
    –He identified leaders among parents and teachers who are parents of kids in the school. "These parents are the ones who participate in PTO and give freely of their time to the school," says Clemons of Birmingham, Alabama. "The teachers I asked to get involved had transferred their own kids here, so they strongly believe in our school.

"These key players, who are officers in the parent/teacher organization, talked up our school to other parents."

– He turned membership in the group into a "package deal" for parents. "A $10 membership fee includes a T-shirt for each of their kids, a folder we used to communicate with the home, and a contribution to their children's classroom party fund.

"The best selling point was the T-shirt," he tells me. "The PTO leaders told parents at registration that we wanted every student to be wearing one on the first day of class. Students in each grade wear a different colored shirt, which gives kids a sense of fitting in from Day One."

- **Hold a raffle for a donated item to increase meeting attendance.**

    "An important PTA meeting was planned for right after the holiday break, and we wanted as many parents to attend as possible," says Principle Guinevere Durham of Bell, Florida.

    "So we raffled off a bicycle. To publicize it, my husband stood in front of the building with me before school one morning handing out flyers. We also offered coffee and cookies to parents who were dropping their kids off at school.

    "Then over the holiday vacation, we mailed letters to parents inviting them to attend. The first Monday after the break, we put a bicycle the PTA donated in front of the school with a sign that said, 'Come win me tonight!' Usually, there are about 20 parents at PTA meetings. For this meeting, though, we had more than 200!"

- **Find out what issues interest parents.**

    An Iowa principal gets parents to come out to PTA meetings when the issues addressed are the really "hot" ones. The key to his success? Parents get to choose the issues themselves.

    "For example, in response to parents' concerns, one meeting was on drug identification," says the principal. "Parents weren't sure how to identify drugs and spot signs of drug use in their kids, so a police officer showed samples of confiscated drugs and drug paraphernalia.

    "After the meeting, I asked parents what other topics they'd like to hear about. Techniques to enhance kids' self-esteem was what they were most interested in. So at our next meeting, a speaker talked about how parents can build kids' self-esteem.

    "Both programs were in response to what parents told me they wanted. More parents than usual attended those meetings."

- **Consider renaming the group to add new life to it.**

    Principal Francine Bullock started a Parent/Teacher Support Group at her school. "Our parents felt they were too busy to belong to an organized group like a PTA, so we renamed the group," she explains.

    "As a result, more parents became involved because they felt less pressure joining it," says Bullock.

    "Besides raising money, the group sponsors a health day and career day. It has even bought books for the school library."

- **Recruit new members.**

    Principal Patricia Ross uses teachers to recruit parents for her school's PTA. "Teachers nominate parents who are involved in their classrooms and list as many as they think are appropriate," she says.

    "From the list, I mail invitations that say, 'Your child's teacher has nominated you as someone who values education.'"

Each year, Ross holds a reception for these parents. This year, it was a breakfast where she displayed sign-up sheets for PTA membership, participation on site councils, and other volunteer opportunities.

"I make it clear from the beginning that the breakfast doesn't obligate parents to join anything," says Ross.

"But once you get them there and they see their neighbors and other parents signing up, it motivates them to get further involved."

- **Have students send written meeting invitations to their parents.**

  Parents tend to show up at events if they know they're important to their children. Here's how one principal got students to remind parents to attend PTA meetings.

  "Our guidance counselor visited each classroom and had students write an invitation to the PTA meeting for their parents," says Principle Guinevere Durham. "A local merchant donated the stamps to mail the invitations. There was no way parents could say they didn't know about the meeting. Usually, we get about 25 people, but 150 showed up that night."

- **Don't let a large meeting overwhelm participants.**

  Principal Phyllis Chastain says the setting for parent organization meetings is important. She moved PTA meetings from her school's gym to avoid the noise and confusion that turns many parents off.

  "No matter how nice your gym is, it isn't good for these types of meetings.

  "Everybody is shouting and yelling to be heard, and everything seems so disorganized. I thought the meetings would proceed much smoother if we divided into smaller groups.

  "So I set up our media center for the people who would be speaking. Then parents sat in their children's classrooms. In each classroom was a monitor, and the speakers were being videoed in the media center.

  "This way, every parent is in a comfortable room and can hear clearly what the speakers are saying. The first time we did this, we presented the budget. For years, the budget meeting was always a shouting match about how to spend the PTA money and what fundraisers to plan.

  "This year, we presented ideas and then asked people to write down their objections or suggestions and return them to the officers. There were no negative reactions. We plan to begin the next meeting with a short program by the children in the gym. Once again, parents will be in the classrooms where they can watch everything on the monitors.

  "Parents have told me that this is a great setup. As long as the PTA officers and myself are available after the meeting to answer any remaining questions, parents enjoy the format."

Invite Parents To Take Part in Decision Making

Many parents don't get involved because they feel they won't have any real say in how schools do things. To correct this, some principals give parents a voice in the decisions that affect their school. Here are five options you can offer parents to encourage them to get active in this area.

1. **Have them complete a survey on parental involvement.**

A Southern principal surveyed parents about the extent of their participation in her school's activities and how they thought they could become more involved.

"A committee made up of parents and staff devised the questions, and a copy was mailed to each family with a student at the school," says the principal.

"The responses have been interesting, and the committee is exploring ways to put the information to use.

"For instance, a small number of parents help out in the classroom. Interestingly enough, many parents surveyed said they would like to do more in this area. The committee has made a list of parents who want to assist in the classroom and is contacting them individually to set something up.

"Many parents also indicated that they help their kids with homework, but almost every parent wanted to do more. Our teachers can now come up with suggestions on how they can help kids at home."

Surveys can also help you get other information. A Minnesota principal sends out an Interest Survey each year to organize his volunteer database—and to learn where parents' educational interests lie. He uses this information to come up with parent education programs.

"It's a two-page survey that parents complete and return to school with their kids," he says.

"We enter the data into the computer and get a printout that tells the parents' names and phone numbers, the type of volunteer work they're interested in, and at what grade levels their kids are."

Principal John Burwell uses survey input in his school improvement plans.

"An accountability committee made up of teachers, parents, staff, and myself conducts the survey," says Burwell of Rifle, Colorado.

"It surveys our students, staff, parents, and other taxpayers. These four groups give us a good cross section of the district."

Once the committee analyzes the survey data, it drafts an improvement plan based on the information. After Burwell's teachers review it, action plans are written to improve the school in the next year.

2. **Establish a parent advisory group.**

Many principals have parent advisory councils. In some districts, these are required by law. Often, though, they exist simply to get parents more involved in their children's school.

Advisory councils can be a great asset to principals because they give you the opportunity to solicit support for the school.

They also offer a controlled forum to answer parents' concerns and questions—and keep parents from meddling in your job.

Principal Perry Hansen has had great luck with parent advisory councils. He shares how his council operates and some of the strategies he uses to make sure his parent advisors stay on his side.

"My parent advisory council includes parents who represent each grade level and one 'at-large' parent representative nominated by my teachers," says Hansen of Spearfish, South Dakota. "Parents serve two-year terms, so the council doesn't turn over completely each year. There's also one veteran teacher on the council. I generally put new teachers on the council, too, because it's a good way for parents to meet them and vice versa.

Hansen's council meets quarterly in the school library over the lunch hour. "It's difficult to get everyone to attend meetings before or after school," he says.

"But people can usually get away at noon. I don't let meetings last any longer than an hour."

During meetings, Hansen and parents cover general information about the school, like how teachers are using new technology, along with specific items like a new science curriculum under consideration.

Hansen also does everything he can to ensure that members of his advisory council support his efforts. Here are a few of the strategies he uses to keep them on his side.

- He establishes criteria for council membership. "One prerequisite is that members have a positive attitude about education," he says. "They don't have to agree with everything we do at the school, but they must be upbeat. This eliminates people who see only what's wrong with schools."
- He stresses to council members that they're ambassadors for education. "This lets parents know that they're representing the school to the community, which helps keep them positive," he says. "I reinforce it by including council members' names and telephone numbers in my newsletter to parents. I invite parents to contact council members if they have questions. This quickly puts them into the role of ambassadors."
- He calls on the council when he needs support at a board meeting. "The board expects me to want certain things for my school, particularly budget items—like more money for a new science program.

  "I convince my advisory group of the need first. Then when the issue comes before the board, I ask members to attend and help me out. Their input packs a punch with the board, and they feel like they're accomplishing something good for the school."
- He lets council members know how much he values them. "When I have an idea I've been tossing around but haven't come to a decision on, I'll ask council members for feedback," says Hansen. "They appreciate this and respond enthusiastically."
- He doesn't let top-notch members slip away after their council term expires. "Several former council members have been elected to our school board," says Hansen. "In fact, I encouraged them to run. It never hurts to have a friendly face on the school board."

3. **Community School Information Councils create involvement opportunities.**

   Principal Marie Ginther's district has a Community School Information Council that meets monthly with the superintendent. The purpose of the group, which has parent representation for each building, is to give parents a chance to share what's happening in their children's school.

   Parents who discuss their ideas, strategies, and problems with other parents and school administrators often end up becoming more involved in schools.

   "The superintendent knows what topics the parents want to address and invites the appropriate staff members to meetings. These could be board members, business managers, teachers, or principals.

   "The parents who serve on the council are chosen by the parent organization at their building. After each council meeting, they report back to their parent organization on ideas that were discussed."

4. **School Improvement Teams give parents a say in education.**

   Some principals offer parents an opportunity to make their schools better by inviting them to serve on school improvement teams.

The payoff is parents who are more involved because they know they're members of a group whose purpose is to enhance education.

"Each building has its own team," says Ginther. "Our team is made up of three parents elected by the parent organization, three teachers, one non-instructional staff member, and myself. We meet monthly to see how instruction in our building can be improved.

"This year, the team decided to focus on teaching values. We surveyed parents through the school newsletter to find out what values they consider important.

"We boiled it down to one value to be emphasized for each month of the school year. Some of the values are honesty, self-discipline, and responsibility and others we could address within the curriculum.

"Then committees were set up to work on each value. We got as many parents involved as we could.

"For example, the parents wrote a good definition of what honesty means. They collected examples of everyday situations that require honesty and wrote activities for students. They also put together a reading list. It was great to see these parents participate enthusiastically in this activity."

The group has also created a phone tree when information needs to get out quickly to parents. Volunteers were recruited and given a list of parents to call.

"Now if we have a program we want to make sure parents know about, we get the phone tree going," says Ginther. "Or we can use it when a budget vote is upcoming to remind parents to get out and vote."

5. **Textbook selection committees solicit parent input.**

Principal Frances Miller of Sierra Vista, Arizona, says that when her school adopts a new textbook, it seeks parents' input on the decision. "We want them to be involved all the way from reviewing the possible new texts to deciding which will be purchased.

"We ask parents to review the texts and let us know what's acceptable or objectionable. We regularly ask parents if they're interested in doing this for us, so we always have a list of volunteers on hand.

"It's just a short-term job, but many parents enjoy looking over the new books and writing brief reviews for us. The superintendent considers their comments before any purchase decision is made."

NOT ALL COMMITTEES HAVE TO BE SERIOUS

Not all parents are cut out for helping choose new curriculum and textbooks or updating a discipline policy. That's why it's important not to overlook the potential for parent involvement in fun assignments.

"I like to give parents some opportunities for fun decision making," says Administrator Stephen Kleinsmith. "For example, I designed a What I Like Best About School contest, where kids could write essays or draw posters to enter.

"Then I formed a committee of parents and teachers to pick the winners. It was just a fun little activity, but parents had a chance to see some positive aspects about the school too."

Build Parent Involvement with School Teams

At Northside Elementary School, soccer and baseball teams are not the only teams that reign. Innovative Principal Bonnie L. Grigg has put each of the school's families on a team led by a teacher—or the principal herself—in an effort to connect parents with their children's school.

About six years ago, Grigg had the idea to take her five-teacher leadership team and put mini-teams of five to six teachers under each one of those leaders—and then put families on each team. On Grigg's team are 13 students and their families. "They're my kids as long as they're at Northside. Their families are my families," she says.

The team program is important because the school is in a low socioeconomic area where the staff have to work to get parents to value education, Grigg says. The program began as a way to reach out to families, "so the school had a connection to these families other than just their classroom teachers. This was somewhere you could form a friendship."

Positive Results

From her team-building project, Grigg sees many good things happening:

- First and foremost, communication with families has increased markedly.
- Kids feel better about themselves and seem happier at school.
- Parent involvement in the school has increased. More parents are seen around school, and more are available to help when called, Grigg says.
- Discipline is improved, with fewer referrals to the office.
- Staff morale is higher, and staff turnover is very low.

Under the program, each staff member has 13 to 15 students representing 10 to 12 families (siblings are automatically on the same team). In all, the school has 30 to 35 teams each year, Grigg says.

Team-Building Activities

Named by color—the yellow team, the purple team, etc.—each team engages in its own team-building activities, such as:

- team lunches
- pizza parties
- ice cream socials at school
- academic nights, including literacy night, science night, and math night, which incorporate discussions about the curriculum with teacher-family activities—for example, in the fall, families carved pumpkins, estimated the number of seeds, counted seeds, and graphed seeds, all in an effort to show parents how the school's math program works
- family heritage night, where families set up their own booths with family foods, slide shows, and other materials

- projects such as designing bumper stickers with the Northside motto, *Caring and Sharing Together*
- "community of caring" service projects

The team leader also acts as a personal liaison for the students and their families. Grigg sends notes to her kids at holiday time, or, "if I hear one of my kids is having a problem with a teacher, I might call the child in to talk."

"The neat thing is that teams have families across age groups. A kindergartner gets to work with his fifth-grade brother on something," says Grigg. In a recent team contest, a brother-sister team won.

No-Cost Program

Setting up teams costs nothing, and the projects undertaken by the teams can be no- or low-cost. While it takes some coordination to get the program going, once all the families are matched up, the hard part is over, Grigg says. The principal tries to keep the teams balanced in terms of numbers, but she doesn't worry about demographics.

When the program began, team leaders made home visits to every family, and now new families are contacted by phone or home visits. A few families found the idea threatening at first, but the feeling quickly dissipated when they gave it a try, Grigg says.

Get Teachers Involved

The teachers helped her plan the program, she says, "so it wasn't anything that came down from me at the top." Now, when the principal and her teachers interview new teacher applicants, Grigg makes it clear that the team program at Northside is "something above and beyond," and asks, "Are you willing to do that?"

Grigg says motivating teachers to participate was not an issue at her school, where staff saw a need for getting parents more involved and saw the team concept as a way to achieve that goal. The principal says her leadership style is about valuing and respecting the teachers for their input, work, and innovations, and then giving back to them in return. She cooks lunch for them on staff professional days or takes over their classes when they need her to. "They know I do these kinds of things, and in return they'll do for me," she says.

Grigg has this advice for principals interested in the project: Get together with your staff and discuss whether you need this program. "It's real important to bring your staff along, and not just have someone hand it down to them."

MATERIALS YOU CAN USE

Survey on Parent Involvement

Survey of Wisconsin Principals on Parent Involvement at the Middle Level, Part 2

Mark as X after the responses that reflect the current situation at your school and estimate the percentage of families affected.

	Often	Sometimes	Seldom	Never	Percentage of families affected 0–25	26–50	51–75	76–100
1. School provides parents with information on adolescent development.								
2. School provides parents information on parenting middle-level students.								
3. School provides parents with special workshops or meetings on parenting.								
4. School lends parents video tapes or audiotapes of parenting workshops or meetings on parenting.								
5. School provides information on developing positive home conditions that support school learning.								
6. School surveys parents to determine the need for assisting them in parenting middle-level students.								

School-home communications (Mark an X for all responses that apply to your school.)

	Always	Often	Sometimes	Seldom	Never
7. Positive messages about students sent home.					
8. Home notified about student's awards and recognition.					
9. The school contacts the homes of students causing classroom disruptions.					
10. The school contacts the homes of students having academic difficulty.					
11. Teachers have ready access to telephones to communicate with parents during the school day.					
12. The school suggests how parents might use home environment (e.g., materials and activities of daily life) to stimulate children's interest in school subjects.					

continues

Survey on Parent Involvement continued

	Always	Often	Sometimes	Seldom	Never
13. The school's mission is communicated to parents.					
14. The school provides organized opportunities for parents to observe classrooms (not help) for part of a day.					

If the school *does not* have a newsletter, *skip questions 15–23 and go to 24.*

15. Frequency of school newsletter
    A.___Weekly   B.___Monthly   C.___Quarterly   D.___Semester   E.___Other _____

The school newsletter contains (Mark an X for all that apply to your school.)

	Always	Often	Sometimes	Seldom	Never
16. Calendar of school events					
17. Curriculum and program information					
18. Parenting information					
19. School volunteer information					
20. School governance information					
21. Tips to help with homework					
22. Information about issues affecting middle-level students and/or parents					
23. The school mission or philosophy					

24. The *primary* vehicle for sending home messages about your school is
    A.___Student   B.___Mail   C.___Weekly student folder   D.___Other _____

Communications mailed home (Mark an X for all that apply to your school.)

	Always	Often	Sometimes	Seldom	Never	Comments
25. Academic progress/grade reports						
26. Newsletters						
27. Notices of meetings at school						
28. Invitations to student activities						
29. Positive messages about students						
30. Student behavior/performance						
31. PTA/PTO information						
32. Disciplinary information						
33. Surveys						
34. Other:						

35. The percentage of teachers and staff sending/calling home positive messages about students is
    A.___Less than 25%   B.___25–50%   C.___51–75%   D.___More than 75%

continues

Survey on Parent Involvement continued

Mark an X after all parent involvement practices that apply to *your* school.

36. Academic progress reports are sent home prior to the end of the grading period.	
37. Grade reports include student social and developmental information.	
38. The school has a meeting room/resource room available to parents.	
39. A parent volunteer program for the school is formally organized.	
40. Parents are employed as part of the school's paid noncertified staff (e.g., teacher aides, assistant teachers, parent educators).	
41. The school has a structured format for lending books, workbooks, and other materials to parents to work with their children at home.	
42. The school has a homework telephone hotline.	

Indicate the methods by which your school obtains parent volunteers and the *effectiveness* of each method with an X after the appropriate response.

	Yes	No	Most	Very	Somewhat	Not
43. Principal contacts with parents						
44. Teacher contacts with parents						
45. Newsletter appeals						
46. PTA/PTO committee						
47. Paid school or district coordinator						
48. Other:						

Write the number of volunteers working at your school in the appropriate space after each statement.

	Regular	Occasional	Comments
49. Noninstructional assistance			
50. Tutoring			
51. Assistance in the classroom			
52. Assistance with cocurricular activities			
53. Directing/coaching cocurricular activities			
54. Career education programs			
55. Fund-raising for school programs			
56. Other:			

continues

Survey on Parent Involvement continued

What is the frequency of the following at your school? (Mark an X for all that apply.)

	Quarterly	Semiannually	Annually	Never
57. The school provides staff development for teachers to work with parent volunteers.				
58. The school has a program(s) to recognize parent volunteers.				
59. The school provides parents with information about goals for student academic performance.				
60. The school provides parents with structured ways to comment on school's communications with the home (e.g., mailed/take-home survey, phone survey).				
61. The school gathers information concerning the level and frequency of parent participation in school programs.				
62. The school has formal parent-teacher conference day(s).				

63. The percentage of parents attending parent-teacher conferences is:
    A.___Less than 25% B.___25–50%   C.___51–75%   D.___More than 75%

What is the frequency of the following at your school? (Mark an X for all that apply.)

	Weekly	Monthly	Quarterly	Semester	Annually	Never
64. The school has a structured program(s) to help parents assist their children with homework.						
65. The school provides parents with information on how to assist their children with learning activities in the home.						
66. The school provides parents with a questionnaire they can use to evaluate their child's progress and provide feedback to the teaching staff.						
67. The teaching staff provide *instruction* for parents to monitor or assist their own children at home on learning activities that are coordinated to the child's class work.						

continues

Survey on Parent Involvement continued

Parents may receive help and direction from teachers for working at home with students in the following subject areas. (Mark with an X the appropriate response for your school.)

	Always	Often	Sometimes	Seldom	Never	Comments
68. Reading/language arts						
69. Mathematics						
70. Social studies						
71. Science						
72. Other:						

73. The percentage of teaching staff providing help and direction to parents to help students with class work is
    A.___Less than 25%   B.___25–50%   C.___51–75%   D.___More than 75%   E.___Don't know

There are a variety of ways in which parents may participate in the governance of a school. (Mark with an X the frequency of the following statements that apply to your school.)

	Always	Often	Sometimes	Seldom	Never
74. Selecting school staff					
75. Assisting with revising school/district curricula					
76. Planning orientation programs for new students					
77. Developing parenting skills programs					
78. Attending school board meetings					
79. Completing surveys on parent advocacy issues					
80. Other:					

81. The principal arranges for staff and parent groups to meet collectively to discuss school issues.
    A.___Weekly   B.___Monthly   C.___Quarterly   D.___Semester   E.___Never

82. The school has a PTA/PTO.   A.___Yes   B.___No

If NO, skip questions 83–86.

83. The principal meets with PTA/PTO officers.
    A.___Weekly   B.___Monthly   C.___Quarterly   D.___Semester   E.___Never

84. Time of PTA/PTO meetings?   A.___Evenings only   B.___Days only   C.___Both days and evenings

85. The percentage of families belonging to the PTA/PTO is
    A.___Less than 25%   B.___25–50%   C.___51–75%   D.___More than 75%

86. Estimate the normal attendance at PTA/PTO meetings.   A.___Parents   B.___Teachers

continues

Survey on Parent Involvement continued

Time Management

In this section rate yourself by marking an X in the appropriate space on the time you devote to each area of parent involvement.

	Should spend less time	Spend enough time	Should spend more time
87. Basic obligations of parents—helping families with basic obligations of parenting middle-level students; helping parents to build positive home conditions that support school learning			
88. Basic obligations of the school—promoting school-home communications about school programs and progress			
89. Parent involvement at school—includes volunteer parents who assist teachers, administrators, and children at school both in and out of the classroom			
90. Parent involvement with learning activities at home—helping parents to assist children at home with school work and learning activities coordinated to child's class work			
91. Parent involvement in decision-making roles at the school level (e.g., PTA/PTO, advisory councils, other committees or groups)			

Additional comments on this survey:

_____
_____
_____
_____
_____
_____
_____
_____
_____
_____
_____
_____
_____
_____

Source: Reprinted with permission from M.J. Dietz, (1992), Principals and Parent Involvement in Wisconsin Middle Level Public Schools. Ph.D. Dissertation, in Madison, WI, University of Wisconsin.

Parent Involvement Survey

To get more parent input about how our school can be better and how to get more parents involved, a new Parent Advisory Committee met earlier this year. We want all parents or guardians to answer the survey below and send it back to the school this week.

For ratings: 1—hardly any, 2—sometimes, 3—about half the time, 4—quite a bit, 5—most of the time.

	1	2	3	4	5
1. How much do you help your child with schoolwork at home?					
2. How much would you like to help at home?					
3. How much do you help in your child's classroom?					
4. How much would you like to help in the classroom?					
5. When requested, how much have you been able to send something to help, even if you haven't been able to come help in person?					
6. How much do you help in the total school program (PTA, clinic, fundraising such as popping corn, etc.)?					
7. How much would you like to help in the total school program?					
8. How much does working outside the home interfere with your involvement?					
9. How much input do you think you have?					
10. How much do you think grandparents would like to be involved?					

Signature (optional) _____

We would like your input! Please express your opinions on the back.

Parent Interest Survey

Dear Parent:

Please take a few minutes to fill out the questionnaire below. This information will assist the District Parent Advisory Committee in formulating services to respond to parent needs. Please return the form to the school with your child or leave it in the school office.

Research indicates that children take learning more seriously when parents show an interest in their education. There are several types of parent involvement. Please check the ones that interest you.

- ☐ Communication (conferences, school programs, home/school contact via phone, notes, meetings, newsletters)
- ☐ Parenting (evening parent meetings, short seminars of interest)
- ☐ Volunteering (helping at school or home)
- ☐ Parent/child evening at school

---

1. Please check any possible seminar topics that would be of interest to you . . . and add any others that come to mind.

- ☐ Outcome Based Education (OBE)
- ☐ Homework hassles
- ☐ Discipline
- ☐ Spending/saving money
- ☐ Bully control
- ☐ Family changes
- ☐ Dealing with teens/pre-teens
- ☐ Overbearing grandparents
- ☐ Child responsibility
- ☐ Health issues
- ☐ Home/school communication
- ☐ Other (add your own suggestions) _____

- ☐ Games/things to do with children
- ☐ Parents as teachers
- ☐ Strangers/street safety
- ☐ Violence prevention
- ☐ Peer pressure
- ☐ Student part-time jobs (good or bad?)
- ☐ Parents teaching sexual values
- ☐ Helping the dyslexic child
- ☐ Working with a hyperactive child
- ☐ Extracurricular (how much is too much?)

Learning Together—A Checklist for Schools

Making Your Family–Community Partnership Work

Following are examples of practices and programs that schools and districts can use to encourage family and community support of children's learning. They are meant to be advisory and should be adapted to each school's or district's needs.

Parenting and Family Skills

- ☐ 1. We sponsor parent education and family learning workshops.
- ☐ 2. We ask families what types of workshops or informational events they would be interested in attending and what session times are most convenient.
- ☐ 3. We provide families with information on child development.
- ☐ 4. We lend families books and tapes on parenting and parent workshops.
- ☐ 5. We provide families with information about developing home conditions that support school learning.
- ☐ 6. We survey parents to determine their needs, assign staff members to help address those needs, and work to link parents with community resources.
- ☐ 7. We have a family resource center or help parents access other resource centers in the community.
- ☐ 8. We have support groups for families with special interests and needs.
- ☐ 9. We train staff members and support them in reaching out to all families.

Communicating

- ☐ 1. We have parent-teacher-student conferences to establish student learning goals for the year.
- ☐ 2. We listen to parents tell us about their children's strengths and how they learn.
- ☐ 3. We follow the "Rule of Seven": offering seven different ways that parents and community members can learn about what is happening in the school and comment on it.
- ☐ 4. Teachers have ready access to telephones to communicate with parents during or after the school day.
- ☐ 5. Staff members send home positive messages about students.
- ☐ 6. We make efforts to communicate with fathers.
- ☐ 7. Parents know the telephone numbers of school staff members and the times teachers are available to take phone calls from parents.
- ☐ 8. We involve families in student award and recognition events.
- ☐ 9. We encourage and make provisions for staff members to talk with parents about the child's progress several times each semester.
- ☐ 10. We communicate the school's mission and expectations for students to parents. The school has a homework hotline or other kind of telephone system.
- ☐ 11. We provide parents with structured ways to comment on the school's communications, for example, with mailed, phone, or take home surveys.
- ☐ 12. We have staff members available to assist and support parents in their interactions with the school (i.e., home–school liaisons).
- 13. We send home communications about
  - ☐ student academic progress
  - ☐ meetings at school
  - ☐ how parents can be involved in student activities
  - ☐ PTA/PTO
  - ☐ student discipline
  - ☐ child development
  - ☐ the curriculum
  - ☐ how parents can be involved as volunteers
  - ☐ how parents can be involved in school governance

continues

Learning Together—A Checklist for Schools *continued*

- [ ] how parents can help with homework and encourage learning at home
- [ ] community resources available to families
- [ ] how parents can communicate with school staff
- [ ] the school's philosophy of learning
- [ ] 14. Staff members make home visits.
- [ ] 15. *Before* a crisis occurs, we speak directly to parents (does not include leaving messages on answering machines) if students are having academic difficulty or causing classroom disruptions.
- [ ] 16. We provide copies of school textbooks and publications about the school to the public library.

Learning at Home

- [ ] 1. We have a structured program to help parents assist their children with homework.
- [ ] 2. We offer learning activities and events for the whole family.
- [ ] 3. We invite parents to borrow resources from school libraries for themselves and their families.
- [ ] 4. We link parents with resources and activities in the community that promote learning.
- [ ] 5. We give parents questionnaires they can use to evaluate their child's progress and provide feedback to teachers.
- [ ] 6. School staff and school communications help parents link home learning activities to learning in the classroom.

Volunteering

- [ ] 1. We encourage families and other community members to attend school events.
- [ ] 2. We offer youth service learning opportunities for students who want to volunteer in the community.
- [ ] 3. We help school staff learn how to work with parent and community volunteers.
- [ ] 4. We *ask* family members how they would like to participate as volunteers at their child's school or in the community.
- 5. We encourage family and community members to become involved as
  - [ ] participants in site-based management councils
  - [ ] presenters to students on careers and other topics
  - [ ] assistants with art shows, read-aloud events, theater workshops, book swaps, and other activities
  - [ ] tutors/mentors
  - [ ] chaperones on field trips and other class outings
  - [ ] instructional assistants in classrooms, libraries, and computer laboratories
  - [ ] noninstructional assistants
  - [ ] from-the-home contributors of baked goods, assembled materials, typing, etc.
- [ ] 6. We have a program to recognize school volunteers.
- [ ] 7. We offer volunteer opportunities for working and single parents.
- [ ] 8. We gather information about the level and frequency of family and community participation.

Governance and Advocacy

- [ ] 1. We encourage parents to attend school board meetings.
- [ ] 2. We assign staff members to help parents address concerns or complaints.
- [ ] 3. We invite staff and parent groups to meet collaboratively.
- [ ] 4. We help families advocate for each other.
- 5. We involve parents in
  - [ ] revising school and district curricula
  - [ ] planning orientation programs for new families
  - [ ] developing parenting skills programs
  - [ ] establishing membership for site-based councils
  - [ ] hiring staff members

continues

Learning Together—A Checklist for Schools continued

Community Outreach

☐ 1. We act as a source of information and referral about services available in the community for families.

☐ 2. We use a variety of strategies to reach out to adults, families, and children of all ages, races, and socioeconomic backgrounds in the community.

☐ 3. We encourage local civic and service groups to become involved in schools in a variety of ways, such as mentoring students, volunteering, speaking to classes, and helping with fundraising events.

☐ 4. We encourage staff and students to participate in youth service learning opportunities.

☐ 5. We open our school buildings for use by the community beyond regular school hours.

☐ 6. We work with local chamber of commerce or business partnership council and public library to promote adult literacy.

☐ 7. We have a program with local businesses that enhances student work skills.

☐ 8. We widely publish and disseminate school board meeting notices, summaries, and board policies and agendas and encourage the feedback and participation of community members.

Source: Reprinted from *A Checklist for Schools: Making Your Family-Community Partnership Work (Appendix)*, with permission of the Wisconsin Department of Public Instruction, John T. Benson, Superintendent.

Decision-Making Table

1. **What learning effects will this proposal have on our children?**

	How important is this? (1=low; 5=high)	Yes	No
a. Will they better learn the skills of writing, mathematics, analytical thinking, etc.?			
Which students will learn these skills?			
b. Will they learn more information?			
Which students will?			
What specific information?			
c. Will they learn more useful values and attitudes?			
Which ones will?			
What specific values and attitudes?			
d. What else will they learn?			

2. **What other benefits will this proposal have for our children?**

	How important is this? (1=low; 5=high)	Yes	No
a. Will they be better prepared for the future?			
To get jobs?			
What kind?			
Who will be better prepared?			
In what way will they be better prepared?			
To *create* jobs? To go to college?			
b. Will the proposal improve their health and safety?			
In what ways?			
How will it do this?			
c. Are there other possible benefits?			

continues

Decision-Making Table continued

3. **What are the costs of this proposal?**

	How important is this? (1=low; 5=high)	Yes	No
a. Has anyone prepared a cost estimate for this proposal?			
Has an independent reviewer checked the cost estimates?			
b. What are the indirect costs of this proposed change in terms of demands for support services?			
c. Does this proposal save money in the first three years over the present system?			
How much?			
Does this proposal save money over the long run?			
How much?			
c. Are there other cost considerations?			
Please list.			

4. **Will this proposal benefit us and other members of this community?**

	How important is this? (1=low; 5=high)	Yes	No
a. Will it result in more or better jobs?			
What different jobs will be created?			
How many jobs?			
What is the quality of these jobs?			
Who will get them?			
b. Will members of this community pay lower taxes?			
Which taxes?			
Tax savings per person: $ _____ ____%			
c. Will we feel better about this community?			
In what way?			
d. As a result of this proposal, will we be better parents?			
In what way?			
e. Are there other benefits for the community?			
What benefits?			

continues

Decision-Making Table continued

5. Will this proposal benefit school administrators, principals, teachers, and other staff?

	How important is this? (1=low; 5=high)	Yes	No
a. Will they be able to do their jobs better?			
Who?			
How?			
b. Will their jobs be easier?			
Whose?			
How?			

6. Will this proposal bring new money into this community?

	How important is this? (1=low; 5=high)	Yes	No
a. In salaries?			
Who will get this money?			
Will it stay in the community?			
b. In construction expenditures?			
Who will get this money?			
Will it stay in the community?			
c. For purchases of supplies, equipment, services?			
Who will get this money?			
Will it stay in the community?			

7. Are there ways to change the proposal to improve any of the above factors?

	How important is this? (1=low; 5=high)	Yes	No
a. Changes at the school level?			
b. Changes at the county level?			
c. Waivers that can be requested from the state?			

Courtesy of the Mountain Institute, 1828 L Street, NW, Suite 725, Washington, DC 20036, www.mountain.org, phone (202) 452-1636; fax (202) 452-1635.

Partners in Learning

Student–Parent–Teacher–Administrator Agreement

(This is a sample. Please feel free to adapt as needed.)

We know that students learn best at _____ School when everyone works together to encourage learning. This agreement is a promise to work together as a team to help _____ achieve in school. Together, we can improve teaching and learning.

As a student, I pledge to

- work as hard as I can on my school assignments
- discuss with my parents what I am learning in school
- respect myself, my family members, and school staff members
- ask my teacher questions when I don't understand something
- use my public or school library frequently
- limit my TV watching and make time for reading

Student signature _____

As a parent, I pledge to

- encourage good study habits, including quiet study time at home
- talk with my child every day about his or her school activities
- reinforce respect for self and others
- be aware of my child's progress in school by attending conferences, reviewing school work, and calling the teacher or school with questions
- volunteer for my child's school or district
- encourage good reading habits by reading to or with my child and by reading myself
- limit my child's TV viewing and help select worthwhile programs

Parent signature _____

As a teacher, I pledge to

- provide motivating and interesting learning experiences in my classroom
- explain my instructional goals and grading system to students and parents
- explain academic and classroom expectations to students and parents
- provide for two-way communication with parents about what children are learning in school and how families can enhance children's learning at home and in the community
- respect the uniqueness of my students and their families
- explore what techniques and materials help each child learn best
- guide students and parents in choosing reading materials and TV programs

Teacher signature _____

continues

Partners in Learning continued

As a principal/school administrator, I pledge to

- make sure students and parents feel welcome in school
- communicate the school's mission and goals to students and parents
- offer a variety of ways for families to be partners in their children's learning and to support this school
- ensure a safe and nurturing learning environment
- strengthen the partnership among students, parents, and teachers
- act as the instructional leader by supporting teachers in their classrooms
- provide opportunities for learning and development to teachers, families, and community members

Most importantly, we promise to help each other carry out this agreement

Signed on this ___ day of _____, 20__.

Courtesy of San Diego City Schools, San Diego, California.

Parent/School Cooperative Checklist

☐ I want my son or daughter to have the best possible education, and I realize that strong school systems are essential.

☐ I will insist on excellent attendance and teach my son or daughter the importance of being prepared and on time.

☐ I will help him or her build self-esteem.
- recognize and reward successes
- criticize with kindness, remembering that we all learn by trying and that we sometimes make mistakes

☐ I will read with my child at least twice a week.

☐ I will help my son or daughter prepare for tests by making myself familiar with the testing schedules, by encouraging him or her to study.
- State Achievement Test, week of _____
- Competency Test, week of _____

☐ I will attend conferences with my son or daughter's teachers on district conference days and as requested by myself or a teacher.
- November 5
- November 10
- November 13

☐ I will discuss interim reports and grade cards with my son or daughter.
- September 21 — Interim Report Week
- October 30 — First Report Card
- November 30 — Interim Report Week
- January 22 — Second Report Card
- February 22 — Interim Report Week
- March 26 — Third Report Card
- May 3 — Interim Report Week
- June 3 — Final Report Card

☐ I will remind him or her of the necessity of discipline in the classroom—especially self-discipline.

☐ I will be visible and active in the school's
- Open house
- PTO
- Evening programs

_____   _____
Student signature   Parent signature

Welcome Family Involvement 1–1:47

School Report Card

We would like you, as parents, to evaluate our progress this year by completing this evaluation and returning it to the school via your child or by mail. It is very important to us as a staff that we continually improve our means and methods of providing a quality educational program for your children. Please take the time to follow through with our Report Card. Thanks for your input.

	Excellent	Good	Average	Unsatisfactory	No Opinion
CURRICULUM AND INSTRUCTION					
The course of study in relation to your child's individual needs	☐	☐	☐	☐	☐
Learning materials in relation to your child's needs	☐	☐	☐	☐	☐
Instructional staff in meeting your child's needs	☐	☐	☐	☐	☐
Instructional methods in meeting your child's needs	☐	☐	☐	☐	☐
Number of students in your child's class (pupil/teacher ratio)	☐	☐	☐	☐	☐
PROGRESS REPORTS					
The school's student report card	☐	☐	☐	☐	☐
Parent/teacher conferences	☐	☐	☐	☐	☐
GUIDANCE AND COUNSELING					
The school's efforts in helping your child become a well-adjusted human being	☐	☐	☐	☐	☐
ATTITUDE					
Your child's enthusiasm for school	☐	☐	☐	☐	☐
DISCIPLINE					
Classroom rules, routines and management	☐	☐	☐	☐	☐
Playground rules, routines and management	☐	☐	☐	☐	☐
COMMUNICATION					
The exchange of information between school and home	☐	☐	☐	☐	☐
ADMINISTRATION					
Your feelings about the operation of the school	☐	☐	☐	☐	☐
Your feelings about the operation of the school district	☐	☐	☐	☐	☐
FACILITIES					
The school building as a good place to learn	☐	☐	☐	☐	☐
The maintenance of the school building and grounds	☐	☐	☐	☐	☐
FOOD SERVICE					
Your feelings about the hot lunch program	☐	☐	☐	☐	☐
BUS SERVICE					
Transportation to and from school	☐	☐	☐	☐	☐
FINANCES					
The district's efforts in getting the most for your educational tax dollars	☐	☐	☐	☐	☐

continues

School Report Card continued

COMMENTS

Please check one response for each question.

What do you appreciate most about the school?

- ☐ The small class size and student/teacher ratio.
- ☐ The course of study and special programs (Chapter I, Special Education).
- ☐ The care and concern shown by teachers, principal, and staff.
- ☐ Good communication between home and school.
- ☐ School and classroom newsletters.
- ☐ Assemblies.
- ☐ No opinion.
- ☐ Other (please specify): _____

What do you believe is the most pressing problem facing the school?

- ☐ Overcrowding and lack of space.
- ☐ Discipline.
- ☐ Busing and behavior on the bus.
- ☐ Lack of communication between school and home.
- ☐ No opinion.
- ☐ Other (please specify): _____

Are there areas of the school program that should receive less emphasis?

- ☐ Too much competition and too many competitive programs.
- ☐ Too many contests and rewards.
- ☐ The schoolwide discipline program.
- ☐ Marks and grades.
- ☐ None, it's great as is.
- ☐ No opinion.
- ☐ Other (please specify): _____

Additional comments you would like to make for our consideration in the improvement of our school:

_____
_____
_____
_____
_____
_____
_____
_____

Parent Satisfaction Survey

What grade would you give the staff of this school?

1. Teachers ☐ A ☐ B ☐ C ☐ D ☐ F ☐ Not familiar with
2. Counselors ☐ A ☐ B ☐ C ☐ D ☐ F ☐ Not familiar with
3. Principal ☐ A ☐ B ☐ C ☐ D ☐ F ☐ Not familiar with
4. Assistant Principal ☐ A ☐ B ☐ C ☐ D ☐ F ☐ Not familiar with
5. Library/Media Center ☐ A ☐ B ☐ C ☐ D ☐ F ☐ Not familiar with
6. Support Staff ☐ A ☐ B ☐ C ☐ D ☐ F ☐ Not familiar with
   (cooks, clerks, secretaries, custodians)

What grades would you give the school in accomplishing the following educational objectives?

7. Preparing students for the next grade level ☐ A ☐ B ☐ C ☐ D ☐ F ☐ Not familiar with
8. Preparing students for middle school/high school ☐ A ☐ B ☐ C ☐ D ☐ F ☐ Not familiar with
9. Preparing students to be informed citizens ☐ A ☐ B ☐ C ☐ D ☐ F ☐ Not familiar with
10. The extent to which the rules of the school are fair and enforced ☐ A ☐ B ☐ C ☐ D ☐ F ☐ Not familiar with
11. The extent to which teachers and parents communicate ☐ A ☐ B ☐ C ☐ D ☐ F ☐ Not familiar with
12. This school in general ☐ A ☐ B ☐ C ☐ D ☐ F ☐ Not familiar with
13. Does this school have positive interaction with its communities and businesses? Explain. _____

_____
_____
_____
_____
_____
_____
_____
_____
_____
_____

15 EASY WAYS
To Increase Parent Involvement

Experts say the best way to improve education on the elementary level is to strengthen parent involvement — by showing parents how to help their children learn and reinforcing their relationship with the school.

We are pleased to offer you 15 proven ways to involve parents as partners in their children's education. Choose what works best for you.

Parent Involvement at School

1 Create a school climate that is friendly, helpful, and open. Start with a "Parents and Visitors Welcome" sign or banner on the front door. If space permits, invite parents to eat lunch with their children. Make new families feel welcome by conducting tours and orientations. Some schools provide names and phone numbers of parents to contact for extra help and support.

2 Set up a "parent cove" in the school — a lounge with comfortable chairs and possibly a "lending library." Provide a variety of books, magazines, cassettes, videos, and other materials on child rearing and education.

3 Develop and support your parent volunteer program. Volunteers are usually the biggest supporters of education. Send out a list of needs the school has and invite parents to volunteer for something that interests them. Typical areas include: media center, clinic, field trip chaperone, preparing materials at school or home, computer lab assistant, reading tutor, playground helper, storyteller, and math tutor.

Consider setting up an area for volunteers to have coffee and get acquainted. Give them special badges to wear or free lunch tickets. Everyone likes to be appreciated, so set aside a time when they can be formally thanked with certificates or awards.

4 Whenever possible, provide opportunities for parents to watch their children perform and take part in special school activities. Whether it's a song or a brief skit, parents are sure to turn out. Try including a performance by students of different grade levels at PTA/PTO meetings. And use these opportunities to deliver important messages to parents.

5 Consider recruiting and training parents for leadership roles in your school. They can take part in advisory committees, school government, or PTA/PTO leadership positions. These individuals can be a valuable source of support, and their opinions carry a lot of weight.

Parent Involvement in Learning Activities at Home

6 Getting parents involved with their children's learning has the greatest effect on school achievement. *MegaSkills* by Dorothy Rich (Houghton Mifflin) is a reference source for at-home activities. Another book, *Parents and Schools: From Visitors to Partners* (NEA Library), contains examples of parent involvement programs in real schools.

7 Research shows that reading aloud to children is the single most important activity in building reading success and enjoyment — and it only takes 15 to 20 minutes a day. Give parents some "how-to" tips,

continues

15 Easy Ways To Increase Parent Involvement continued

including a list of high-quality children's literature for various grade levels. A presentation at a PTA/PTO meeting by a reading specialist or media center individual could help inspire parents to get started. Pizza Hut's BOOK IT reading incentive program is a popular way to get this type of program off the ground. For details, call 1-800-4-BOOK IT. For other ideas, see *The Read-Aloud Handbook* by Jim Trelease (Penguin).

Communicating with Parents

8 Set up an "early warning system" for academic, behavior, and attendance problems. Parents often get irritated when they receive bad news about their children's school performance long after problems have begun. They will appreciate the concern and effort, and teachers will be more apt to gain parents' cooperation.

9 Keep parents informed with frequent, clear communications — newsletters, flyers, and memos. Be brief and write in a simple, conversational style. An eye-catching format entices parents to read what you have to say.

10 At the beginning of the school year, give parents a school activity calendar. Include important dates, in-service days, holidays, special events, and even important telephone numbers.

11 Consider providing information to parents through computerized phone messages. Parents can call a special number and select information on a specific topic of interest — for example, school policies and procedures, special events, or other important news parents need to know about.

12 Most parents want to stay informed about their children's progress in school. Special "good news" notes and phone calls are appreciated. Since many parents cannot attend conferences or meetings during the day, you may want to offer evening conferences as well. Also, consider sending home folders of students' work on a particular day each week — parents will be more likely to see it.

13 Encourage your teachers to stay in touch with parents. Surveys show that more than one-third of parents do not meet with their children's teachers during the school year. In fact, approximately 60 percent of parents surveyed have never even talked to the teachers by phone. When parents don't show up for conferences and special meetings, suggest your teachers contact them by telephone. After all, a phone conference is better than no conference.

14 Give parents a clear picture of the curriculum being taught to their children. Provide them with an overview of each content area, including specific objectives and skills. One idea is to have one or two teachers give a mini-lesson on a specific subject. Students may enjoy demonstrating something they've learned, for example, a simple science experiment. You may also want to show a video of students and teachers in action.

And Remember the Basics

15 Parent involvement begins at home. But, according to research, many parents need help with the basics. They need to understand the importance of providing for their children's health, safety, and well-being. Also, they must learn practical ways to create a positive home environment that provides security and stimulation and supports their children's learning and behavior.

Parent newsletters and articles, special reports, parenting programs, workshops, and PTA/PTO meetings provide parents with information that can promote student success.

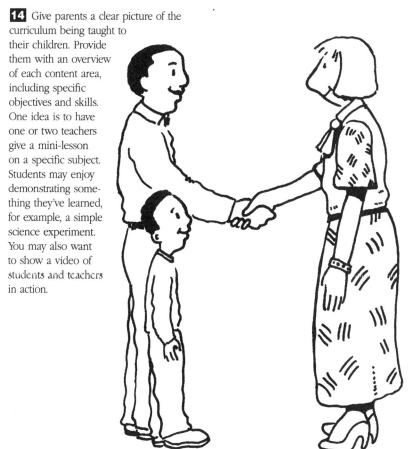

Parent Involvement
Starting Today!

Q: What sets one school apart from another?
  a. The principal
  b. The teachers
  c. The parents

A: All of the above!

Your administrators and teachers are crucial to your school's success. So are your students' parents. But in today's hectic world, it's not always easy to get parents involved. We've put together a list of ideas you can put into action immediately. They'll encourage even the busiest parents to become willing partners in their children's education.

❶ Create a parents' drop-in time. Designate a time each month that parents can drop by to chat with the principal. Rotate the times to accommodate busy parents' schedules — from early morning to daytime and evening hours. Publicize the drop-in time through letters sent home and notices in your school newspaper.

❷ Host monthly parent events. Vary your programs to include speakers on parenting topics and fun social events. Remember, the best way to draw in parents is to showcase their children. Open your programs with a student talent show, display of student work, band concert, or video production. *Example:* "This month at Main Street Elementary School."

❸ Send home schedules. Busy parents need frequent reminders of what's happening at school. On the first of each month, send home a calendar with school events filled in—everything from standardized testing dates to field trips, PTA meetings, and school events. Supplement the calendar with weekly, one-page "Monday Memos" reminding parents about what's coming up each week.

❹ Encourage regular contact between teachers and parents. Have each child keep a parent-teacher journal (a small spiral notebook works fine) in his backpack. At least once a week, teachers write a brief entry about the child's progress, something special the child did that week, or something that needs work. Parents respond and students carry the journals back to school.

❺ Welcome parents who speak other languages. Send home notices in their language. Find staff members and community volunteers to translate during parent-teacher conferences and school meetings. Plan an international night featuring food and displays about countries represented in your school community.

❻ Survey parents. Start and end each year with a parent survey. At the beginning of the year, ask parents about their goals for the year, programs they would like offered, and their feelings about the school. As the year ends, survey parents to gauge their satisfaction. Parents who are asked their opinions—and see that their opinions count—are more likely to get involved.

continues

12 Easy Ways To Increase Parent Involvement continued

12 Easy Ways to Increase Parent Involvement

7. Distribute a "Who's Who" list. At the beginning of the school year, send home one-page "Who's Who at Main Street Elementary School" sheets. List teachers and staff members, including school telephone numbers, fax numbers, e-mail addresses, and the school Web site. Laminate the sheets as a handy year-long reference for parents.

8. Give kids incentives to bring home notices. Include a line for a parent signature on each school notice you send home, and give children a point for each signed notice they return. Children can accumulate the points for individual rewards, like stickers, pencils, or books, or class rewards such as an ice cream party.

9. Have teacher "call-in" hours. Ask your teachers to designate an hour each week when they're available for parent phone calls. Teachers can announce their "office hours" at back-to-school night, then send home reminder notices. Having regular call-in times makes your teachers more accessible and your parents more likely to communicate with them.

10. Involve everyone. Research shows student achievement is highest when both parents are involved in their children's education. Try these ideas to target moms, dads, and grandparents in your community. Hold monthly Early Bird Book Breakfasts, where parents and grandparents read to children while they enjoy breakfast together. Ask for help with fall and spring school grounds cleanups. Try parent-staff or parent-child basketball and softball games.

11. Distribute volunteer forms each quarter. Offer many opportunities for volunteering in your school. To accommodate everyone's schedules, list activities like helping in the classroom, working in the media center, making phone calls from home, and going on field trips.

HELP ON THE WEB

These Web sites offer information on how to get parents involved in their children's education.

http://pfie.ed.gov Find information on the national family involvement initiative, a calendar of events, and a list of publications available from the Partnership for Family Involvement in Education. The partnership is sponsored by the U.S. Department of Education.

www.pta.org The Web site of the National Parent-Teacher Association includes PTA news, links to local PTAs, bulletin boards, and program information.

www.cpirc.org This site, from the Colorado Parent Information & Resource Center, includes resource information in various languages, information for parents on how to be involved in their children's education, parent interviews, and parent involvement research.

www.npin.org Find a virtual library and a question-answering service on parent involvement and other topics at this site from the National Parent Information Network. The Network is part of the ERIC system administered by the National Library of Education.

www.ncpie.org This National Coalition for Parent Involvement in Education site includes resources, guidelines for schools on developing family/school partnerships, and a listing of NCPIE organizations and board members.

www.handinhand.org Look for "What's Working Where," links to related Web sites, and an online brochure for parents, families, and teachers. This is the site of "Hand in Hand: Parents, Schools, Communities United for Kids," a program sponsored by the Mattel Foundation and coordinated by the Institute for Educational Leadership.

Include a place for parents to suggest activities they'd like to do. *Tip:* Ask each family to donate at least 10 hours a year, and award certificates to families who meet that goal.

12. Open a Parent Center. Make your school a gathering place for parents. With donations from parents and your community, stock a room with parenting and education books, magazines, and newsletters. Add a television, VCR, and videos, if possible. Include a binder with the curriculum for each grade and another binder with staff biographies and a personal letter from each staff member. *Tip:* Local businesses may be willing to contribute items, such as furniture or money, to get your center started.

How to get PARENTS to attend SCHOOL Functions!

What if you held a back-to-school night and no one came?

While it's unlikely that no one would come, you often don't get the attendance you'd like at back-to-school nights, open houses, parent meetings, or parent-teacher conferences. What can you do to attract more parents to these events? How can you make your school more parent-friendly?

With these questions in mind, we've put together a list of creative ways to get parents more involved. Try some or all of these ideas. We think you'll fill more seats at your next event!

Have students perform.
Who can resist seeing their children on stage? The next time you plan an open house or other school event, arrange a performance of the chorus or band to coincide. Or schedule a meeting to follow the school play or spring talent show.

Give rewards for 100% parent participation.
Nothing succeeds like an ice cream party! Give a round of ice cream pops to each class in which all the parents attend parent-teacher conferences or the school's open house.

Advertise your events.
At the beginning of the year, send home a notice announcing the dates of all school events. As each date approaches, send home reminders. Also, announce the programs over the loudspeaker, so children will remind their parents when they get home. Post large signs throughout the community about your upcoming events and place an item in your community newspaper.

Arrange for rides.
Sometimes transportation is the only thing keeping parents from attending. Post a list in the school office of neighbors willing to drive, and advertise that it's there. Try to arrange for a school bus to pick up parents who need rides.

Show videos of children.
Lights, camera, action! Start school programs with a video of students in action at school. Videotape kids in the classroom, on the playground, and at lunch. You can do the taping yourself, ask your school media center coordinator to do the honors, or have a crew of fifth- or sixth-graders handle the job.

Provide babysitting during meetings.
It's often hard for parents with young children — especially single parents — to attend after-school or evening meetings. They either can't find or can't afford sitters. Why not arrange for in-school childcare during school events? Recruit local high school students to provide free babysitting in exchange for community service hours, which many states now require for graduation.

Require attendance at parent-teacher conferences.
Make it a school policy not to release report cards until parents have attended a conference. Ask teachers to call parents who don't attend.

Overcome language barriers.
If your parents speak languages other than English, make your programs bilingual. Print materials in different languages. Provide an interpreter at parent-teacher conferences and at school programs.

MORE ▶

© Copyright 2001 Resources for Educators, Inc.
a division of Aspen Publishers, Inc.

continues

How To get Parents to Attend School Functions continued

How to get PARENTS to attend SCHOOL Functions!

Offer parents incentives to attend.
Remember door prizes? Hand out numbers as parents file in, and when the program ends, pick numbers from a hat and give out prizes. You can ask local businesses to donate items or gift certificates. Or make the prizes child-oriented, such as free ice cream at lunch, a line-leader pass, or pizza with the principal.

Call parents before events.
With the help of your PTA or PTO, put together a list of parents who usually do not attend events — and call them! Divide the list among PTA/PTO officers, teachers, and staff. Just remind parents about an upcoming event and encourage them to attend. Mention any special incentives you have planned.

Hold parenting workshops.
Before or after school meetings, host workshops on hot parenting topics. You can usually find a nearby professional or someone from a local college to speak for free. Try these ideas: effective discipline, computer literacy, getting kids to eat right, handling ADHD, or challenging gifted children.

Help parents feel secure.
If parents feel unsafe coming out at night, ask your local police department to station a patrol car at school when you have evening events. Send a notice home letting parents know that a police car will be out front.

Stage an authors' tea.
Many classes work all year on writing stories. Make your end-of-the-year event an "authors' tea," with students proudly displaying their books. Serve punch and cookies, while parents wander from table to table seeing what their young authors have written. Tie this in with a speaker on literacy or a review of your school's language arts program.

Host family evenings.
Make your school events a family affair. Offer meals, games, and learning activities. For example, throw a potluck dinner before the PTA meeting. Or plan a Family Math Night or Family Science Night, where parents and children play math games or do science experiments together.

Vary program days and times.
Try to accommodate parents' busy schedules. Make times available for parent-teacher conferences before, during, and after school, or even in the evening. Vary your program schedule so events are held at different times and on different days of the week.

Appeal to all parents.
Reach out to all parents with such ideas as a pre-meeting staff/parent basketball game, a technology talk, or a workshop on financial planning for college.

10 Ways to Make Your School More Parent-Friendly

1. Post a friendly sign on the front door.
"Welcome to Main Street Elementary School. We are so happy you are here. Please come to the office so we can personally greet you."

2. Make your telephone greeting parent-friendly.
A person answering the phone is the best. If you do have recordings, make your taped message an inviting one. And make it bilingual if you have non-English-speaking parents.

3. Whenever possible, encourage teachers and staff to greet parents warmly in the halls.
Learn their names. Mention something nice about their children.

4. Line the walls with snapshots of your students.
Take pictures of children in class and at play, and display them in school hallways. Put pictures of the teachers and staff near the office. Parents will know who the teachers are, and they'll love seeing photos of their kids!

5. Invite parents to volunteer in whatever way they can.
Make parents feel welcome to help out in the office, media center, health room, classrooms, playground, or cafeteria. Encourage working parents to help, too, by collating book orders, preparing classroom materials, or making telephone calls at home.

6. Make home visits.
It helps to meet parents on their own turf. Encourage your teachers to do so, also. Parents will see you and your teachers as people first, authorities second.

7. Communicate with parents regularly.
Send home regular news from the principal. You could even write a column for your community newspaper.

8. Involve parents in school decision making.
Put together a parent advisory committee to help you develop school policy. Publicize the results of the committee's work.

9. Have a parent resource room in your building.
Do you have an extra room, office, or corner somewhere in your school? Ask parents or local businesses to donate sofas and chairs, a VCR, and parenting books, magazines, and videos. Parents will have a place to congregate and feel welcome in your school.

10. Host parent clubs.
Make your school into a community resource. Offer meeting space for book clubs or senior citizens' groups. Or suggest parenting clubs, such as one for parents of learning-disabled children or gifted and talented children.

© Copyright 2001 Resources for Educators, Inc.
a division of Aspen Publishers, Inc.

Successful Parent Involvement Programs

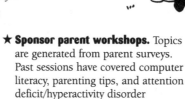

You can help your students be more successful in school. How? By getting their parents involved. As you know, research shows that children do better in school if their parents are familiar with the school and participate—at any level.

Here's the problem. How do you get today's busy parents to take time from their hectic schedules to get involved? Try these creative ideas your colleagues have dreamed up. They're suggestions that you can implement starting today!

Reach Out to Parents

Merritt Elementary School, located in a low-income neighborhood in the nation's capital, has achieved an astonishing 100 percent parent membership in the PTA. The school also has high attendance at school meetings and a group of parents who volunteer on a regular basis. How do they do it? The answer is a wide range of ideas that reach out to parents and bring them into the school.

★ **Offer incentives.** The school gives away food and gift certificates to parents who come to PTA meetings.
★ **Help with transportation.** The principal asks parents to volunteer to drive neighbors to school meetings.
★ **Hold parent nights.** Both parents and children attend these quarterly events where teachers go over class activities and parents can see their children's portfolios of schoolwork.
★ **Sponsor parent workshops.** Topics are generated from parent surveys. Past sessions have covered computer literacy, parenting tips, and attention deficit/hyperactivity disorder (ADHD).
★ **Require parents to attend parent-teacher conferences.** The principal personally calls parents who don't show up for the quarterly conferences and withholds report cards until they do.
★ **Involve teachers.** Teachers send home notices encouraging parent involvement and call parents to discuss their children's progress.

Contact: Dolores Abrams, Vice Principal, Merritt Elementary Extended School, Washington, DC, (202) 724-4618

Serve a Diverse Community

Is your school one of the growing number with a diverse community of parents? If so, take a page out of the book of Bailey's Elementary School, a Virginia school with children from 47 countries who speak more than 20 languages. By offering community services and opening the school to parents for various programs, the school has become a key part of its community. Here are some examples:

★ **Parent volunteers** collect and sort donated clothing and once a week hold a "boutique" where parents can shop for clothes at no cost. Volunteers also collect canned food and stock a food pantry that is open to needy families.
★ The school has high school students or parents act as **interpreters** for back-to-school night and other school events. Staffers who speak other languages are available during parent-teacher conferences.
★ Regular **evening events** run the gamut from family literary night to math night, dances, and karaoke parties.
★ Parents meet for **breakfast** and either have a roundtable discussion or listen to a speaker.

Contact: Jean Frey, Principal, Bailey's Elementary School for the Arts and Sciences, Falls Church, VA, (803) 575-6800

continues

Successful Parent Involvement Programs continued

Host Family Events

Getting parents excited about a big school event is a great way to keep them involved in your school all year long. Here are the programs that Northside Elementary School in Colorado has offered its students' families.

Each spring they host an **academic fair,** open to parents and the community at large. For two days and nights, the gym is filled with samples of student work in many subjects, including writing, art, and computers. In the evenings, parents are treated to student performances.

Other **family nights** vary from year to year. They've had "Art in the Park," where the school auctioned off about $1,000 worth of student-painted old wooden chairs. Also, they sponsored "Put Your Best Foot Forward," an auction of student-decorated old shoes. Another time the school hosted "Starry Starry Night." They set up large telescopes in a field and a "star tent"—which kids could crawl into and see "stars" all around them—in the gym. Families rotated through various stations, including a library station with books about stars and an art station with supplies for drawing pictures.

Contact: Bonnie Grigg, Principal, Northside Elementary School, Montrose, CO, (970) 249-2554

Open Your Doors

Some principals figure the best way to get parents involved is to make it easy for them to drop by and visit. Moline Elementary School in St. Louis offers "muffins and donuts" to entice parents.

They host monthly **"Donuts with Dad"** or **"Muffins with Mom"** mornings. These are informal events, staged as alternatives for parents who are too tired or busy to attend evening meetings. The morning schedule also brings in parents who work at night.

While the morning drop-ins began simply as a way to get parents into the school, other components may be added. There may be a brief talk to parents about reading with their children or a plug for attending upcoming parent-teacher conferences. By the way, the events are not limited to Mom or Dad—any "caring adult" in the child's life is welcome to attend.

Contact: Sarah Riss, Principal, Moline Elementary School, St. Louis, MO, (314) 868-9829, ext. 4811

Chapter **1–2**

Strengthen Communication

Improving Communication with All Families	1–2:1
School–Home Communication	1–2:1
Communication Can Increase Involvement	1–2:2
Supply Information Through Handbooks	1–2:6
A Handbook Can Make a Big Impression	1–2:7
19 Ideas for a Parent-Friendly Handbook	1–2:9
Craft Quality Newsletters	1–2:10
Tips To Improve Your School Newsletter	1–2:13
Does Your Newsletter Meet Parents' Needs?	1–2:13
Hear What Parents Have To Say	1–2:12
Use Phones Creatively	1–2:15
Idea Cards Yield Parent Input	1–2:17
Increase Communication with Technology	1–2:16
Web Site Ideas	1–2:18
Neighborhood Meetings	1–2:18
Orientation Video for Incoming Families	1–2:19
Students Must Take Communications Home	1–2:20
Reward Improves Teachers' Efforts	1–2:21
Providing Urgent Info via News Releases	1–2:21
Establishing Individual Contact	1–2:21
Communicating in Crisis Situations	1–2:22
Improve Media Relations	1–2:23
Materials You Can Use	1–2:25
Let's Communicate	1–2:25
Let Us Hear from You	1–2:26
Report to Parents	1–2:27

Principal's Positive Phone Calls 1–2:28
Thanks Bank Checks 1–2:29
"Beginning the New School Year" Letter 1–2:30

Chapter **1–2**

Strengthen Communication

IMPROVING COMMUNICATION WITH ALL FAMILIES

SCHOOL–HOME COMMUNICATION

The importance of quality, two-way communication between schools and parents cannot be overstated. Partnerships that lead to higher student achievement are difficult, if not impossible, to establish without it. Given this, it is ironic that so much time is spent teaching students listening and communication skills but that school leaders themselves do a mediocre job of listening and communicating with the community. Some examples are schools with multilingual families that make information available in English only; schools that dismiss or fail to follow up on parent and resident suggestions; schools that hesitate to cooperate with the media; schools that deliver predominantly "bad" news about students rather than "good" news; and schools that don't emphasize teacher communication with parents.

A study of Iowa school districts by Stephen Kleinsmith, assistant superintendent at the Millard Public Schools in Millard, Nebraska, shows that effective communication skills are the most important quality a school administrator can possess. The study asked school board presidents and superintendents to prioritize a list of 10 leadership qualities. The qualities ranked were stated as follows: values-driven work ethic, champion team builder, communicator, enthusiastic optimist, high expectations of self and others, lifelong learner, one who overcomes adversity, progressive change agent, visionary goal achiever, and willingness to take risks. Both superintendents and board presidents ranked communication as the most important trait a school leader could have.

"I consider this [these results] a clear reflection of the demands on school leaders and the need for them to work with the community around them," Kleinsmith says.

Communication Can Increase Involvement

It's essential to let parents know what's going on in school and what they can do to help you and their children. This is where effective home/school communication comes in.

Parents simply won't get involved if you don't keep them updated and informed about school activities. Any communication with parents should be clear about what is happening at the school, how parents are already helping out, and what other activities parents can do to get involved.

You also should repeat over and over again that you encourage parents to play a role at your school. Here are some ways you can make your parent communication more effective.

- **Make sure they read your printed materials.**

    Just about every school I know of has a school newsletter. This newsletter typically includes calendars, menus, and reports about activities happening at school. The challenge you face is to make sure parents read your newsletter.

    Here's a problem Principal Phyllis Chastain encountered and how she solved it. "I was at an aerobic class with a couple of parents," says Chastain of Winder, Georgia. "I asked them what they thought about the changes to our school's Christmas program this year. Their faces went blank. Then I realized these parents knew nothing about the program.

    "To make sure parents were actually reading our newsletter, I worked out a deal with the owner of a steak house. We now hold a monthly drawing for a free steak dinner for a family. The restaurant owner and the school go halves paying for the dinner. Parents enter the contest by having their children return the ballot from the school newsletter that goes home once a month. "Now parents call me to say they're disappointed after their ballot didn't get returned because it was lost in the pocket of their child's book bag!"

    A school newsletter is also an excellent tool to get feedback from parents. On the back page of her school newsletter, a Southern principal includes a Let's Communicate form that encourages parents to communicate with teachers.

    The form asks parents to list the name of the teacher they'd like to speak to, their names, their kids' names, and a telephone number the teacher can call. It also asks parents to say when they want to be called. This eliminates phone tag between parents and teachers.

    After parents fill out the form, they tear it off and mail it to the school.

    "When I receive a Let's Communicate form, I photocopy it and personally deliver it to the teacher," says the principal. "Then I ask the teacher to tell me when he or she makes the call to the parent."

    Principal Chris Hetzel of Waunakee, Wisconsin, asks parents to send information for her to use in the newsletter. "Our newsletter has a special brag section. Parents can let us know about anything their children have done that they want others to know about, and we share it in our newsletter. For example, a mother wrote that her daughter was one of the first in the state to pass a test in ice skating. Other parents write that their son earned a new badge in Cub Scouts or that one of their kids won an event in a youth swim meet."

An Eastern principal designed a two-part Let Us Hear from You! insert for his school newsletter.

"The form is intended to give me as much information as I can get about what parents like and don't like about my school," he says. "The first part of the form lets parents ask questions.

"It also allows parents to tell me any rumors they've heard about the school. I always have parents who contact me and ask, 'My child told me this. Is it true?' One parent was up in arms because her kid said that 100 kids at the school had lice. I want to nip rumors like this in the bud before they get out of hand. On the second part of the form, I ask parents to share an idea that might help the school. The Let Us Hear From You! form helps me keep my finger on the pulse of my parent community."

- **Take to the air waves to reach parents.**

In home-to-school communication, don't limit yourself to newsletters! Take advantage of radio or television also. Principal Stuart Hott of Shelbyville, Illinois, makes good use of a public access program on the radio. "Our local radio station has a Talk of the Town feature," says Hott. "The PTA simply asked the station manager if we could use it to get out the news of our school.

"I've appeared on the show to talk about specific programs and to remind parents to attend parent/teacher conferences. Teachers and students also discussed activities we planned for American Education Week.

"Since I started doing this, there's been a real change in the tone of parent communication. Instead of just the standard 'negatives,' I'm hearing a lot more positive things about our school. This I can live with."

Don't overlook the potential for reaching parents through local access television channels. Vice Principal John Lee hosts his own half-hour cable TV talk show.

"One of the things I try to do on the show is correct inaccurate statements people make about education in general and our district in particular," says Lee of New Milford, Connecticut.

The weekly 6:30 P.M. show, sponsored by the local school administrator's association, also features guests who discuss the issues with Lee.

"It's an opportunity for educators to talk intelligently to the public—without interference from people whose mentality is just, 'Lower my taxes, and I don't care what programs you cut.'"

So far, shows have focused on the district's budget, special education programs, and the school accreditation process. Lee tells me he used the first show to explain why today's schools are different from those a generation ago.

"This is always a point of contention with some district residents," he says. "So we discussed how changes in society have affected schools by looking at the impact broken families, drugs, and violence have had on education.

"The point I wanted to communicate was that things have changed since the '50s when chewing gum was the Number One discipline problem in schools."

The show's format typically consists of three, eight-minute segments. Guests have included the district superintendent, other principals, subject-area coordinators, and a former school board member.

"A high school student volunteers to run the camera," says Lee. "All I have to do is sit at a table and talk education with my guests."

Getting on the air presented no problem, he adds. "The administrators' association contacted the cable company to ask if it was interested. The first thing the coordinator of public access wanted to know was when we could start!

"I know for a fact that district residents watch the show. Whenever I go to the bank or the post office, I hear comments and reactions to the show. Students talk to me about it the next morning too."

- **Send positive information about the student home.**

Do you get the maximum mileage out of your classroom visits? A West Virginia Principal does. His parent communication reports on the favorable things he sees in the classroom. Then he sends parents a letter about their kids.

"I visit my school's classrooms every day. To let parents know about the positive instruction going on, I complete a form that tells them what I've seen," he says. "Then I run off a copy for each student, so he or she can take it home."

"I mention to parents that I visited their kids' classroom," says the principal. "Then I share one or two activities I witnessed during the visit.

"For example, I've told parents about a science teacher who used a ball-and-incline exercise to explain a principle of geometry, or a P.E. teacher who uses an obstacle course to develop students' motor skills."

He closes the letter with a message to parents about how important home/school cooperation is in their kids' educational growth.

He says the form is a great way for parents to hear good news about what's going on in their children's classroom.

"The benefits we reap from this strategy are satisfied and informed parents and teachers who appreciate my recognition of their top-notch work," he says. "These far outweigh the cost of paper and photocopying. Most parents call me after they receive a letter to say, 'I never knew my son or daughter was learning such interesting material in school!'"

- **Let your fingers do the walking.**

These days, it's easy to use technology to improve your communication with parents.

Principal Fred Ortman's Starline (from his school's nickname) lets parents call 24 hours a day for up-to-the-minute information about what's happening in their son or daughter's classroom.

One of the big pluses of the system is that Pacific Bell Telephone of California makes the service available to schools for a nominal fee—$50 a month. "It's Pac Bell's contribution as a good corporate citizen to education," he explains.

The system requires little work or technology on the school's part and is operated from Pac Bell's offices.

The real beauty of Starline, however, is that it gives parents direct access to information from their kids' teachers. "Parents can dial in a code and number and receive a message from a teacher about homework assignments or events like an upcoming field trip. We even have an extension number for our bilingual teacher."

To make sure parents use the service, Ortman put together a directory that each student is required to take home.

"This is modeled after a telephone book and instructs parents on how to use Starline," he says. "In addition, it gives them each teacher's extension number.

"The need for communication between school and home has never been more crucial. I believe Starline has been a tremendous way for us to improve ours."

Action: It might be worth a call to your telephone company to see if it offers a similar service to schools.

You can also use this type of phone service to shoot down rumors that always seem to plague schools. Principal John Beaty of Winston-Salem, North Carolina, tells this story . . . .

"Last year, there was a verbal confrontation involving two boys—one black and one white," says Beaty. "It was resolved by a staff member, the students went home at the end of the day, and everything was OK—so we thought.

"The next morning, the community was buzzing with rumors that a race riot was brewing. The word was out that armed KKK members were even planning to show up at school! Our absentee rate the following day was 11 percent higher than average. Many parents called to tell me that they feared for their kids' safety and weren't sending them to school.

"When the news media get their teeth into something like this, they just don't let go—and in this case, they didn't. There's no way I could control what the media said."

The solution to the problem? Simple. Beaty used the school's Phonemaster Notification System to give parents the real story.

"If there's an incident that could spawn rumors, we program our automatic calling system to start calling immediately and into the evening.

"The next morning, I review a printout of parents who haven't answered calls, and we phone them.

"Now when a rumor surfaces, parents call to say, 'I heard something about the school. Since I didn't hear from you, though, I dismissed it as a rumor.'"

- **Set up a room in your school to encourage teachers to communicate with parents.**

    If your school doesn't have the resources for a telephone in every classroom, take heart. Assistant Principal Kevin Davis set up a Parent Communication Room to encourage parent and teacher communication.

    Teachers now have access to a room for the express purpose of contacting parents.

    "By designating it our Parent Communication Room, we show teachers that we're serious about the importance of regular parent contact and that we expect them to make the effort," says Davis of Carmel, Indiana.

    "The room has several telephones, along with samples of positive and negative letters teachers can use and envelopes. The school pays teachers' postage. Telephone records and mailing addresses are also handy to make the job of communicating with parents easier.

    "In a sense, we're telling our teachers, 'If you have a problem with a student, don't dawdle—let parents know about it. If you have something positive to share with parents—don't put that off, either. Go to the Parent Communication Room and make contact."

    Davis expects the room to improve the school's existing parent communication program. "We also have a computer calling system to let parents know what's happening with their kids," he says. "It's been successful and useful, but it's still somewhat impersonal.

    "Now, however, if a parent gets a computer call from the school and a personal phone call, note, or letter from a teacher, communication packs an extra punch."

Supply Information Through Handbooks

Handbooks are one of the most efficient ways for schools to communicate information about programs, facilities, policies, and procedures. Generally, two styles of handbooks exist: the school–parent handbook distributed by individual schools and a district handbook available through the central district office.

A strong parent focus makes parent handbooks most appealing, says Assistant Principal David Jordan, of Henderson, Kentucky. His school's handbook begins with a letter inviting parents to participate in school activities, followed by pages about education and family-related topics, including helping children succeed in school, helping children adjust to a parent's remarriage, learning to talk with children, and guidelines for setting rules. "Parents read this section more closely than they do the information geared to students [that appears later in the handbook]," he says.

Principal Nancy Renfro, of Indian Head, Maryland, summarizes important policy-related information on two pages in her handbook that she calls the Quick Reference Section. Parents enjoy the convenience of having policy details in one place, she says, rather than having to use an index to locate specific information.

Other handbook practices that can set the tone of the parent–school relationship include:

- a passage in the welcome letter emphasizing parents' roles and responsibilities in children's success or failure in school
- information on school contacts that is prominently displayed (front cover, back cover, boldface type)
- an open letter from faculty inviting parent dialogue
- information on contacting staff members, organized by department and grade level, including guidance counselors
- dates of parent–teacher conferences, a summary of their importance, and expectations for them
- an introduction to the volunteer program and volunteer opportunities
- a building map to guide visitors
- a calendar of school activities
- handbooks available in languages other than English

Like parent handbooks, district handbooks are an excellent means of communicating with the community at large, as well as families that are new to the district and trying to choose a school. And, like parent handbooks, these publications can be put together in a variety of ways.

The Fort Wayne, Indiana, school district publishes a handbook annually as a guide to its School Choice Fair, a one-day event open to the public, in which all of the district's schools promote curriculum and activities to parents and community members. The 28-page booklet for the fair begins with information about each school in the district, including the school address and telephone number, the name of the principal, and unique features of the school listed in bullet form. In the outside margin area of each page are snippets of information, such as the process for applying to a school. Also included in the booklet is a matrix providing an at-a-glance summary of the location and features of each school, a district map, enrollment forms for both elementary and secondary schools, and short synopses of other district programs, including adult and continuing education, career education, alternative learning, special education, and community programs.

The fair is an outstanding way for schools to promote involvement by telling their stories through a variety of media. Conversely, it is an excellent means for parents and residents to ask questions and communicate with the schools. The event also addresses growing concern among public schools about competition from private schools, because it is an opportunity to advertise the strengths of the public schools.

All handbooks should be updated annually. To help identify specific items that need clarification or that were previously omitted, Principal Patricia Andrews, of Wausau, Wisconsin, each year asks parents who are new to the school to keep a running list of school-related problems, questions, and subjects they wish they had known about. She uses this information as a guide to rewrite the handbook.

At a Rochester, New York, elementary school, parents receive a new handbook each year. Principal Marie Ginther inserts a letter in the handbooks that asks parents how the publication can be improved. "They often tell us they feel something has been overlooked or ask us to clarify some policy for them. This feedback has made our handbook more understandable," she says.

A Handbook Can Make a Big Impression

A school student handbook can either be a powerful tool that inspires parents to get involved in your school—or just another piece of junk information that gets thrown away.

Many schools mail their handbook to parents or have their kids take it home with them. However you get yours to parents, be sure it makes them feel that they're an important part of your school.

A school handbook should do more than just explain your school's policies and procedures. Here are ways you can use your handbook to motivate parents to take an interest in school activities.

- **The handbook should begin with a parent focus.**

    "The first page of our handbook is an open invitation to parents to take an active role in their kids' education," says an Eastern principal. "For instance, it suggests that they discuss school with their kids daily, visit classrooms, and participate in parent/teacher conferences. This message is a reminder to parents that we value their involvement all year long."

- **It should ask parents for ideas to improve the handbook.**

    "We give parents a new handbook every school year," says Principal Marie Ginther of Rochester, New York. "It covers our school policies and procedures from when a child is absent to volunteer opportunities for parents.

    "We also send a letter with it that asks parents how the handbook can be improved. Parents often tell us they feel something has been overlooked or ask us to clarify some policy for them. This type of feedback has helped make our handbook more understandable to parents."

- **The handbook must be usable.**

    Many parents scan school handbooks and then banish them to the old magazine file. That's not what you want them to do! You want parents to use their handbooks throughout the school year.

    "To make sure parents refer to our handbook over and over, we combine it with the school's events and activities calendar," says Principal Francine Bullock.

    "The calendar includes all our policies, procedures, and expectations. Every month, parents learn something because they use the calendar to find out what's going on at school."

- **It must have information just for parents.**

    "Several years ago, we added a parent section to our handbook that really gets parents' attention," says Principal David Jordan of Henderson, Kentucky.

    The section begins with a letter from administrators encouraging parents to participate in school and in their children's activities. Then it deals with specifics, like how to help a child succeed in school, how to talk with children, and how to set reasonable rules at home. Parents can also read about report cards, curriculum, standardized tests, clubs students can join, severe weather rules, etc.

    "We've discovered that parents read this section more closely than they do the information geared to students.

    "Parents will see tremendous changes in their children as they go through school, and we want to prepare them by explaining how they can help their kids succeed."

- **Parents need to sign a statement that they've read and understood your handbook.**

    Remember, the most painstakingly written and designed handbook is useless unless parents read it. Here's a way to make sure your handbook is read: At Principal Shirley Eye's school, students don't receive a locker assignment until a form verifying that they and their parents have read the handbook has been signed and returned to the classroom teacher.

    "Since this is a 'something for something' exchange, most students return the forms," says Eye of Appomatox, Virginia. "After all, kids don't want to carry all their books and coats around the school for the entire year."

    The form Eye uses doubles as the back page of her handbook. This makes it easy for parents to tear it out when they've finished reading the handbook.

    No matter what incentive you use, Eye says it's always a good idea for parents and students to sign something that says they've read and understood the information in the handbook.

    "Verification forms are especially important when enforcing rules and regulations with students," she says. "A lot of kids try to shirk responsibility by saying, 'I didn't know.' When you require parents and students to review the handbook and sign a form, kids can't say this. It's also support for me in case a parent objects to my actions.

    "For example, we recently confiscated a student's pocketknife under our weapons policy. His parents appealed to the district, but the school board backed me up. A major factor in its decision was that both the parents and the student were aware of the policy because they had reviewed the handbook."

19 Ideas for a Parent-Friendly Handbook

Here are 19 strategies other principals use to make their school handbooks more parent-friendly and at the same time, encourage parent involvement:

1. **State school policies on the inside covers.** Principal Nancy Renfro's handbook of Indian Head, Maryland, has two pages that highlight important information for parents. Because of its convenience, she calls it the quick reference section. It explains student attendance, book return policy, dress code, and the school's policy on student telephone calls.

2. **Add a closing note from faculty and staff.** Renfro's handbook ends with a note encouraging open communication between the school and home by inviting parents to bring their concerns to the school's attention.

3. **Include a statement of the school's educational philosophy.** A South Carolina high school lists its 10 areas of responsibility, including "to provide each student with an opportunity to explore individual talents and interests," and "to establish a program of education that will enable every student to develop individual potential."

    A good variation on this is to list your school's objectives for students. An Indiana school, for example, includes four goals under its skills and knowledge objective.

4. **Add a welcome to parents.** At Associate Principal Mike Hertting's school in Wausau, Wisconsin, the first page of the student/parent handbook welcomes parents and explains what's in store for them and their children.

    A twist on this idea is a message to parents that explains their responsibility to participate actively in their son or daughter's education.

5. **Make it easy for parents to contact the school when their son or daughter will be absent.** At the top of an Iowa school's attendance policy is a phone number parents can call if a student will be absent.

6. **Print school contact information where it can't be missed.** On the back of the cover of his school's handbook, Principal Tony Fieder of Cambridge, Ontario includes the school's address and telephone number.

7. **Give the school's office hours.** Many schools forget to include this in their handbooks. A short statement that the building is open on school days from 7:45 A.M. to 3:45 P.M. is all you need.

8. **Include faculty credentials.** I like this idea, but it's something few schools do. A Indiana school has two pages on its teachers' academic credentials. A sample entry reads: Teacher Jane Doe, B.S., XYZ University, M.S., XYZ University, English Teacher and English Department Chairperson.

9. **Feature quotes about education on the cover.** Principal Bob Arp of Columbus, Nebraska, includes quotes from Ralph Waldo Emerson and Carl Sagan in his handbook. Quotes can also be used throughout the handbook!

10. **Use photographs of students on the cover.** A Missouri school has a great cover for its student/parent handbook. It features pictures of the student council president, vice president, secretary, and treasurer.

    You can take this a step further by using photographs of students in action throughout the handbook. A New Jersey school includes pictures of graduation ceremonies, assemblies, and school field trips.

11. **Include a map of your building.** The layouts of many large schools can be confusing to visitors. At Assistant Principal George Chandos' school in Phillipsburg, New Jersey, a map of the building is on the inside back cover of the handbook.
12. **Personalize the handbook by adding an "issued to" statement on the handbook's cover.** Principal Randy Pratt of Butler, New Jersey, puts this on the cover.

    It "personalizes" his handbook by asking kids to write in their names and those of family members.
13. **Include a welcome to students and parents from the student council president.** A New Jersey principal prints the president's message on page three of his school's handbook.
14. **Feature staff contact information by grade level.** An Eastern school's handbook makes it easy for parents to contact teachers by listing their phone numbers by the grade level they teach.
15. **Share positive results from the previous year.** A New York school's handbook reports on improvements made after the school implemented its new attendance policy.

    An example of positive results: "Average student attendance increased from 90 percent to 96 percent last school year."
16. **Print a calendar of school activities for the year.** The key here is not to cram school activities into the dates on the calendar. Instead, print this information by the side of the calendar to increase readability.
17. **Include a welcome message from teachers.** This is an excellent opportunity for teachers to encourage parents to get involved in their kids' education.
18. **Mention parent/teacher conference on page one.** A Wyoming school runs this note about the school's parent night: "The purpose of parent night is to strengthen parent/teacher relationships, to encourage parental input, and to conduct conferences. We look forward to meeting with you."
19. **Share your school's history.** An Illinois school devotes one page of its handbook to the school's history. This is a particularly effective way to give parents new to the school information about its historical role in the community.

Craft Quality Newsletters

Newsletters are the most common way schools communicate with external audiences. Principal Michael Dietz reports that they also are considered the most reliable source of information, according to a telephone survey of parents at Lake Shore Middle School in Mequon, Wisconsin. Every fourth individual listed in the parent registry was asked what he or she liked best about school communications. The school's monthly newsletter scored consistently well.

What makes a first-class newsletter? Good information, yes. But Superintendent Jon Rednak says appearance is as important as content. "If teachers and educators want to be looked upon in a more professional manner, they need to provide top-quality, professional looking information to parents and community residents."

Dietz, however, says newsletters don't have to be flashy and polished to get the job done. "They simply need to have the information in them that parents want."

The best newsletters strike a balance between these two positions. They also follow general publication rules.

Know the audience. All communication must be tailored to the audience and its information needs. Technical jargon, which often peppers internal communications to faculty and staff, means little to parents and community members.

However, it is equally important not to oversimplify communications. "Talking down to people puts them off as much as talking above them," says Kleinsmith. Both he and Rednak say optimum readability is best achieved by asking members of the target audience to review a draft copy of communications.

If a written report isn't communicating what you actually mean, it must be changed," says Rednak, "or people will be left to make assumptions about what it means. And assumptions often turn into rumors, which can have a tremendously negative effect on the district's relationship with the community." He describes a past district report outlining an elementary school reorganization as "so unclear, [that] people completely misunderstood what we were thinking of doing." The board reacted by dismissing the entire idea.

Review of draft copy is especially valuable when communication is related to a controversial issue. Kleinsmith says, "Readers can provide extremely valuable insight as to whether the content of the communication will be inflammatory. Once you go public with something, you can't go back—so you need a variety of people to look at communications prior to their final draft."

To assess readers' specific communication wants and needs, Kleinsmith conducts focus groups. He randomly invites members of a given publication's target audience to participate, then sends them copies of the publication and preparation instructions in advance of the meeting. During the session, he compares information currently provided in the publication with information that participants described as most important.

In combination with focus groups, Kleinsmith invites wide-scale reader feedback on school publications by placing in all communications a standing invitation for readers to communicate their opinions. A variety of response methods, including telephone, fax, mail, or electronic mail (e-mail), are encouraged.

Publish in more than one language. Part of meeting audience needs is making communications available to everyone in the audience, not just those who speak English. Principal Fred Ortman says his school in the Los Angeles area produces all communications, whether sent to parents or the media, in both English and Spanish.

"Our school is 70 percent Hispanic, and we need to be welcoming to all parents, many of whom speak only Spanish," he says. "By making our communication user friendly, we're doing our best not to exclude families from our school."

Principal Brenda Dykes provides Spanish translators at meetings of the Parent–Teacher Organization. Because of this practice, she says more than 200 parents often attend the meetings.

Include only essential information. Long work hours for parents and busy extracurricular schedules for students mean that "the shorter and sweeter a story is, the better it is," says Kleinsmith. "People will read something that makes its point quickly and clearly, but they probably won't read a lengthy piece unless it's about a really hot topic."

To hold readers' attention, he recommends using bullet-style lists and short summaries of what administrative decisions mean to parents, instead of in-depth descriptions of problems and issues. Repeated features, such as lunch menus and calendars of events, should always be placed in the same place in the publication. Readers who always look for specific information become accustomed to looking in the same location for it. Moving those features is both frustrating and inconvenient to the reader.

Balance attention to people and policy. Many school newsletters tend to be very procedure oriented, as opposed to stressing student and teacher achievement, says Amy Friedman, communications coordinator at Millard Public Schools in Millard, Nebraska. "This is not to say that newsletters shouldn't be used as vehicles to pass along procedural information. But people like to read about people."

Use an easy-to-read format. Large quantities of information are not necessarily what the audience wants, says Friedman, especially if it is difficult to read. "There's a misconception that a lot of communication is the best communication, so [schools] develop 10- to 12-page newsletters full of blocks of copy."

The problem, however, is that to readers with low reading skills and readers who did not enjoy school, this format may appear intimidating and difficult. Consequently, these individuals may only skim the information or, more likely, she says, not even look at it. "Our [district] goal is to use more graphics in our publications and to present information in a two-column format. We're also trying to use more white space," says Friedman.

Plan ahead. Appeal is broadened by mapping out which topics will be part of each newsletter (e.g., even balance of emphasis on academics and athletics). This approach also gives the administrator additional control over each issue's content, especially when writing and/or production is turned over to staff or parent volunteers. "When I require staff to write stories about their areas of responsibility, I tell them which month I plan for the article to appear and give them a specific date that I want the completed story turned in," says Kleinsmith.

Proofread. Although it may seem like a small, commonsense detail, proofreading is easily sacrificed to meet deadlines. But few things can make a school look as unprofessional as misspellings and incorrect sentence structure. (Those are, after all, things schools are supposed to be teaching.)

Include the school logo. This technique is a lesson that schools can learn from businesses, says Friedman. "[Businesses] make sure their logos appear on everything associated with them. The audience learns to recognize the logo and, as that happens, the organization's identity strengthens."

Hear What Parents Have To Say

As a principal, you have to make the time to listen to parents if you want them to get involved. Here are six strategies to get their input.

TIPS TO IMPROVE YOUR SCHOOL NEWSLETTER

If you spend the time and effort to publish a newsletter for parents, make sure it's interesting to look at and read. Here are some easy-to-implement tips on how to make your newsletter a must-read:

- **Give a student Page One coverage.** "Our newsletter always runs a story about a student's accomplishments on the front page," says Principal Samuel Brewer of Muscle Shoals, Alabama. "For example, it recently featured a second-grader who held her own vocal recital. This is a great PR tool because it helps build rapport with parents, kids like the recognition, and students enjoy reading about their classmates."

- **Have kids pick student work for publication.** "A four-student editorial board selects student work to showcase in each issue of our newsletter," says Principal Susan Mawhiny of Guelph, Ontario. "The students on the board are chosen by their peers and teachers. We've trained them to judge work on its merits, not on the basis of who did it. We also ask them to pick something from each class."

- **Make parent involvement opportunities a high point.** If you want parents to be more involved, focus on specific activities for them. Include several articles on how parents can get involved, the importance of being involved, and how children appreciate their parents taking an active role in their education.

DOES YOUR NEWSLETTER MEET PARENTS' NEEDS?

An Illinois principal uses a quick survey to find out if his newsletter is meeting the needs of parents. On a regular basis, he includes this one-page Now It's Your Turn survey on the back page. Here's what it asks:

1. Do you read the (name of the publication)?
2. Is the newsletter worthwhile?
3. What do you like about (name of the publication)?
4. What don't you like about (name of the publication)?
5. What would you like to see included in future issues?

Be sure to give parents instructions for returning their responses to you by including your school's address or asking them to send it to school with their son or daughter.

1. **Use the telephone effectively.**

    A Southern principal uses the phone to get to know parents and their needs. But with a large student population, it takes a personal commitment on her part to reach everyone. Here's how she does it:

    "I give one grade level a form each week and ask the chairperson to route it to his or her teachers," says the principal.

    "Each teacher writes in the names of two students, their parents' home and work phone numbers, the parents' names, if different from the students', and what the kids did that was positive.

    "The chairperson returns the form to me by Thursday, and I make five to seven calls to parents by Sunday. My assistant principal also calls parents. Last year, we made nearly 400 calls. Sunday afternoon is the best time to call parents because they're usually home. But it's fun to call parents at work to relay positive news, so they can tell coworkers.

"Teachers have been willing to make more phone calls to parents because they know the assistant principal and I are doing the same thing. Plus, I've got 1,050 students here, which makes it tough to get to know parents. The positive phone calls really help."

2. **Have lunch with parents at their workplace.**

   Principal Stuart Hott's Lunch with the Principal program gives him the opportunity to meet regularly with parents.

   "A majority of our parents work for a single employer," he tells me. "So once a month, I visit them there over lunch.

   "As parents come in to eat, I introduce myself and give them a copy of my parent newsletter," says Hott. "This is a great way to reach parents—I've even snared volunteers to help with events like our academic honors banquet!

   "Parents appreciate the informality of these lunch visits because they can voice their concerns and get things off their chests."

3. **Hold town meetings with parents.**

   Offering parents a forum to express their opinions and ideas can be a great way to hear what's on their minds.

   "When I was a principal in a school where five small towns had consolidated, I set up town meetings in every community," says Administrator Stephen Kleinsmith.

   "I usually picked three or four topics to put on the agenda to give people an idea of what we would be discussing.

   "These were things like discipline, another school policy, or a topic parents had expressed an interest in, like the curriculum.

   I made sure I listened to parents' input and then put it to use. Parents want to know their opinions and suggestions are important. Otherwise, they'll stop coming and stop talking to you."

4. **Hold monthly principal coffees.**

   Parents should have the opportunity to bring their concerns to you informally if they don't like the idea of large group meetings. For these parents, a Midwestern principal holds a monthly coffee that might be just the ticket.

   "Their concerns may be something that is going on in a specific classroom or a schoolwide policy that they have questions about," he says.

   "You need to make sure all parents feel welcome to attend. I ran announcements in the school newsletter and used word-of-mouth advertising. I would personally invite some parents and ask them to tell their neighbors and friends."

   If you want more people attending your coffees, try Principal Joyce Williams' strategy.

   - Meet in a "welcoming" part of the school. "We use our school's media center," says Williams of Corydon, Indiana. "It's an open, cheery area with plenty of windows and a relaxing feel to it. Teachers are often in the media center reading stories to their students. It's a place where parents feel comfortable, not intimidated."
   - After the meeting, let parents know what's happening at school. "We typically wrap things up by showing parents our new computers and how they work or by visiting classrooms to see student learning," she says.

"I meet with the group from 8:45 A.M. to 9:30 A.M. and bring parents up-to-date on what's going on at school. Then I open the session up for questions. There is only one rule: We don't talk about individual kids or individual teachers.

"These meetings are very helpful. Anytime you can make parents feel you're accessible and they're welcome, you'll have fewer problems with their kids."

5. **Ask parents to host meetings in their homes.**

    "Our district now has CLASS meetings," says Principal Marie Ginther. "These meetings give parents a chance to host meetings in their homes. (CLASS stands for community learning about students and school.)

    "For example, if several parents have questions about the budget, I'll bring together the relevant staff to answer them.

    "Then parents set up a date and time and invite other parents to their home to discuss the budget."

6. **Parent Advisory Link gives parents an outlet for participation.**

    Principal Bill Freeman's school came up with a way to give parents a major voice in the education process. Parents can join a group called the Parent Advisory Link.

    "This group was set up so parents would have a direct link into the ongoing areas of education like fine arts, discipline policy, and curriculum," says Principal Bill Freeman of Braidwood, Illinois.

    "At the first meeting, I asked parents how they'd like these meetings to be run. They told me they didn't want any officers for the group and asked me to lead meetings. They also insisted that no teachers attend meetings, so they'd feel free to voice their opinions."

    Here's how Freeman runs the meetings.

    - He sets a flexible agenda. "I always have a couple topics I want to explain to parents—for example, recent test scores or our school improvement plan. Then I focus on what they have to say."
    - He makes sure everyone has time to contribute to the discussion. Freeman goes around the room and gives each parent 24 seconds to speak. Anyone can say whatever he or she likes. Parents often make suggestions like holding a meeting to discuss violence in school.
    - He gives parents an assignment. "Before we end the meeting, I give parents a 'homework' assignment for the next meeting.

        "This could be asking their son or daughter how the school year is going. I might ask them about what they've heard downtown about the school system or ask them for their input on specific classes."
    - He finds out what parents learned at the meeting. "I give them an exit quiz about what they learned at the meeting and how I could improve the next one. I always supply refreshments and make it a special night out for parents."

Use Phones Creatively

At Principal Jim Wheeler's school, parents can call in and find out what TV programs are recommended by the school. "Our media coordinator reviews TV listings for programs that are appropriate for students," says Wheeler. "Then she spends a few minutes each day recording her recommended programs on our hotline."

Many of the programs are on The Discovery Channel or PBS, Wheeler of Winston-Salem, North Carolina, says. "We think educational programs are the best for students. We're trying to get parents to keep their kids from watching undesirable programs. This is one way we encourage them to do this."

Another way you can use phones to your advantage is to give your teachers instant access to them, so they can call parents for any reason.

Principal Patty Madison has phones in every teacher's room in her school. "Teachers keep a list of their students and their parents' phone numbers right by the phone," says Madison of Tom Bean, Texas. "They've done a wonderful job of calling parents the minute their child does something great.

"For example, a teacher can phone a parent and say, 'John has something to tell you.' The student gets on the phone and tells his parent that he just scored 100% on a math test."

Madison was worried that parents would be upset if they received phone calls at work, but they've been very supportive. "I've had no complaints about the phone calls. In fact, I've received many calls to thank me for what we're doing.

"Not only do the phones help teachers solve discipline problems and communicate positive news better, but they also cut down on paperwork and phone duties for my office staff. Plus, it really wasn't very expensive to do because much of the labor and supplies were donated."

Increase Communication with Technology

Increased computer resources, including access to Internet and World Wide Web and modernized telephone systems, are expanding the communication of schools with both internal and external audiences. For example, e-mail allows school administrators to send and receive information 24 hours a day. The World Wide Web allows schools to post and update information that can be accessed from any computer with an Internet navigation program. Remote-access video can link students in different locations for a single classroom presentation and discussion.

These and other technologies should be as much a part of a school's communication repertoire as newsletters, newspapers, radio, and television. As people become more sophisticated with home computers and other new technology, they will look to these sources of information as much as they have relied on traditional communication methods in the past. Many districts already use e-mail to keep staff apprised of school news and to dispel rumors.

For obvious reasons, e-mail works best with small, well-defined audiences, such as staff members, board members, Parent–Teacher Organizations, and individual clubs. To reach more global audiences, such as parents or the community at large, it is more effective to use a home page on the World Wide Web.

For high usability of a Web site, only a few photos should be used, and the page should be kept current. The time needed to download multiple photographs will frustrate users who want to get in and out of the Web site quickly.

IDEA CARDS YIELD PARENT INPUT

Parent surveys don't have to be long to be effective. Brief, simple ones often work well. And parents appreciate the time saved by a short survey. Take it from an Eastern principal:

"Once a year, I send home Here's an Idea postcards to parents," she says. "On one side is a space to write a response and lightbulb in the top left corner.

"I ask parents to give me one idea to improve the school and return the cards to school with their kids. I respond with a letter to each one who sends me a card. It's a good way to let parents know that we value their opinions.

"Suggestions run from procedural to curriculum issues and have included ideas on how to revise the foreign language curriculum to how to improve food in the cafeteria."

To browse school home pages, consult the School Home Page Registry on the World Wide Web. Most schools with home pages are accessible alphabetically by state. The address is <http://web66.coled.umn.edu/schools.html>. For a list of potential items for a Web site, see the Web Site Ideas, which enumerates more than 20 ideas that other school home pages have included.

Internet access also makes schools excellent community resources for computer information and training and is an effective vehicle for bringing nonparent residents into the school. The Beachwood Public School District in suburban Cleveland, Ohio, is promoting communitywide computer literacy through beginning and intermediate computer courses for senior citizens as part of its Elderclass program. The program, which offers services in addition to the computer courses, has wide appeal to older adult community members and generates a large amount of school support from that group.

Superintendent Rednak's Pennsylvania district opens its high school library as part of the Second Shift program that makes school facilities available to the public after normal business hours. The library is one of the few places where any member of the public can use a computer and access Internet resources. Volunteers from the school's coaching staff, Parent–Teacher Association, booster clubs, and faculty supervise the library during late-afternoon and evening hours, when students, parents, and community residents can take advantage of the technology available.

Video technology should also be considered a valuable communication tool, says Andrew Thomas, community relations coordinator at the Canandaigua City Schools in Canandaigua, New York. His district created a videotape for elementary school orientation that gives newcomers a first-person look at the building's layout, a summary of rules and procedures, and a glimpse of the school's atmosphere.

"We felt that with VCRs in every home and more people turning to video as a way of gaining knowledge, many parents would have a real use for a product like this," he says. "In the past, when someone inquired about the school, we sent him or her a map and some literature. That's valuable. But with video you have a medium that shows pictures of what the school actually looks like and how daily events happen. We believe that if parents and students can watch together in the comfort of their own living rooms, students will feel a lot better about coming to school on their first day."

WEB SITE IDEAS

Consider the following elements when developing your school's home page on the World Wide Web:

- School activity calendar
- Staff directory with individual telephone numbers and e-mail addresses
- Main telephone number and street address of school
- List and contact information for school administrators and department heads
- Student–parent handbook
- Recent editions of school publications (e.g., school newsletter, school newspaper, school-oriented news stories)
- Lunch menus
- Event and activity notices
- School calendar
- Building map and virtual tour
- Volunteer opportunities
- Samples of student work from unique programs or award-winning projects
- Parenting tips and strategies
- Mission statement
- Scholarship opportunities
- E-mail communication opportunities
- District information
- Links to other education-related sites
- School history
- Student government news
- Children's activities
- Alumni news and updates
- Department news (e.g., athletics, academics, drama, and band)
- Club information
- PTA/PTO information
- Awards and scholarship updates
- School neighborhood and city information
- Principal's message
- Homework and discipline policies

Neighborhood Meetings

To maintain awareness of school activities, Superintendent and High School Principal John Metallo conducts regular, informational meetings for parents and community residents in the heart of their comfort zones—their homes. Members of the Fort Plain Central School District's Parent–Teacher Organization in Fort Plain, New York, organize the gatherings, where attendees can talk with school staff and parents about specific issues and/or concerns.

"We wanted to foster support for our school programs and, at the same time, generate input from parents and community members," says Metallo. "The neighborhood meeting idea is an effective way to do this."

The meetings have been particularly effective in the dissemination of program-specific information. Past topics have included state financial aid and other resources, student grouping, ability tracking, cooperative learning, services available through the school, and the high school's reading lists, as well as how parents can contact teachers and how students can conduct college searches.

Rumor control is an added benefit of the meetings, says Metallo. "Even when people don't truly know how things work, they think they do. These meetings give us a chance to tell people how the school district actually does things."

Preparation and Participation

The team of school representatives varies from one meeting to the next. Metallo typically attends, as does the district's other principal; others including teachers, guidance counselors, and school nurses participate as relevant topics are discussed. These participants give short overviews of current events in their respective areas at the meeting's start. Audience questions follow.

Metallo estimates that 10–40 people attend each of the six to eight meetings each year. Additional meetings are held as situations warrant. "The most important factor in getting maximum participation is that we conduct meetings when the community wants us to," he says.

Volunteer hosts and hostesses, who are solicited by the Parent–Teacher Association, prepare refreshments and develop the guest list. They may invite everyone from the neighborhood, or the meeting may be organized only for parents who have children of a certain age.

The home atmosphere, says Metallo, improves attendance and participation. "The informal atmosphere of a neighbor's home is attractive to parents and residents, especially those who are uncomfortable in the school's formal setting. People are less intimidated by school staff and more at ease with themselves," he says.

Although the neighborhood meeting is a simple idea, it is not one Metallo will easily give up. "The meetings are well attended and very positive. Participants all express interest in the opportunity to do it again," he says.

Orientation Video for Incoming Families

Program Description

To ease the transition to a new school, the Canandaigua City Schools in Canandaigua, New York, developed a 20-minute orientation videotape for parents and students new to the district's primary school. The video presentation, "Discover the Excellence," is narrated by two third-grade students. This videotape outlines school rules and practices and is available for checkout at the local library.

The project won a 1995 Pinnacle Award for excellence in education in the board and district operations category.

Community Relations Coordinator Andrew Thomas says the videotape provides parents and children, whether new kindergarteners or transfer students, with a friendly, nonthreatening orientation session that they can review and discuss at home.

"We believe that if parents and students watch together in the comfort of their own living rooms, students will feel a lot better about coming to school on their first day," says Thomas.

Benefits

The primary benefit of the videotape is that it provides another vehicle for explaining school policies and practices. The school handbook includes the same information, says Thomas, but parents don't always realize which information in it is most important.

"And some information that's important when people first come to the school is not part of the handbook," he says. "They want to know what the various programs are like, what the people look like, where the cafeteria is in relation to the student's room, that sort of thing. Parents can get [some information] from a map, but it's tougher to visualize. The video shows actual parents and students doing things."

One of the practices depicted in the videotape is the district's rotating, 6-day schedule of "specials." "We're always questioned about that, so we made sure it was addressed in the video," says Thomas.

The video presentation format also contributes to students' sense of security. "The tape isn't always slick, but you don't want slickness. You want something that speaks the truth and appeals to parents and to their children," he says. "When the video tour guides say, 'Let's go visit the classroom,' it's friendly [and] engaging, and the students watching feel like they're being spoken to personally, because students like themselves are leading the tour. This is far more appealing than if the tape featured an administrator talking about policies."

Production Process

The idea for the videotape was conceived by a school board subcommittee focused on community relations. It is patterned after a tourism video presentation that featured a cab driver narrating a tour of the city with the camera as the passenger. It gives viewers a first-person look at the school building's layout and explains common rules and procedures. Producing the videotape involved several subcommittee members, including school board members, students and staff, and Thomas, who has a background in television production.

Two third-grade students served as tour guides. As they walked through the school, they described where they were and explained rules and procedures. When all video footage was collected, the tape was professionally edited. The entire production process took about one year, at a cost of approximately $1,000; most of the cost was due to the editing process.

Although videotape has proved to be an informative and convenient way to deliver information, Thomas cites two specific problems with the medium.

1. *Accepting mediocre quality.* "When you're making a video, you need to be as good as you can be. Poorly done video looks really bad. And people are used to seeing high-quality video on television and in movies," he says. Thomas says that parents don't expect the school district to be Steven Spielberg. If schools want people to respond to tapes, however, they "can't look like a home video."

2. *Using the video too long.* Clothing, hairstyles, furniture, and language often give away the year of production and can actually distract from the videotape's message if it is used too long, says Thomas. "We will need to update the tape in a few years so it doesn't start to look dated, and [we will need] to make sure the policies are up to date. We're expecting each video to have a shelf life of about four to five years."

Students Must Take Communications Home

Every principal knows this story. You go to the trouble of preparing newsletters or other communications, only to have students end up losing them on the way home. So why not give Principal Nancy Renfro's idea a try?

She uses large clasp envelopes to make sure information actually makes it home to parents. The envelopes also give kids a handy way to organize the information parents need to see.

REWARD IMPROVES TEACHERS' EFFORTS

While looking for a way to emphasize teacher communication with parents, Principal Michael Kinnamon hit on a great idea.

He gives his staff members rewards when they make five positive telephone calls to parents, make one home visit, or send 10 positive notes home. Teachers receive a coupon that's redeemable for 30 minutes of free time—with Kinnamon covering their classes!

"The incentive helps teachers build rapport with parents—which means fewer problems for me," says Kinnamon of Frankfort, Ohio. "Teachers responded better than I expected. Almost 100 percent earned the coupon.

"They're eligible to earn one coupon a year because I have only so much time to fill in for them. Teachers also have to arrange the time they want me to cover for them a few days in advance."

"We bought 7×10-inch brown clasp envelopes for every student," says Renfro. "We emphasize that the envelopes are important and that we expect the kids to use them to take home information about school.

"The school always sends federal forms and progress reports home for parental signatures.

"We tell the kids that this kind of information must go home in the envelopes. The envelopes are three-hole punched, and kids keep them in the front of their three-ring binders.

"The envelopes help, especially with kids who have poor organizational skills. They're easy to keep track of, and students know the importance we place on using them.

"Teachers have reported fewer problems to me this year getting homework and forms returned from home. This means I haven't had to deal with many complaints from teachers or student referrals to the office."

Providing Urgent Info via News Releases

When information must be communicated quickly, Stephen Kleinsmith, assistant superintendent at the Millard Public Schools in Millard, Nebraska, recommends using news releases to parents. These one-page documents are different from news releases sent to the media and from other communications between school and home, which lends urgency and importance.

However, parent news releases must be used sparingly and must contain timely and important information. Anything related to student safety and security, for example, is fair game for a parent news release. "If there's a change in how students will be dismissed during bouts of inclement weather and it's the middle of winter, we put that in a news release, because it may apply the very next day," says Kleinsmith.

Establishing Individual Contact

In addition to the general dissemination of information via newsletters, individual communication with parents is also necessary. A specially designed parent communication room reminds teachers of this responsibility and provides them with resources to follow through with it, says Assistant Principal Kevin Davis, of Carmel, Indiana. The room includes several telephones, samples of both positive and negative letters that teachers may use as models, envelopes, mailing addresses, and telephone records.

"We're telling our teachers, 'If you have a problem with a student, don't dawdle. Let parents know about it. If you have something positive to share, don't put that off either. Come here and make contact,'" he says.

At a Tom Bean, Texas, elementary school, each teacher has a telephone and a list of parents' telephone numbers in the classroom. "Not only do the phones help teachers solve discipline problems and communicate positive news, but they also cut down on paperwork and phone duties for the office staff," says Principal Patty Madison.

Communicating in Crisis Situations

Facing the media during a crisis is always awkward for school leaders, says Amy Friedman, communications coordinator at Millard Public Schools in Millard, Nebraska, but not answering reporters' questions likely will worsen an already bad situation.

"I can't stress enough that people not wait for reporters to go away, because they won't. The media [are] very persistent, and if you won't talk, they will find someone who will talk. And it may not be from your point of view. It's very important to speak soon so you don't lose the public's trust," she says.

Information should be presented calmly, systematically, and as it becomes available. Generally, Friedman says administrators should give the facts of what happened and what actions were taken and conclude with the steps the school is taking. "It's important that you be seen as someone who is taking charge and accepting responsibility. This is how you maintain people's trust," she says.

As soon as school officials learn of a problem, they should begin gathering facts and informing the media of when they plan to make a formal statement about the situation. Scheduling a press conference buys time to find out what happened and minimizes media-related distractions during the fact-gathering process. "Reporters will understand if you say you will get back to them when you know more and then follow through," says Friedman.

Delaying a meeting with the media or refusing to comment, however, are serious mistakes that fuel the public rumor mill. In crisis situations, says Friedman, some comment is almost always better than none. "Whatever you do, never say, 'No comment.' What this means in the public's eye is that you're hiding something."

Despite the inherent negativity, a crisis is actually an opportunity for a school and its leaders to shine in the public eye, says Friedman. "Everyone is watching. A school district can use that time to demonstrate its organization, professionalism, and resiliency." She adds that ongoing media communication is also essential to the healing process a school must experience after a crisis.

"It's important to continue to sell yourself and talk about what's good in the schools. This helps the public reconnect with what they knew was good about the schools before anything happened," she says. Periodically informing the media of progress on long-range plans to solve the crisis-provoking situation is also strong follow-up strategy. When possible, the media should be encouraged to produce a follow-up story about how the school or district has been improved since the original incident.

Improve Media Relations

Of all external audiences, the media are perhaps the most threatening to school administrators. But that fear is overblown, says Amy Friedman, communications coordinator at Millard Public Schools in Millard, Nebraska. "The media [are] very accessible and willing to cover both the good news and the bad news. It's a misperception that [they are] only interested in schools when there's an incident of violence," she says.

Ongoing communication with reporters can help administrators ensure that their schools receive fair, even news coverage. An easy way to begin building, or refining, a cooperative relationship is to keep the media updated on school activities through news releases. For optimum results, these documents should have the following four qualities.

1. *Succinctness.* The time and space allotted to school news likely will be limited, Stephen Kleinsmith, assistant superintendent at the Millard Public Schools in Millard, Nebraska, says. Economy of language is essential. To provide detailed information without short-changing the opportunity for coverage, Kleinsmith recommends writing news releases in two parts. On the first page, write the bare bones summary. Then attack a more lengthy, detailed message. "If [reporters] have time or space, they can elaborate," he says.
2. *Newsworthy content.* Friedman says principals should apply the "what, so what rule" before releasing information to the media. She advises teachers and administrators to ask themselves, "What is going on?" and follow that question with "So what? What makes this different or important, and why should others be interested?"

   "If [teachers and administrators] come up with a good answer to both questions, then the event is probably newsworthy, and a release should be drafted," she says. "Items also have to be things that aren't standard school activities. Writing that parent–teacher conferences are coming up, for example, is not something the media [are] interested in."
3. *Adequate contact information.* News releases should feature at least two people whom reporters can contact for further information, says Kleinsmith. "If a reporter can't reach the first contact, your school won't automatically lose the opportunity for exposure. The reporter already has the name and number of a second contact person."
4. *Suited to the medium.* Administrators with media savvy tailor messages to the appropriate medium, says Friedman. "Television likes things with visual appeal. Some events [that] don't seem groundbreaking are things that television really jumps on because they can get vivid, interesting pictures," she says.

Friedman cites local television stations' "huge" response to beach party lunches held at several district locations, where students bring beach towels to sit on in the gymnasium or cafeteria during the lunch period. "[Television stations] liked the visual appeal of this event in contrast with the winter weather outside," she says.

School officials must realize that news coverage won't always be rosy, says Rednak, but openness and a cooperative attitude yield dividends in the long run. He says the local media's attitude toward his school district changed almost immediately after he discontinued his predecessor's practice of never giving out copies of the school district's proposed budget. "Reporters had a lot of questions the first year [I gave them this information]. But the second year they just accepted the information and wrote a very positive story about the district."

MATERIALS YOU CAN USE

Let's Communicate

We recognize that school schedules create many unique circumstances. It is our desire to communicate as often as necessary to benefit your child.

It may be difficult, with the varied schedules of our community, to contact your child's teacher. Please note from whom you wish a call, and this form will be forwarded immediately for a response.

Please have _____ contact me _____ regarding
        (teacher)   (parent)

_____ at _____. The best time to
   (student)   (phone number)

contact me (parent) is _____.
          (time of day).

Let Us Hear from You

We want to hear from you! As a valued part of our school system, your ideas and concerns are being solicited. Two forms are included below. One form is designed for you to ask questions about our school, and also to ask about any rumors you may have heard. The other form asks you to give us any ideas you may have that could make our school a better place for children. Please take the time to fill out one or both forms. If you wish to have a reply, please list your name and address.

I have a question . . .

I have a question about our school. I would like to know:

I heard a rumor about our school and would like to know if there is any truth to it:

☐ I am a parent of a student.

☐ I am not a parent of a student.

_____
Signature (optional)

_____
Address (optional)

I have an idea . . .

I have an idea to improve our school. Here it is:

☐ I am a parent of a student.

☐ I am not a parent of a student.

_____
Signature (optional)

_____
Address (optional)

Let us hear from you! Clip and send your ideas or questions to school.

Report to Parents

School Name
Address
Telephone

Name of Principal:

Date:

Dear Parents:

I had the opportunity to be in _____ classroom recently. You should be very proud of _____ and his/her classwork. He or she is really doing some good work. While I was in the classroom, I saw the following activities:

-

-

-

Your child's teacher had some terrific ideas that I observed during my visit. I saw creative thinking and lots of responsiveness by _____.

Please support _____ educational growth. You are very important to your child's growth and our work as co-educators for _____.

Sincerely,

Principal

Principal's Positive Phone Calls

Student's name: _____ Teacher: _____

Parent's name if different than student's: _____

Phone   (home): _____

       (work): _____

What's positive: _____

_____

_____

Student's name: _____ Teacher: _____

Parent's name if different than student's: _____

Phone   (home): _____

       (work): _____

What's positive: _____

_____

_____

Student's name: _____ Teacher: _____

Parent's name if different than student's: _____

Phone   (home): _____

       (work): _____

What's positive: _____

_____

_____

Thanks Bank Checks

Thanks Bank
The Bank That Pays Daily Interest and High Dividends

It is a pleasure to _____ _____ 20____

PAY TO THE ORDER OF _____

_____ THANKS

Thanks for _____

_____

GOOD DEEDS AVAILABLE
FOR MUTUAL PROFIT   1:008100459   PERSONAL ACCOUNT

Thanks Bank
The Bank That Pays Daily Interest and High Dividends

It is a pleasure to _____ _____ 20____

PAY TO THE ORDER OF _____

_____ THANKS

Thanks for _____

_____

GOOD DEEDS AVAILABLE
FOR MUTUAL PROFIT   1·008100459   PERSONAL ACCOUNT

"Beginning The New School Year" Letter

Dear Parents,

This week, we become partners in one of the most important jobs there is—helping your child become all he or she can be. It's a scary, exciting, and challenging task but a terrifically rewarding one too. As we form a partnership this year, we would like to make a contract with you.

We promise to greet students each morning with the expectation that the day will be important. Will you learn about the school program, so you can show the same enthusiasm?

We promise to prepare exciting lessons. Will you help your son or daughter come to school on time and well-rested to appreciate them?

We promise to assign worthwhile class work each day. Will you check daily to see that your son or daughter has completed the work to the best of his or her ability and review those areas causing difficulty?

We promise to encourage students to take part in school activities. Will you see that your child is properly dressed to participate fully?

We promise to work to make the school day an intellectually stimulating one. Will you ask questions and encourage discussion, so your child can share his or her educational growth with you?

We promise to call home whenever we feel a student needs extra help in getting along with others, growing in responsibility, or working harder. Will you call us if you hear a report about school that bothers you?

One of our goals this year is to encourage students to participate in school work and school fun. You can help by sharing school life. Children learn what they live. When your son or daughter sees his or her life surrounded by caring and attentive parents and school staff, he or she will surely join with us to help make this the best year possible.

We are looking forward to an exciting year and a rewarding partnership with you.

Sincerely,

Chapter **1–3**

Recruit Family Volunteers

How Volunteers Can Help	1–3:1
Offer All Kinds of Volunteer Opportunities	1–3:1
Reaching Volunteers	1–3:2
Recruiting Takes Thought and Effort	1–3:2
Try Personal Testimonials	1–3:4
It Takes a Special Effort To Recruit Fathers	1–3:4
Offer At-Home Opportunities	1–3:5
Raise Your Expectations	1–3:5
Use the Right Tools	1–3:5
Offer Parents a Benefit for Volunteering	1–3:6
Recognize Their Efforts	1–3:7
Materials You Can Use	1–3:9
Volunteer Flier #1	1–3:9
Volunteer Flier #2	1–3:10
Volunteer Availability Form	1–3:11
Volunteer Application Form #1	1–3:12
Volunteer Application Form #2	1–3:14
Volunteer Interest Survey	1–3:16
Recruitment Letter	1–3:17
Volunteer Want Ads	1–3:18
Guidelines for Volunteers	1–3:19
75 Ways Volunteers Can Help	1–3:20

Chapter **1–3**

Recruit Family Volunteers

HOW VOLUNTEERS CAN HELP

OFFER ALL KINDS OF VOLUNTEER OPPORTUNITIES

With all the demands busy schedules place on parents, it's no wonder that many of them can't find the time to volunteer in schools.

Yet volunteering is a vital part of parent involvement—and a vital part of your school. With more and more schools strapped for resources to keep programs and activities, it makes sense to tap parent help, instead of making cutbacks.

Many schools use volunteers for clerical help and helping in the classroom—and this is great. But don't limit yourself to these activities. Parents can also run reading programs, raise money for extracurricular activities, and chaperone school trips.

Here is a sampling of interesting volunteer opportunities you could offer parents.

- **Special program sponsors.** A Midwest principal tells me that volunteers made it possible for her students to participate in a national reading incentive program. "This program is co-chaired by a member of the parent/teacher organization board and the school librarian," says Principal Betty Replogle of Beatrice, Nebraska. "We call parents in and go over the theme and instructions for the program. Then they take over. No teacher, administrator, or staff has to do any work connected with the program."

    Kids read books and then watch as their name tags are moved along a chart as the number of books they read increases.

    "Volunteers make the bulletin board and laminate students' name tags," says Replogle. "They also collect score sheets once a week, calculate moves along the chart, and award prizes when kids reach significant points on the chart."

- **Classroom assistants.** "We use volunteers for tutoring students who need special help," says Community Education and Public Relations Director Elaine Sander of Seiling, Oklahoma. "They also perform chores for teachers, like making bulletin boards or working in the library."
- **Office helpers.** Principal Ian Patrick of Rothesay, Nebraska, uses volunteers in his attendance office. "They telephone the home of every student who doesn't report to school, so it doesn't take long for us to track down absent students!"
- **Special project supervisors.** Principal Allan Reyer of Natrona Heights, Pennsylvania, tells me his school wouldn't have a yearbook if parents didn't give their time and talents. "In addition, they help us organize a party for students who will be moving on to another building next year," he says.
- **Fundraisers.** "Our 34-member PTO executive board holds several fund-raising activities each year," says Principal Charles Scott of Caramel, Indiana.

  "Members designate the money for school improvements and staff development. This year, for instance, they earmarked $3,000 for sending teachers to professional conferences and workshops."
- **Additional "staff" members.** There would be no computer lab at Principal Eli Baker's school if it wasn't for volunteers. "A retired businessman organized the room, ordered software, and then scheduled businesspeople to monitor the lab on a rotating basis," says Baker of Sumter, South Carolina.

  "Volunteer help and donations save the school district the cost of hiring a staff member to operate the lab."
- **Extracurricular activity boosters.** Principal Glenn Frank of Moretown, Vermont improved his band program by using volunteers. "Instead of adding more staff to help with lessons, we advertised via our school newsletter, and the newspaper for volunteers with backgrounds in music."

REACHING VOLUNTEERS

Recruiting Takes Thought and Effort

The first rule of recruiting is to let parents know what your needs are and how they can help out. It's important to spread the word in many different ways—even at the risk of repeating yourself.

"Active volunteers tell me that they know people who want to help out but aren't sure what they can do," says Volunteer Coordinator Brenda Valentine. "So we need to keep reiterating the basic message."

Valentine of Charleston, West Virginia, asks parents to volunteer four different ways.

- **Personally.** "At the first PTA meeting of the year, I stage a big welcome for parents," she says. "While I have a captive audience, I give a talk on how much we need them to help at school."
- **Through teachers.** "On PTA night, parents go to individual classrooms and meet with teachers," says Valentine.

"This is when teachers emphasize how important parents can be in the classroom. For instance, a teacher will say, 'The kids really enjoy being read to, and they like reading to someone else. I don't have time to do this, but I'd love to have volunteers fill the need.'"
- Via the student handbook. "Our student handbook expresses our appreciation for volunteers and explains that parents' time and talents are important to the school. Then we tell readers how to go about getting involved."
- Through the parent group. "Our PTA appeals to potential volunteers by sending parents a list of things that teachers need help with," Valentine says.

Simply getting the word out, however, isn't enough to bring in all potential volunteers. Sometimes, specialized recruiting is in order. Here are eight things other schools are doing.

1. **Have students perform at a PTA/PTO meeting.** "One of the best ways to get parents involved in the PTO is to have their kids give a band or drama performance," says Principal Eli Baker. "Whenever we do this, there are always more parents than places to sit. To make sure parents stay for the entire meeting, the performance is always last. Otherwise, people will leave after the show and never hear about volunteer opportunities."
2. **Make it easier for parents to volunteer.** "Many parents don't volunteer because they can't get here—or because no one is available to take care of their kids," says Parent Coordinator Debbie Smith. "We provide free transportation from central locations, so parents who don't have cars can volunteer. We also use volunteers to provide on-site child care."
3. **Recruit volunteers at an open house or back-to-school night.** "You can't just put information on a table, though, and hope that parents notice it," says Principal Charles Scott. "At our open house, I make sure that every teacher distributes volunteer forms to parents."
4. **Promote volunteerism at a special parents' program.** "During the first month of school, we have a series of parents' evenings," says Principal Barb Patrick of Olympia, Washington.

    "Parents visit their kids' classroom to learn about the curriculum and general school programs. This is an opportunity for me to make a pitch on volunteering and pass out volunteer application forms."
5. **Send fliers or letters home with students.** "Ours include a list of jobs volunteers perform at school," says Teacher and Volunteer Coordinator Dena Wheeler of Afton, Iowa.

    "Parents check what they feel most comfortable doing. They can also indicate whether they'd like to volunteer on a regular basis or just for special projects."
6. **Include a special Volunteer Opportunities column in your school newsletter.** "I borrowed the idea from the Help Wanted ads in the newspaper," says a Canadian principal.

    "The volunteer column runs in our June newsletter to inform parents about the school's needs for the next academic year.

    "This eases some of the volunteer attrition rate every year by allowing me to tap into the school's parents. I also distribute 'job' listings at parent/teacher nights."

7. **Make a personal contact.** Form letters and fliers alone aren't going to get the job done, says Principal Chet Hubbard of Lubec, Maine.

    "I've found that the best way to get people to volunteer is to approach them personally," he says. "You'd be surprised how often you call somebody to ask if he or she will help with an event and get 'yes' for an answer."

8. **Provide volunteer information at registration.** "When parents register their kids for school, we ask them to fill out a Volunteer Availability Form," says a Western principal. "We always get a good group of volunteers this way because parents' enthusiasm for the school year is at its peak."

Try Personal Testimonials

Here's a great parent volunteer recruiting strategy: Ask a volunteer to describe the satisfactions of volunteering to other parents. After all, they're more likely to respond to another mom or dad than to a form letter!

At her school's open house, Principal Karol Sonnamaker has a volunteer talk about the emotional rewards of volunteering.

"This year, a mother described different opportunities and how volunteering changed her view of the school," says Sonnamaker of Eunice, New Mexico. "Then she mentioned how much students look forward to seeing her. The few times she was unable to come in, the kids later told her that they really missed her!"

It Takes a Special Effort To Recruit Fathers

Getting fathers to volunteer at school functions has always been a chore for principals. Many dads have the attitude that volunteering is a mother's responsibility or that they don't have the time for it because they have to work.

Fathers should be more involved in their kids' education! The "secret" to bringing dads into schools is to tailor volunteer activities to fit their interests and schedules.

Here's what a Texas principal does to attract fathers.

- A Saturday morning work detail. "The past two springs, we've sent a note home to fathers explaining that 'grounds work' needs to be done at the school. Projects have included painting, pulling weeds, and pest extermination.

    "We provide coffee and donuts, and fathers work from 8 until 1 P.M.—and get the rest of the day off. The program has been a great success! Many men bring their kids, and the sense of accomplishment is high for everyone. Every time a father drives by the school, he can say, 'The school looks sharp, and I helped make it that way.'"

- A Dads are Special People reading program. "Since we asked fathers to help with maintenance, we're now trying to get them involved in the classroom. So we sent another note home inviting dads to school for before-school reading sessions.

"The cafeteria staff serves breakfast. Fathers read to their kids for 15 minutes in the classroom."

"These sessions have really increased fathers' participation with their children at my school."

Note: When fathers participate in programs like these, ask them to fill out a volunteer availability form. Once they're having a good time, they'll be much more likely to sign up to volunteer again.

Here's what Principal Jim Wheeler does to get male volunteers at his school.

"Our goal is to get more men into our school, so we've set up a male role model program," he says.

"The men don't necessarily have to be fathers. There are students in our school who don't have a male presence in their homes, and they really need to see some positive role models."

"Even the kids who do have fathers at home still need to see more men in the school because there seems to be a lack of them in almost all school systems."

"We ask the Masons and church groups for volunteers who can be at school over the lunch break. These men then visit and talk to the students."

Offer At-Home Opportunities

While some parents can't volunteer during the day, they still have talents you can tap into. The key here is to provide opportunities when they're most convenient for parents.

"One of the problems we have is lots of single moms or two-career families who just don't have the time to volunteer," says Principal Lynn Redden of Coldspring, Texas. "So we started our Brown Bag volunteer program. We called it this because the jobs are things students can carry home in bags for their parents and then return to school.

"We've found that many parents are more than willing to do things at home, like collating papers, coloring, or cutting out materials for classroom use.

"Students take a packet home that includes instructions for parents. Brown bags send a message that school is important. Even if parents can't be there to help, they can still do something."

Raise Your Expectations

Principal Fred Ortman tells parents up front that they're expected to help out in the school in whatever way they can—and gets a great response. "We expect our parents to get involved in some way with their child's classroom," says Ortman.

"Parents can work in the school by tutoring students, having students read to them, and helping the teacher. Outside the classroom, they can donate things like paper or building materials. For example, one father is in the construction business, and he built some holders for student work. Other parents have made props for school plays."

Use the Right Tools

Many principals tell me that surveys and application forms are an effective way to get the names of potential volunteers. If your school does this, take a good look at the forms you use.

Then ask yourself these questions: What information do I request? Do I give volunteers a choice about what they can do? Is the language friendly and inviting?

Creating or fine-tuning a volunteer recruitment form may be the most important step in your parent recruiting process. There are two reasons for this.

1. **Its format can influence whether some parents will volunteer at your school.** For example, if the form is too long or too detailed, many prospective volunteers just won't fill it out. Or if they feel the form categorizes them in a way they're not entirely comfortable with, they'll just throw it away.

2. **It helps you do a better job of assigning volunteers.** Prospective volunteers' interests and availability are good things to base their placement on. An effective form gives you the information you need to make the right fit.

A volunteer application form should include this standard information: The applicant's name, address, telephone number, his or her children's names, and availability.

After this point, however, applications take on their own unique identities.

For example, Parent Coordinator Debbie Smith says that, instead of grilling applicants about their professional background and personal history, her application focuses on their interests.

"It gives a whole inventory of ways they can help in schools," says Smith. "In addition, the form asks them to describe any hobbies that might be put to use at school."

Principal Barb Patrick takes a similar approach to volunteer recruitment. Her form includes space for applicants to indicate their special interests and involvement preferences. "It also asks for the names of two non-family members as references," she tells me.

What form is best for your school? It depends on how you plan to use your volunteers.

Offer Parents a Benefit for Volunteering

At Principal Patricia Baker-Benally's school, volunteers are rewarded in a unique way. Through the school's Parent Academy, Baker-Benally gives parent volunteers employment skills and experience they can add to their resumes!

"Many parents involved in the Parent Academy want a second income, so they're looking for work experience," explains Baker-Benally of Wainwright, Arkansas. "Through the academy, we obviously use parents' talents and abilities. But we also help them improve their communication skills and teach them how to operate office equipment and computers—which is all valuable work experience.

"The academy gives something back to parents who volunteer. After they complete the academy, I write a letter of recommendation for them. The parents leave with a sense of accomplishment and something concrete for their job searches." Here's how the academy works.

Parents complete 11 instructional activities to earn a "degree." Each of the 11 activities must be performed a pre-set number of times to receive "credit" for the experience. "For example, one activity is 'art materials and bulletin board preparation,'" says Baker-Benally. "This involves identifying, securing, locating, and setting up material that students will need for art periods or classroom displays. The parent must complete four experiences in this activity.

"The program can take from 40 to 75 hours and may be spread out over a two-year period. Each parent is given a checkoff sheet of the 11 instructional activities. As each activity is completed, a teacher, Parent Academy coordinator, or school secretary signs and dates the appropriate space.

During the year, Baker-Benally meets regularly with parents in the Parent Academy. The first meeting is during orientation when she explains the program, gives a tour of the building, and demonstrates the different tasks parents will be doing.

"Midyear, I meet with parents who are halfway through the academy and recognize them with certificates of service," she says.

"In the spring, I hold graduation for parents who complete the academy. The PTA provides a plaque for each graduate, and a lunch is served. I present parents with the letter of recommendation and thank them again for their work."

Baker-Benally says many graduates are getting jobs. "One woman is now working at a pet store. She credits the academy with giving her the customer service skills she needs for the job."

The school's only expenses are recognition plaques and certificates. Baker-Benally estimates she spends $1,000 to $5,000 a year on these. "The overall benefit of the program, however, far outweighs its cost," she adds.

Recognize Their Efforts

Recognition is a key part of any volunteer program. Many schools honor their volunteers at a tea, luncheon, or brunch. There are any number of ways, however, that you can turn these mainstays into very special occasions.

"At our school, the teachers work with cooks and serve our brunch—and volunteers love it!" says Principal Marc Boyd of Goffstown, New Hampshire.

Here are more twists to traditional recognition events.

- Invite the media and district officials to the ceremony. "I notify the newspaper and the district's media relations specialist about our volunteer luncheon," says Principal Eli Baker.

  "Volunteers receive a gift in token of our appreciation and have their pictures taken for the paper."

  Note: Many principals invite superintendents and school board members to volunteer recognition ceremonies. It's a great idea because these individuals enjoy seeing who is making a difference in education.
- Remember volunteers with gifts during the holidays. "I make sure all volunteers get a Thanksgiving or Christmas card," says Community Education and Public Relations Director Elaine Sander. "I also give them a gift. This year, it was a gold-colored address book the size of a credit card."
- Invite parents to all-school recognition assemblies. "We give gifts to volunteers at our last all-school awards assembly," a Wisconsin principal tells me. "Almost all parents attend this event, so it's a great opportunity to thank volunteers in front of a large group."
- Send personal "thank-yous." Three times a year, Principal Chet Hubbard sends his volunteers Hubbard-grams, which are brief messages of praise. "I pick two or three contributions a volunteer has made and recognize him or her for them," he says. "For instance, a recent Hubbard-gram said, 'Your work in the Valentine Program was superb, and I commend you for your patience during the field trip. You're becoming an important part of our school system, so I'd like to thank you personally for caring for our students.'"
- Go "public" with volunteer recognition. Principal Perry Sandler of Jackson Heights, New York, tells me that his district doesn't hold volunteer recognition events at school. "Instead, the school board sponsors a ceremony at city hall to recognize the outstanding efforts of our volunteers."
- Give volunteers immediate recognition for outstanding work. "I like to give volunteers on-the-spot recognition," says a Florida principal. "Usually, I present them with a performance award, which is good for dinner at a classy restaurant, or I give them some small item they probably wouldn't buy for themselves. I note

the things volunteers like—a particular type of music or hobby, for instance—and then brainstorm ideas for gifts."
- Thank volunteers in print. "Our school publishes a newsletter through the parent group," says a Midwest principal. "For this month's issue, I'm working on a special thank-you for volunteers who contributed to a spring event—and I'm going to name names!" This principal says he also recognizes volunteers in the school newspaper and in weekly letters home.
- Thank parent volunteers through their kids. "I've found that this is the best way to recognize volunteers," says Principal Marc Boyd. "For example, I told a student how much I appreciated his father helping to reserve a room at a college for our health curriculum committee meeting. This makes students feel good about their mom or dad, because they know that he or she really cares about education."
- Go "high-tech" to get teachers to show their appreciation to volunteers. Principal Barb Patrick uses electronic mail to send periodic reminders to teachers about thanking volunteers. "The teachers then have kids create a picture or poster recognizing those individuals," she says.
- Include volunteers when you recognize faculty. "Whenever we show our appreciation to teachers or other staff, like during National Education Week, we make sure our PTA is part of the 'celebration loop,'" says Principal Israel Bordainick of Thiells, New York. "This is also an opportunity for me to acknowledge the PTA's contributions.

MATERIALS YOU CAN USE

Volunteer Flier #1

We would like to again thank all the volunteers who helped our students during the past school year. Your assistance made the school experience much smoother and more enjoyable for all concerned. We would like to set up another volunteer program for the coming year. Volunteers may choose specific times to work or be available on a call-in basis. Please fill out this form according to your preferences.

☐ No, I am not interested in volunteering.

☐ Yes, I am interested in the following way(s):

- ☐ morning session (9 to 11:30 A.M.)
- ☐ afternoon session (12:30 to 3 P.M.)
- ☐ all day
- ☐ call-in basis only
- ☐ call-in basis in addition to above
- ☐ once a month
- ☐ twice a month
- ☐ once a week
- ☐ twice a week
- ☐ other (please specify) _____

_____ ( ) _____
Name   Phone

_____
Address

Volunteers help in the classroom, tutor and read to students, check papers, help develop classroom materials, bulletin boards, and assist with other student-related activities. All-day volunteers may ride their children's bus to and from school on their volunteer days.

Volunteer Flier #2

Farming
Woodcrafts
Visited a foreign country
Authors
Recycling
Energy
Water quality
War experience
Transportation
Math
Space
Space travel
Presidents
Disabilities
Mapping
Electricity
Cultures
Visits to other states
Foreign languages
Ecology
Occupations
Health
Weather
History
Holidays

Do you have a talent or specific knowledge about any of these areas or any others that you would be willing to share with our students to enhance their education?

If so, we would like to hear from you. Just fill out the form below and return it to the school.

Do you know someone else who would be interested? Just jot down their names and their topic areas also!

Name: _____

Phone: (____)_____

Topic area(s): _____

Friend's name: _____

Phone: (____)_____

Topic area(s): _____

Volunteer Availability Form

VOLUNTEERS NEEDED

We need your help in the coming year to have a top-notch school. Will you please volunteer? You will be called to set up a time to help that will be at your convenience.

☐ I will work in the school health clinic.

Phone: (_____) _____

Signed: _____

☐ I will help in the office or wherever I'm needed most.

Phone: (_____) _____

Signed: _____

Volunteer Application Form #1

PLEASE PRINT

School: _____

Name: _____ Date: _____

Address: _____

City: _____ State: _____ ZIP: _____

Day telephone: (____) _____ Evening telephone: (____) _____

Preferred day(s) of the week (circle):   M   T   W   Th   F

Hours available   Mornings: _____

                                Afternoons: _____

                                Evenings: _____

                                Weekends: _____

Type of volunteer: ☐ Parent   ☐ Student   ☐ Business partner   ☐ Community

Special skills: _____

_____

Children in this school:

Name	Teacher
_____	_____
_____	_____
_____	_____
_____	_____
_____	_____

continues

Volunteer Application Form #1 continued

Interest and hobby list for volunteers

What I Like To Do	A lot	Some	None	Comments
Reading				
Writing				
Speaking to groups				
Meeting new people				
Dancing and singing				
Sorting papers				
Keeping records				
Typing				
Fixing machines				
Drawing and sketching				
Camping outdoors				
Swimming				
Hiking				
Working math problems				
Selling things to people				
Teaching				
Cooking				
Presiding at meetings, events				
Acting in a play				
Directing a theater production				
Driving a car				
Computer data input				
Using the telephone				
Crafts				
Taking responsibility				
Research and analysis				
Experimenting with mechanical things				
Making things, repairing them				
Making decisions				
Leading a discussion group				

Other:

Volunteer Application Form #2

Name: _____   Student's teacher: _____

Phone Number: _____   Hours/days available: _____

===

☐ OFFICE HELP   Hours are flexible

☐ CLASSROOM   Individual help for the teachers. Duties range from
                                 making copies and helping with special projects to
                                 listening to new readers. Hours determined by
                                 volunteer and teacher.

☐ LIBRARY   With the help of volunteers, the library is available to
                                 students five days a week. Please circle one of the
                                 following times: 9-11 A.M.; 9 A.M.-12 P.M.;
                                 11 A.M.-1 P.M.; 12-3 P.M.; 1-3 P.M.

☐ PUBLISHING: ☐ TYPISTS   People willing to volunteer for one to two hours a
                                 week, anytime. A training session will be help for
                                 those unfamiliar with the word processor.

                 ☐ CLASS LIAISON One to two people per class to represent a single
                                 class and assist with binding (sewing pages together
                                 and gluing covers on typed pages). Training sessions
                                 will be held. Work can be completed at home.

☐ NURSE   Volunteers to assist the nurse.

☐ CAFETERIA   Helping serve lunch to students on pizza and
                                 chicken-nugget days, and on special occasions.
                                 11:50 A.M. to 1 P.M.

☐ POPCORN   Rotating teams of two will pop and distribute pop-
                                 corn one morning monthly. Wednesdays 8:45 to
                                 10:30 A.M.

continues

Volunteer Application Form #2 continued

☐ RECESS — Assisting a teacher monitoring playground activities one day per week, 9:40 to 10:30 A.M.

☐ VIDEO/PHOTOGRAPHER — Taking snapshots or videotaping happy times at school for the bulletin board.

☐ SPECIAL EVENTS
- ☐ BOOK FAIR
- ☐ ARTIST IN RESIDENCE
- ☐ CELEBRITY READERS

☐ FUNDRAISING — Volunteers are needed to help staff fund-raising events throughout the year.
- ☐ ICE CREAM SOCIAL
- ☐ BREAKFAST WITH SANTA
- ☐ CANDY SALES

☐ HEALTH SUPPORT COMMITTEE — Composed of people with or without health service backgrounds. The group works to support and enhance the existing health curriculum by facilitating the use of community resources; e.g., water safety, dental health, head lice prevention.

Please return this form as soon as possible. Our coordinator or another volunteer association member will contact you in the near future. Thank you!

Volunteer Interest Survey

You are invited! As a volunteer, you can help children learn.

Please share your time, skills, or interests with our students. You need not be experienced in teaching, just willing to share. The gift will help our students develop positive attitudes toward learning and motivate them to achieve their potential.

On the form below, please indicate how you are willing to help. We have provided a list to give you some ideas. We welcome your suggestions. This form may be returned in person or by mail to any school office. We will contact you regarding future involvement. Thank you!

Your name | Telephone (Area/No.)
(Daytime)
(Evening)

Address

Names and grades of your children, if any, attending our schools

I am willing to help students by

☐ coming to school ☐ working from my home ☐ no preference

I prefer to work at (name of school)

I prefer to work at (name of school)

I prefer to work with the following students

☐ elementary ☐ middle school ☐ high school ☐ no preference

I have the following skills to share:

☐ sewing/needlecraft
☐ working with one child
☐ typing/word processing
☐ working with a small group
☐ making phone calls
☐ making a presentation to a class
☐ cutting paper shapes
☐ installing/designing bulletin boards
☐ working with simple carpentry

☐ shelving/cataloging books
☐ filing
☐ posting fliers in the neighborhood
☐ making posters/banners
☐ providing child care
☐ reading stories to children or listening to them read
☐ bookkeeping
☐ keeping score at athletic events
☐ working on publicity

☐ helping with math or science skills
☐ providing transportation
☐ organizing school events or fundraisers
☐ chaperoning field trips, bus trips, or dances
☐ writing grants
☐ school decision making or advisory committees
☐ talking about career

Other ways I could help

My other hobbies/skills (e.g., camping, architecture, Swedish cooking, local history, calligraphy) are

I have access to

☐ typewriter or word processor ☐ pickup truck or van ☐ audiotape recorder ☐ video camera

Source: Reprinted from *Survey of Interest for Volunteers (Appendix)*, with permission of the Wisconsin Department of Public Instruction, John T. Benson, Superintendent.

Recruitment Letter

Dear Parent,

Most of us think education is important. We know that our children's future success and happiness depend on the education they receive today. That's why we're asking for your help. You can be part of this learning process—as a volunteer.

Why should you volunteer? There are many reasons:

Your kids will benefit. Even if you're not in their classrooms, your children will know you are in school. They'll see that you believe learning is important.

You'll get to know your children's teachers. Knowing the teacher makes it easier to ask for help when your child needs it.

The school will benefit. The time you spend in school will allow our staff to do more things for more kids. That means better learning for all.

The community will benefit. You'll learn more about our school, and you'll be able to share what you know with friends, neighbors, and coworkers.

Volunteering is easy. We'll be glad to train you for your job. Many of them can be done at home or in school, during the day, or on the weekend.

Volunteering is satisfying. You'll meet other parents. You may learn new skills. And you'll get a good feeling from knowing that you're a part of something important.

Please help us help your kids. Be someone who makes a difference. Be a volunteer. It's easy to get started. Just call me right now at _____ and tell me that you're interested. I look forward to working with you!

Sincerely,

Principal

Volunteer Want Ads

Parent Volunteer Opportunities

From time to time we require some extra assistance at the school in various areas. If you can help in any one of the following positions, please contact the appropriate supervisor through the school office. Telephone _____.

Job title: Band assistant
Supervisor: Band instructor
Number of volunteers needed: 1 to 3
General job description: Assist in general operation of band program
Duties and responsibilities: Filing, clerical, depositing funds, photocopying, phoning volunteers for supervision at concerts, festivals and workshops, van/truck transportation of equipment, fundraising organization (bake sales, candy sales), assisting with trip organization (making performance bookings, hotel and restaurant reservations)
Skill level required: Ability and willingness to assist in any or all of the above
Time commitment: Your choice—work is ongoing and any assistance is appreciated
Approximate date/time of year required: Throughout the school year
Other notes/comments: Guidance and help available from band director

Job title: Library volunteer
Supervisor: Tom Johnson
Number of volunteers needed: Several
General job description: Assist in general operation of the school library program
Duties and responsibilities: Clerical tasks such as filing, shelving, repairing books, etc. and some bulletin board or other design work
Skill level required: Attention to detail
Time commitment: Your choice
Approximate date/time of year required: Throughout the school year

Job title: Selling bus passes
Supervisor: Jane Doe
Number of volunteers needed: 1
General job description: Assist in selling bus passes to students
Duties and responsibilities: Receive money, write student name on bus pass
Skill level required: Ability to print legibly and pay attention to detail
Time commitment: 45 minutes two mornings each month
Approximate date/time of year required: Last day and first day of each month, September through June
Other notes/comments: Assistance available from office staff as needed

Guidelines for Volunteers

Welcome to our school! We appreciate your gift of time and energy. The benefactors are the students, and on their behalf, thank you! We hope that you will benefit from your experiences. To help make your visits enjoyable and productive, we offer these tips:

1. **Sign in.** Sign in at the office and wear a volunteer button. Indicate your location, so we may find you in the event of a message. All who sign in are eligible for our monthly door-prize drawing.

2. **Where is it?** The floor-plan map is in the orientation handbook and indicates where the classrooms and workrooms are. Please ask for a mini-tour.

3. **For your comfort.** A refrigerator and microwave are in the commons area for your convenience at lunch. There are adult rest rooms off the commons area. There are two soda machines in the staff lounge.

4. **Supplies.** Room X is stocked with supplies.

5. **Workrooms.** Room X is the parent VIP workroom. This is the room we have designated for parent and community volunteers to work. The library and Room X are first choices for making photocopies. There is a copier in the staff workroom, Room X, but we ask that it be used as a last resort. Courtesy directs volunteers to interrupt use of the copy machine for a staff member on a tight schedule between classes.

6. **Pre-school children.** Pre-schoolers are welcome in the parent VIP workroom but must not be left unattended. Pre-school children must be under your close supervision at all times.

7. **Safety.** Regular volunteers should obtain a TB test from the school nurse. Everyone is to evacuate the building during fire drills.

Further questions? Please stop by the VIP workroom or office.

75 Ways Volunteers Can Help

Looking for new ways to get parents involved at your school? Take a look at this list, compiled by the Association of California School Administrators. You're sure to find some new ideas for using volunteers at your school.

1. Tell stories to children.
2. Listen to children read.
3. Conduct flash card drills.
4. Provide individual help.
5. Assist in learning centers.
6. Set up learning centers.
7. Help contact parents.
8. Reproduce materials.
9. Work in clinic or library.
10. Check out audiovisual equipment.
11. Practice vocabulary with non-English speaking students.
12. Make instructional games.
13. Play instructional games.
14. Play games at recess.
15. Assist with visual tests.
16. Prepare visual materials.
17. Develop programmed materials.
18. Grade papers.
19. Prepare bulletin boards.
20. Help with book fairs.
21. Work with underachievers.
22. Reinforce Dolch words.
23. Assist with field trips.
24. Make props for plays.
25. Set up a book exchange.
26. Gather resource materials.
27. Help children learn to type.
28. Help children with arts and crafts.
29. Help with cooking projects.
30. Check out books from public library.
31. Set up experiments.
32. Take attendance.
33. Collect lunch money.
34. Escort children to bathroom, library, cafeteria.
35. Work on perceptual activities.
36. Make list of library resources.
37. Visit a sick child at home.
38. Work with a handicapped child.
39. Prepare teaching materials.
40. Record grades.
41. Supervise groups taking tests.
42. Discuss careers or hobbies.
43. Show a filmstrip to a group.
44. Help children with walking on balance beam, jumping rope, or skipping.
45. Reinforce learning of alphabet.
46. Reinforce recognition of numerals.
47. Drill recognition of color words.
48. Talk to children—be a friend.
49. Help children with motor skill problems.
50. Help children learn a foreign language.
51. Play a musical instrument.
52. Help students who play instruments.
53. Make puppets.
54. Dramatize a story.
55. Help with handwriting practice.
56. Set up "grocery store" to practice math skills.
57. Drill spelling words.
58. Make reading carrels from boxes.
59. Tell stories with puppets with flannel board.
60. Assist with sing-alongs.
61. Show slides.
62. Discuss care and training of pets.
63. Demonstrate different artistic abilities.
64. Discuss life from the viewpoint of a person with a handicap and the importance of understanding others.
65. Discuss different handicaps.
66. Discuss attitudes, feelings, and emotions.
67. Share ethnic backgrounds and experiences.
68. Discuss farm life and farm animals.
69. Demonstrate gardening skills.
70. Help prepare assembly programs.
71. Discuss holidays and special occasions.
72. Discuss aspects of safety.
73. Share information about local history.
74. Demonstrate pioneer crafts.
75. Assist in preparing courses.

Chapter **1–4**

Deal with Difficult Situations

Handling Discipline and Other Tough Issues	1–4:1
Dealing with Difficult Parents	1–4:1
Communicate with Difficult Parents	1–4:1
Parent Development Helps Educate Parents	1–4:3
Working on Discipline Issues	1–4:3
Parents Must Know the Rules	1–4:5
Educating Parents on Attendance	1–4:6
Sample Attendance Sticker	1–4:7
Q & A about Attendance Policy	1–4:7
Parents Harm Children in Custody Battles	1–4:8
Reach Out to Difficult Parents Even More	1–4:8
Materials You Can Use	1–4:10
Midterm Progress Report	1–4:10
Student Status Report	1–4:11
Parent Notification Form	1–4:12
Discipline Plan Letter	1–4:13
Discipline Brochure	1–4:14
How To Deal with Difficult Parents	1–4:16

Chapter *1–4*

Deal with Difficult Situations

HANDLING DISCIPLINE AND OTHER TOUGH ISSUES

DEALING WITH DIFFICULT PARENTS

If all parents were angels, school would be a little bit of heaven, wouldn't it? Unfortunately, some parents will be angry, frustrated, disappointed, or just plain worried. An important part of parent involvement is knowing how to handle these difficult parents.

In fact, these are the types of parents that you need to work with the most. They become your biggest supporters and allies if you can channel their energy into positive feelings about the school.

Difficult parents require more communication from you and your teachers. Why? Because they're usually not getting the whole picture from their children. As a result, they're often unaware of the school's efforts to help their kids do better.

Communicate with Difficult Parents

Whether you're dealing with parents who think you're doing nothing for their children or parents who claim you never told them about any problems, the antidote is the same: communication and lots of it. Here are three ways you can begin:

1. **Regular personal meetings help ease tension.**
   "Parents of a boy in our school said we weren't doing enough for him," says a Canadian principal. "They complained to the superintendent, the board, and the regional office of education. They even wrote a letter to the Prime Minister of Canada!

"It was a clear situation, however, where parents weren't giving their son support at home. Their view was, 'Teaching is the school's job, not ours.' The only kind of parent involvement we could get out of them were accusations that we were a 'do-nothing' school.

"So I decided to make a personal commitment to keeping the student's parents informed on a monthly basis about what the school was doing for him. The boy's teacher, a central office staffer, and I met with the parents each month.

"We reviewed his progress, set goals, and revised his program to make sure we were meeting his needs. This is much more than we'd ever done in the past for a student.

"During meetings, I pointed out what we were doing and where we were experiencing problems. Then I suggested ways the parents could help at home—for example, by making sure homework is completed. After each meeting, I wrote a letter to the parents highlighting areas of agreement between us and them. I also thanked them for their participation.

"This helped a lot. Even if they disagreed with some of our actions, I could prove that we were doing everything in our power to help their son succeed in school."

2. **Written communication supports your case.**

An Illinois principal uses two forms to help her keep parents up-to-date on their child's progress in school. Both forms must be signed by parents and returned to the school.

This is ready-made documentation that protects her and her teachers from "you-never-told-me" parents.

In addition, she says the forms force parents to monitor their kids' academic performance—and to take responsibility for helping improve their school performance. Here's how they work.

- "The first form I use is our Midterm Progress Report," she says. "It keeps parents (and students) informed about progress or lack of progress. Parent conferences and teacher contact just aren't enough. We send out the Midterm Progress Reports between each report card.

    "Teachers make great use of the form's Recommendations for Improvement section to specifically state students' needs—for example, 'work on grammar.' We print the forms on three-page carbonless paper to make them teacher-friendly—teachers only have to fill out a single sheet. This provides documentation for the teacher, school, and parents."

- "I also use a Student Status Report," says the principal. "Even with four report cards, four Midterm Progress Reports, and two parent conferences, we still need another method that quickly informs parents of problems.

    "The Student Status Report allows us to tell parents of their kids' status on an 'as needed' basis."

    "The report lets teachers request parents' help in specific areas—like completing missed assignments or improving grades. Once parents sign and return the forms, we have proof that they did see them. We'll even mail them if we suspect kids aren't taking them home.

    "Teachers don't mind the extra work the forms require because they know that documentation by the school is more important than ever," she says.

    "Some parents are only looking for a reason to jump us. But the forms are just as helpful to the majority of parents who are interested in knowing about their kids' performance.

"Also, the forms aren't necessarily negative. Teachers can use them to praise parents and students by saying, for example, 'Your child raised her grade to a B. Congratulations!'"

3. **Get teachers and parents talking about discipline.**

Most principals would prefer to see teachers working with parents to resolve discipline problems their kids cause. Here's how an Eastern principal reinforces this to his teachers:

"We've always had a Parent Notification Form to use for discipline steps," says the principal. "But we recently added a section that says, 'If you wish to contact me (the teacher) about this incident, I will be available at the times and phone numbers below.'"

"This seemingly minor change has really opened up communication between parents and teachers who hesitate to make the first move," says the principal.

"Some teachers have always resisted calling parents—probably out of shyness or fear of what parents might say," he explains.

"When kids are having trouble in school, though, their parents almost always want to talk to the teacher."

"Now if the teacher doesn't contact them, parents know when and where they can reach the teacher—and they take advantage of it."

"As a result, teachers who wouldn't have called in the past can often work out some plan of action together with parents—and my involvement is minimal."

Parent Development Helps Educate Parents

Parents who haven't been in a school for years can present special problems because they don't understand what's going on, says a Connecticut principal.

"After several years as a university professor, I came back to the principalship, and it's just a different world now. Parents wouldn't recognize our schools if they've been out of touch with them for any length of time."

You can avoid banging heads with parents who have outdated ideas about schools by using a little "parent development."

Just as you would with teachers, spend time face-to-face with parents to introduce new ideas. When parents are educated about changes going on in your school, they're a lot less likely to oppose your innovations.

"When we have inservices for teachers on curriculum topics, I schedule time for the speaker to present the same material to parents," says the principal. "This is an excellent way to update parents about what we're doing.

"In fact, we're bringing in a consultant to talk to teachers about changes in children's literature. I've planned two hours for him to talk to parents.

"We're also having a teacher workshop on the use of new math materials. That speaker will talk to parents about how they can help their children with math."

Working on Discipline Issues

Working with parents on their kids' discipline problems can take up a good chunk of your time.

Admittedly, it isn't the ideal form of parent involvement, but here are some strategies principals use to get parents to support their discipline policies:

- **Hold a conference with the parents.**

When students are experiencing trouble with their behavior or grades, Principal Priscilla Martinez sends a letter to parents inviting them to a Saturday morning conference at her school.

Martinez uses the meeting to emphasize the importance of good behavior and academic performance—and parents' responsibility to help their kids.

"I meet with the student's teacher during the week to determine the problem," says Martinez. "On Saturday, I sit down with the parents and their kids to discuss the problem.

"If the kid is failing a subject, I explain why—maybe he or she isn't turning in homework assignments."

"Then I'll work with the parents to devise a plan to make sure the student completes his or her homework."

When parents don't respond to her letter, she approaches them directly. "I'll visit their home and let them know that the problem is serious," she says.

- **Call a parent at work to get a response.**

Principal David Hillmer of Sycamore, Illinois, solved the problem of parents who don't respond to his requests for assistance: He calls them where they work.

"I get more activity from parents when I call them at their offices," he says. "They move a lot more quickly to discipline their kids or to respond to my requests."

"Parents don't like to take calls at work. For one thing, they don't want their supervisors to know that there's a problem with their kids. This puts uncomfortable pressure on the parents."

Hillmer's method recently worked with a mother whose son was a real troublemaker. "She insisted that if I ever had a problem with her child, I was to call her at work," he says.

"So when I couldn't get her son to stop causing problems, I called her office. She came to school and smoothed over the problem."

"The next day, he was at it again—the mom hadn't been tough enough with him. So I called her, and she was a little miffed. But she came to the school to talk with her son."

"The next day—another problem with the kid. The third time I called the mother at work, she was mad. She started yelling that I was bothering her at work."

"But you know, after that third telephone call, the kid never caused any more problems."

"When you call parents at work, their first response is, 'Is this an emergency?' I always say 'yes.' If it has reached the point where I have to call them at work, it's an emergency."

- **Require parents to attend school with their child.**

Principal Lynn Redden isn't opposed to radical solutions to serious discipline problems involving students.

"When there's a persistent problem, like poor attendance, and I would otherwise consider suspension, I'll call the parent and require him or her to attend school all day for three days with the student."

"I believe that the student's behavior is ultimately the parents' responsibility, so they should be with their child to improve it. This has been effective because parents realize the problem is severe enough for me to ask them to take off work for three days and follow their child around the school."

"Parents usually don't like the idea at first. Afterwards, though, they admit it was time well spent. If a parent refuses to go along with the plan, I say that I'll contact a judge and report the parent for violation of state compulsory attendance law. In Texas, if we make this ruling because of discipline problems, the only way a child can get back into school is with his or her parent. If the parent refuses to participate, he or she is breaking the law."

- **Get parent support for your discipline plan.**

Discipline just won't work unless you have parent support. That's why Principal John H. Connell took his school's new discipline plan straight to parents and asked for their support. Here's how he did it. . . .

"Our School Improvement Team developed a new discipline plan that uses rules based on assertive discipline and teachers' individual classroom rules," says Connell of Lovington, New Mexico. "We believed it was going to work well. Since it was new, though, we wanted to tell parents about it—and get their support."

Connell sent a full-page letter to parents describing the plan's expectations, consequences, and positive reinforcements.

"At the bottom of the page was a space for parents to sign, indicating that they supported the program," he says. "We also added a note stating that if the form was not returned, we would assume that they agreed."

Connell says that getting parents' approval means that there are fewer questions when there's an actual disciplinary situation involving their kids.

He adds that all but a handful of parents indicated they would work with him to make the discipline plan a success. "A few parents disagreed with parts of the plan, so I called them, and we worked out a compromise.

"For example, some kids live 50 miles from school. So instead of staying after school, they serve detention in in-school suspension."

Getting parents involved by asking them to approve the new discipline plan has paid off, Connell says. "In the past, a lot of kids felt they could push us a little bit further and get away with a lesser punishment than they deserved.

"Now the kids don't do that so much. They know their parents are backing us—and that Mom and Dad would probably agree that they deserve whatever punishment we give them."

Parents Must Know the Rules

While parent support for discipline is important, it's no guarantee that parents will read the information on discipline that you give them. Many principals (and parents) agree that the discipline section of school handbooks often goes unread.

If parents aren't aware of how your discipline policy works, it can cause problems later on when you apply it to their kids.

Principal Rosemarie Green of Warren, Pennsylvania, says that many parents of her students were skipping over her handbook's discipline section. As a result, they would often call her to question the way their children were being disciplined.

To fill this obvious communication gap, Green asked her teachers for help. They responded by creating a tri-fold brochure specifically about discipline. To make sure it caught parents' attention, it was printed on neon pink paper and sent home separately from the parent/school handbook.

"The brochure is simple and to the point. It lists rules for the cafeteria, the playground, and the hall. It also includes general classroom rules that all teachers enforce. Asking teachers to create the brochure forced them to evaluate their expectations—and boil down their rules to only the three or four most essential ones."

"Following the lists of rules are the consequences of breaking them. The brochure also has a coupon that parents sign and return to the classroom teacher. This indicates that they've read and discussed the brochure with their kids."

Green says that 100 percent of the coupons were returned last year—and that the brochures helped teachers deal with a lot of misunderstandings.

"Every once in a while, a cranky parent would call to ask why a student was removed from the cafeteria and forced to eat alone. The teacher would read from the brochure, 'The student violated cafeteria rule number four, keep your table area clean. The consequence is that the student is removed from the cafeteria.'

"If parents get really cantankerous, you can remind them that they signed off on the discipline brochure. Once you recite a rule, though, they usually don't have much to say."

Educating Parents on Attendance

Associate Principal Rodney H. Henke of Wisconsin Rapids, Wisconsin, tells me his school gives parents a practical tool designed to drive home the importance of their children's regular attendance at school.

"Our attendance process is computerized, so kids know they can't beat the system," he says. "But we still felt we needed to educate parents about the rules."

That's why the school mails an attendance brochure to every home before school begins in the fall. "The brochure covers attendance rules—what we consider excused or unexcused absences—and gives parents directions on calling the school when a student is absent.

"It also includes frequently asked questions about attendance, and everything in the brochure is in 'parent-speak language,'" says Henke.

The brochure also comes with a handy sticker parents can place near the telephone. The sticker (see graphic below) gives the attendance phone number and information parents need to have ready when they call the school.

Even though the sticker tells parents where to call, they don't always follow through on the information. If they don't call by the specified time, Henke calls them, then sends another sticker home.

He also reminds students that they have to be responsible too. "If they were on the job, they would need to clear a day off with their boss—they couldn't just skip out," he says.

"Since the kids can't call in their own absences, I tell them that they might have to remind their parents to call in.

"Many take this seriously and really help us educate their parents about what to do."

So far, results of the brochure approach have been positive, and Henke tells me that the school's attendance rate has gone up from 90 percent to 95 percent.

SAMPLE ATTENDANCE STICKER

Lincoln High School **ATTENDANCE NUMBER:** **422-6350** Wisconsin Rapids Public School District	1. Call by 9:00 A.M. on the day of the absence. 2. Be prepared to indicate: • parent/guardian name • telephone number • reason for absence • student name • date(s) of absence 3. If you need further assistance, call: Lincoln High School Office at 423-1520 between 7:30 A.M. and 4:00 P.M. **Thank you for your cooperation!**

Q & A ABOUT ATTENDANCE POLICY

Associate Principal Henke offers a question and answer section in his attendance policy brochure. Here's a sampling...

Question: Why should parents/guardians call the attendance line instead of sending a note the day after the absence?

Answer: The attendance line helps the school do a quicker and more efficient job of monitoring attendance and absences of a student. Another reason is if a parent/guardian is going to be absent from work, the parent or guardian would notify his or her employer prior to their absence.

Using the same practice, the school has established this policy to help prepare students for the world of work. More importantly, the attendance line also builds better and faster communications between the home and school.

Parents Harm Children in Custody Battles

There's nothing more heart-wrenching than a child caught in the middle of a custody battle. Unfortunately, schools are also getting caught in this middle-ground. This means that principals sometimes have to take extra precautions to protect kids in their schools.

A Florida principal who faced a frightening situation shares this story.

"I was in my office when an upset mother called me," she says.

"It seems that her ex-husband had started wearing battle fatigues and was talking about guns. He was also using drugs heavily.

"The woman said she had no idea what her ex-husband might do if he suddenly decided he wanted to see his daughter in school."

Alarm bells started going off inside the principal's head. She'd heard enough horror stories about distraught parents who suddenly went berserk.

"I informed the police of the situation," she said. "Then I planned a secret phrase to put my staff on alert. If I got word that the father was headed our way, I'd get on the intercom and say, 'Popcorn will be served on Wednesday.'

"We always have popcorn on Friday, so teachers would know we had a problem if I changed the day. They were instructed to lock the doors to their classrooms when they heard those code words."

Parents involved in custody battles often force principals to assume the difficult role of visitation arbitrator. "A father recently called to ask if he could see his daughter over the noon hour," says the principal.

"I called his wife to see if it was OK with her. She angrily refused. Then I had to call the father back and tell him he couldn't come to the school."

The principal says he struggled to cope with this uncomfortable situation. "I had to say 'no' to a crying man who was on the phone begging me to let him see his daughter. It wasn't easy."

Reach Out to Difficult Parents Even More

Most principals would agree that difficult parents' attitudes can often be traced to their own negative experiences of school.

Here are four steps you can take to show parents that school isn't an intimidating or threatening place.

1. **Work with them in a setting where they're comfortable.** "Many parents I speak to don't want anything to do with school because they're still carrying scars from their school days," says Principal Lynn Redden. "If I want to reach out to them, I have to go to their homes.

    "When I visit them in their homes, they're comfortable and more open to talking about their children."

2. **Always keep your focus on the child.** "I can't stress enough the importance of having something positive to say about the child," says Redden.

    "I always try to do what will help the child, which is what parents want too. We just need to work together to give the student a positive school experience."

3. **Let parents "get it off their chests."** Many parents want to unload their problems on you, and they can get pretty angry. "I find that what works best is to let parents say all they have to say," says Principal Ivan Kershner of Gypsum, Colorado. "Typically, they start out strong but just as quickly run out of steam. Then I can jump in and begin answering some of their complaints and statements."

    "I try to show parents that I'm willing to consider their points," says Principal Glenn Babbitt of Oak Lawn, Illinois. "I repeat their concerns to make sure I understand correctly. I also ask if they have questions about any other issues."

4. **Get social service agencies involved when necessary.** "We always start with the premise that parents want their children to succeed," says Principal Dot Moran. "But some parents have basic survival needs like housing, nutrition, and medical help. You have to address these first because if kids are hungry, they're not going to be able to focus on learning."

    Social workers, nurses, and counseling agencies are also available to help families of students, Moran says.

    "For instance, we had some parents with alcohol problems whose children weren't receiving the proper care at home. We connected the parents with an agency in town. This led to a trusting relationship with the parents. They started to open up to us, so we could help them get the assistance they needed."

    Moran also helped a mother who couldn't read. A first-grade teacher worked with her, and then the school put her in touch with a literacy program in town.

    "Now she can read with her child and, of course, her child is doing better in school."

MATERIALS YOU CAN USE

Midterm Progress Report

Student: _____   Date: _____

Teacher: _____   Grade: _____

This report is to inform you of your child's progress at this point in the grading period and is provided in order to assist you in helping your child achieve his or her best.

S = Satisfactory   **U = Unsatisfactory**

___Readng   ___English   ___Social studies
___Spelling   ___Math   ___Classroom behavior
___Penmanship   ___Science   ___Homework

In order to improve, your child needs to:

☐ Complete required work   ☐ Come to school more regularly
☐ Complete work on time   ☐ Hand in written homework
☐ Other _____

Recommendations for improvement: _____
_____
_____
_____
_____

This report has been discussed with your child.

Do you desire a conference? _____

Please discuss this report with your child, sign the yellow copy, and return it to the school.

_____   _____
Signature   Date

Deal with Difficult Situations   1–4:11

Student Status Report

Date: _____

Our goal is to provide each of our students with the high quality educational program and support that he or she will need to become a successful and responsible citizen in the world of tomorrow. In order to accomplish this task, we need our parents' support and cooperation.

This report requests your help in assisting _____ in the area(s) indicated below.

- ☐ Complete assignments (listed below) missed during the period of his or her absence.
- ☐ Finish work (listed below) not completed during school.
- ☐ Complete homework assignments (listed below).
- ☐ Improve his or her grades in the following subjects (listed below).
- ☐ Other. _____

If you have any questions, concerns, or suggestions, please feel free to write a note or call me at school between _____ and _____.

Thank you for your assistance.

_____   _____
Teacher signature   Parent signature

Parent Notification Form

Date: _____

Dear Parents,

This is to notify you that your child, _____, was sent to the office today for misbehavior in school. Please discuss this infraction with him or her. It is our hope that, with your help, we can bring about a change in your student's behavior that is more socially acceptable and will help to develop responsibility and a respect for himself or herself and the rights of others. Please sign the form below and return it to school with your child tomorrow.

Reason for being sent to office: _____

_____

This infraction, as defined by the school discipline code, is: ☐ Major ☐ Minor

An accumulation of 3 points will result in In-School-Suspension; 4 points will result in Out-Of-School-Suspension. (Reference: Student Handbook, page 11) A major infraction results in a student receiving 1 point on his or her discipline record.

If you wish to contact me about this incident, I will be available to speak with you at the time(s) and phone number(s) listed below:

Phone: (___)_____ Date: _____ Time(s): _____

Phone: (___)_____ Date: _____ Time(s): _____

Teacher's Signature _____ Date: _____

Action taken:

1. Discussed the incident with your son or daughter.
2. Assigned your student to after-school detention _____ to be served from 3:10 P.M. to _____ P.M. It will be necessary for you to provide transportation home for your student on that day.
3. Other
4. Your son or daughter has accumulated _____ points this year.

_____   _____
Administrator signature   Parent/Guardian signature

Discipline Plan Letter

At this school, we believe every teacher has the right to teach, and every student has the right to learn.

Students will be treated in a friendly, fair—but firm—way. Teachers will handle most discipline in their classrooms. This includes, but is not limited to, asking the student to:

1. Be assigned to study hall over noon hour.
2. Stay after school.
3. Write extra assignments.
4. Be in time-out in another classroom or office.
5. Contact his or her parents (The teacher may request a conference).

If the actions of the student warrant being sent to the office, discipline in the office may include, but is not limited to:

1. A principal conference with the student.
2. Either a written or phone contact with the parent.
3. Parent, pupil, teacher, and principal conference.
4. Detention at noon or after school.
5. In-school suspension.
6. Suspension from school (reinstatement requires a parent conference).
7. Other._____

Please check whether you agree or disagree with this plan. Then sign and return the lower portion of this sheet to your child's homeroom teacher. If you disagree with the discipline plan, be aware that you may be required to pick up your child from school if his or her actions cause harm to or disrupt the education of others.

**If this form is not completed and returned by _____, it will be assumed that the parent(s) or guardian(s) are in agreement with the provisions of this school discipline policy.

☐ I agree with the discipline plan.

☐ I disagree with the plan and understand that it's my responsibility to pick up my child should his or her actions cause harm or disrupt the education of others.

_____   _____   _____
Student Name   Parent Signature   Date

Discipline Brochure

Dear Parent/Guardian(s),

This pamphlet contains the discipline plan for this school. Its purpose is to keep you well-informed of rules and consequences. In order to maintain a high standard of excellence, we feel that consistent rules and enforcement of those rules by staff are imperative.

Please do what you can to be sure your child understands our school rules. These rules are our way of providing a safe, educational environment for your child.

After you have read through the pamphlet, please sign and date the section below, tear it out, and return it to school with your child. This will signify to us that you have read our discipline plan.

I have read the discipline plan and discussed it with the student(s).

Parent/Guardian:
Date:
Comments:

COUNTY SCHOOL DISTRICT

The school district board of education believes that in order for an individual to be a contributing member of society, he or she must possess certain values. The board also feels that the school should embody certain values as part of its reason for existence.

The board recognizes the importance of these values and encourages students to adopt them so they can develop the self-discipline necessary to be contributors and responsible members of the community. The board feels that these values are based on community standards and, if not accepted, will result in the enforcement of consequences that will protect the rights of the community to maintain the standards it considers acceptable.

Human rights and equal opportunity are intended for every citizen according to our Constitution. Laws are designed to protect individual and group rights. They work well if:

1. Everyone knows the rules.
2. Everyone respects and obeys the rules.

The board intends that these rules be distributed to every student and his or her parent/guardian(s).

Classroom Rules

1. Treat others with respect.
2. Stay in your seat unless you have permission to leave it.
3. Keep hands and feet to yourself.
4. Raise your hand to speak.
5. Sharpen pencils before or after class.
6. Be respectful of the teacher's desk.
7. All homework must be neat and on time.
8. Only one boy and one girl at a time will be excused for restroom privileges.
9. Follow directions the first time.

Hall Rules

1. Walk.
2. Whisper.
3. Keep hands off the walls.

Lunchroom Rules

1. Wait for teacher before entering lunchroom.
2. Sit in assigned seats.
3. Raise your hand if you need something.
4. Clean your table area.
5. Clean your floor area.
6. Exit quietly.

Playground Rules

1. Walk on the stones; keep stones off equipment.
2. One person on slide at a time.
3. NO flipping over bar on silver slide.
4. NO banging feet on silver slide.
5. Go in one direction on the rings and monkey bars.
6. No more than three people on tire swing.
7. Persons are to climb through tunnels, not over the top.
8. Touch football only.

Dismissal

Dismissal of students is at 3 P.M. Dismissal begins with a teacher bringing students downstairs and permitting students to exit from the front entrance only.

Any student not going home in the usual manner must have a parent note. This note must be given to the teacher/principal and then given to the bus driver. Without a note, no students will be permitted to walk somewhere if they usually ride a bus, or to ride a different bus. Please remember that if someone other than the legal parent/guardian is to pick up a child, we must have written permission.

continues

Discipline Brochure continued

If you must meet your child after school, please wait outside the front doors. This is a very busy time of day, and if you are upstairs, or in a hall, you will interfere with dismissal. Parents should not meet children in the building. The exception to this is parents meeting children after morning kindergarten.

Please remember that teachers are happy to talk with you, but make an appointment. Discussing your child at dismissal time or in the morning makes it difficult for the teacher to give you his or her full attention.

School rules

1. Students may ride bikes to school. Bikes must be placed in racks upon arrival.
2. Students are not permitted in school after dismissal unless supervised.
3. No hats in the building.
4. During fire drills, students should exit quietly and quickly.
5. Students are permitted to go home for lunch only when they have a note signed by a parent.
6. Students must obey the crossing guard, bus driver, and teacher on duty.
7. Students should be positive, respect school property, and represent themselves well.
8. Students are responsible for the care of their textbooks, library books, and all other school property. Non-returned or damaged books must be paid for.

Consequences for all rules

1st offense—Warning

2nd offense—Time-out (length determined at teacher's discretion)

3rd offense—Loss of recess

4th offense—Note and/or contact with parent or guardian(s)

5th offense—Conference with building principal

(BLANK)

Market Street Elementary School

Discipline Plan

How to deal with difficult parents
Tips for administrators and staff

Mr. and Mrs. Carter storm into the school office—angrily demanding to see you immediately. They say they're "sick and tired of having Joey picked on and treated unfairly!"

What do you do when difficult or angry parents like these show up at school? How can you transform a potential confrontation into a constructive dialogue?

There are no easy answers. Each situation is different. But given the level of violence in schools and the constant threat of lawsuits, it's extremely important to deal with these awkward situations effectively. Here are a few general principles that will help you.

Use the personal approach

Research shows that parents respond best when spoken to in a *personal* way rather than in a businesslike, professional way. So, talk to them as equals, respecting their efforts at the difficult job of parenting. Often the first step in dealing with these parents is to put yourself in their shoes. Ask yourself, "How would I like to be treated?" or, "How would I like someone to speak to me about my own child?" Let parents know you need to work together—as partners—to help their children.

See parents as caring—not just angry

It helps to remember that most parents—even angry ones—are concerned about their children's education. Although their approach may be misguided, their motives are often good.

Remind parents that children's accounts of what happened are often inaccurate or exaggerated and that one purpose of the meeting is to determine the facts together. Just as you expect parents to see your side of the story, you should be prepared to see things from their perspective. When the parent and the student are right, admit it and express your strong desire to help the child.

Schedule appointments for visits

Most schools have the policy that conferences need to be scheduled in advance. But if parents show up unannounced, try to greet them graciously—with a warm smile and a pleasant "hello." If possible, stop what you're doing to listen for a few minutes. Then, let them know that although you'd like to meet with them, their concerns are too important to discuss without preparation. Schedule a time they can come back—after you've had time to prepare.

over, please

continues

How To Deal with Difficult Parents continued

How to deal with difficult parents: *Tips for administrators and staff*

Stay cool under fire

Parents who are angry and unreasonably critical may blast you with an irrational tirade. Try to remain calm yourself, even in the face of outright hostility.

If you feel you're "losing it," silently repeat soothing words to yourself, such as, "I am cool. I am calm." Your controlled, quiet, and firm tone of voice will often be enough to soothe an irate parent to the point where rational discussion can begin.

Turn arguments into discussions

Your goal is to transform an argument into a discussion. In order for this to happen, parents have to feel that their viewpoints are being respected and heard without bias.

Acknowledge parents' anger by saying, "I can see that you're angry. Let's take this one step at a time." It often helps to ask parents what they would like you to do. This shows you take their feelings seriously and that you want to resolve the problem—together. Let them talk without interruption, even when you believe they're wrong.

Finally, acknowledge any points they have made which are true. Admitting your mistakes—or those of a staff member—may be uncomfortable, but it can diffuse parents' anger. Result: You'll pave the way for further constructive communication.

Outline parent concerns—in writing

Taking good notes helps document your meeting and prevents future misunderstandings. If possible, break down parents' complaints into key points and discuss them individually. Ask questions to clarify complaints that are unclear. When you finish, summarize the main points to make sure they're accurate—and to let parents know you heard them. If appropriate, ask if they have any suggestions or solutions to propose.

Invite a colleague if you expect trouble

If you expect any trouble, invite another staff member to the meeting. Always hold the conference in the school, during hours when other staff is still in the building. This is especially important if safety is a concern or you think it will be helpful to have witnesses to what is said.

When you take the team approach, discuss in advance with other teachers or administrators how you will handle the situation and what roles each of you will play. If more than one of you is in the room, be careful not to seem like you're ganging up on the parents—or you'll never diffuse anger. No one likes to feel threatened or "set up."

If you feel abused...

Suppose, in spite of your efforts, a parent's anger continues. In a firm, controlled voice, say, "I'm very uncomfortable with the way you're speaking to me. It's making it impossible for us to work together for the good of your child. I'll be happy to continue if you stop cursing" (screaming, etc.). If this doesn't work, it's time to end the conference. Simply say, "It's not going to be helpful for us to continue today. I'd be glad to set up another meeting when everyone is calmer." If you feel physically threatened, don't hesitate to get help or even call the police.

Speak the truth—tactfully

One of the toughest things to do when dealing with parents is to get them to see their children's shortcomings. It's especially hard for parents to hear anything negative about their children. They may feel it reflects on their parenting abilities and that they are powerless to do anything about it. That's why it's important to also mention some positives about their children's abilities, work, or attitudes.

End on a positive note

At the end of the conference, summarize the discussion and what actions you and the parents have decided to take. Many educators have found it helpful to have parents sign an agreement that describes what will happen at school and at home to resolve the issues. Sometimes the next step is to schedule another meeting so that issues brought up at the first meeting can be looked into. Parents need to feel that something has happened, or they'll just stay upset. If possible, save at least one encouraging comment for the end of the conference.

Practice prevention

One of the best ways to reduce the number of difficult encounters with parents is to have an ongoing relationship with them. Regular parent-teacher conferences, school visits, or phone conversations can head off trouble by establishing trust and letting parents know about their children's progress and behavior *before* a crisis occurs.

Make an effort to contact parents when their children do something *right*. When parents hear good news, they realize you care and will be more receptive if you have to tell them about a problem.

What's the bottom line? Try to see all parents as partners. Then, work together with a spirit of cooperation for the good of their children!

Part 2

Teachers

Chapter 2–1   Build Parent–Teacher Teams 2–1:i

Chapter 2–2   Work Together for Student Success 2–2:i

Chapter 2–3   Improve Parenting Skills 2–3:i

Chapter 2–1

Build Parent–Teacher Teams

Keeping Parents Informed	**2–1:1**
Informed Parents Get Involved	2–1:1
Telephone Schedules That Work	2–1:1
Use the Telephone Effectively	2–1:2
Written Communication Is Vital	2–1:3
Newsletter Improves Parent Communication	2–1:3
Items To Include in Your Newsletter	2–1:4
Communicate Your Educational Plan	2–1:4
Speed Letters Save Time	2–1:5
Use Communication Folders	2–1:5
Idea Folder Lets Parents Help Kids Learn	2–1:6
Happy-Grams Are Good Icebreakers	2–1:6
Journals Increase Parent Involvement	2–1:6
Communicate More Than Just Grades on Report Cards	2–1:7
Mark Statement Gives Feedback on Math	2–1:7
Keep Parents Updated on Homework Status	2–1:8
Connect with the Right "Parent"	2–1:8
Thank Parents for Helping	2–1:9
Home Visits Develop Personal Relationships	2–1:9
Teachers Answer Parents' Questions	2–1:11
Use Positive Communication Ideas	2–1:11
Strategies To Reach Difficult Parents	2–1:12
Case Conference Forms To Handle Angry Parents	2–1:13
Materials You Can Use	**2–1:15**
Speed Letter	2–1:15
Monthly Mark Statement	2–1:16

Monthly Mark Statement (Blank)	2–1:17
Good Homework Notice	2–1:18
Bad Homework Notice	2–1:18
Test/Quiz Slip	2–1:19
Case Conference Form	2–1:20
Building a Strong Parent-Teacher Partnership	2–1:21

Chapter **2–1**

Build Parent–Teacher Teams

KEEPING PARENTS INFORMED

Ensuring effective family involvement is too big a job for principals to handle alone. You need the active support and participation of the teachers in your school. If your staff communicate regularly with families, conduct useful parent–teacher conferences, foster at-home learning support, and partner on discipline, students can achieve their best—in and out of the classroom.

INFORMED PARENTS GET INVOLVED

Telephone Schedules That Work

Telephoning parents is easy and quick—if you don't try to do too much at once. Here's two things teachers recommend to avoid telephone burnout.

1. **Make one call a day.** Telephone one parent every weekend of the school year and make regular communication with parents easy on yourself.
   A Michigan teacher says you'll be surprised at how quickly you can make contact with all students' parents.
   "One daily contact is an easy goal to meet," he says. "The hard part isn't spending three minutes communicating with a parent but finding a school telephone that's available.
   "The tone I use with parents is, 'It's going fine, and I just wanted you to know.' This kind of call is short and sweet and requires a minimum amount of time."
2. **Set aside a specific time for calling parents.** Of course, the key to making this work is self-discipline.

A Texas teacher uses a regimen to force himself to communicate good news about his students to their parents.

Every Wednesday evening, he blocks out two hours to make positive phone calls to parents. "As far as I'm concerned, there's nothing good on TV Wednesday night anyway," he says. "I simply call parents and tell them some good news about their kids. For example, I recently called the parents of a boy in my class to praise his behavior, telling them, 'You must have brought him up very well.'

"I take my grade book home each Wednesday because it has parents' names and telephone numbers in it. The book also contains information that I can use to praise students—like good marks and attendance records.

"I keep the calls brief and usually reach six or seven homes during the two-hour period. I find that making seven phone calls a week lets me communicate with each parent several times during the school year.

"Students never know in advance that I will be calling their parents. In fact, the news that I've called spreads like wildfire the next day.

"Kids say, 'He called my house, and I didn't do anything wrong.' Students now come up to me and ask why I haven't called their parents."

Use the Telephone Effectively

The telephone is a great way to get in touch with parents. Here's how other teachers use it effectively.

- **Keep track of the phone calls you make**

  Keeping a log of which parents you call and when is important. It's easy to say you'll remember phone conversations, but this gets tougher as the school year goes on. And you want to make sure you aren't calling only a small group of parents.

  This is why you need some method of tracking phone calls. Here's what a Montana teacher does:

  "I use my seating chart and write a date by each student's name when I make a phone call home," she says.

  "This lets me know at a glance that I'm getting in touch with all parents. The seating chart also gives me a mental picture of the classroom and what happened that day. That often jogs my memory about what I want to tell parents about."

  Another method of keeping track is to set up a chart where you record the phone calls you need to make and then date them when you make the call. It's a good idea to leave some space on the chart to record what was discussed too.

- **Require students to call their parents**

  Sometimes, a phone call carries more weight with parents if it comes from their children. Teacher Judith Whitehead found that when students are required to call their parents to explain a problem situation, the problem usually clears up quickly.

  "Having a student make the call is often a quick wake-up notice to the parents that they're really needed," says Whitehead of Moneta, Virginia. "For example, one of my students wasn't doing homework.

  "I told him that if he didn't have his homework done for the next day, he would have to call his mother. Well, the homework wasn't completed, so he called his mother. He said, 'Mom, Mrs. Whitehead wants to talk to you because I haven't done my homework.'

"Then I got on the phone and told his mother that it was time she knew her child was not completing assignments and that this would result in poor grades," says Whitehead.

The problem was cleared up the next week. Whitehead says she almost always solves problems with these phone calls.

- **Suggest parents call you once a week to discuss progress**

   Don't forget about the flip side of the phone—parents can use it to reach you quickly too. One Illinois teacher isn't afraid of asking parents to call him to help work out their kids' attitude problems.

   "I give parents of struggling students my home and school phone numbers and ask that they call me once a week," he says. "At-risk kids can really drain a teacher's energy. If you plan on making any progress with them, you simply have to have the ongoing support and help of parents.

   "Some parents are good about calling weekly, while others aren't," he adds.

   "But at least they can't tell me later that they weren't given the opportunity to work with me on improving their kid's performance. And I find that the kids of parents who are willing to communicate with me frequently do improve."

- **Call with only good news**

   A Maine teacher calls parents early in the year to share good news about their children. "Once we're settled into a routine, I make an effort to call parents to ask how school has been going for their kids," says the teacher. "I'll ask, 'Has your child said anything that you think I should know about?'

   "I also try to tell the parents something positive about their kids. We've been in school long enough that I can come up with good examples for each student.

   "I often discover information about kids that helps me—like one student who acted up in my class because of a conflict in another classroom.

   "The calls are a good way to build parents' trust because I'm not calling for a 'bad' reason. I just call to ask how it's going."

Written Communication Is Vital

Parents also need written reminders that they can help their children succeed in school. You can accomplish a lot with letters, newsletters, postcards, progress reports, and report cards.

If you aren't sending information home to parents or if you need to try some new strategies, here are some successful ideas other teachers use.

Newsletter Improves Parent Communication

Teachers at a Missouri school wanted to strengthen communication between themselves and their students' parents. So they started something new at their school.

Each of the teachers now writes a newsletter to parents. The beauty of teacher-produced newsletters is that they let you reach parents directly with the information that concerns them most—what's happening in their child's classroom.

It's always tough to add another duty to your already busy schedules, so here's what the teachers did to make it easier to get the process going.

- **They chose how often to write the newsletter.** Even though the teachers have to write a newsletter, they can do it on either a weekly or monthly basis. If a teacher feels overwhelmed, he or she can choose the monthly option.
- **A reasonable length for the newsletter was set.** Teachers know their newsletter doesn't have to be long and involved. One page is plenty. Some teachers write their newsletter by hand, while others use the computer.
- **Teachers shared samples of successful teacher-to-parent newsletters.** This gave the teachers a variety of options, and they picked and chose elements from different newsletters that appealed to them the most.

    For example, some teachers include what they'll be covering in class for the upcoming week or recognize individual students for accomplishments.

Communicate Your Educational Plan

Teachers at a Canadian school write individual long-range plans for their classes and mail them home to parents each year.

This is an excellent way for parents to know from the start what their kids will be expected to master during the year.

The plans go home during the first month of school. Some teachers write lengthy plans, but most are about two pages in length.

In addition, teachers indicate on their plans how they'll evaluate student performance—noting methods they'll use, like class presentations that are different from written exams.

ITEMS TO INCLUDE IN YOUR NEWSLETTER

If you're not doing a newsletter to your parents, you're probably wondering what you should write about. Here's what other teachers are doing . . .

- "I include a complete calendar page for the upcoming month in my newsletter," says Teacher Lisa Crowton of West Boylston, Massachusetts. "This way, parents know when all our activities take place, and I don't have to keep reminding students."
- Teacher Peggy Staib of Riverhead, New York, uses photos in her weekly newsletter. "I take a photo of something that happened during the week, and it goes in the next newsletter," she says. "Parents really like to see their kids in action in the classroom or on field trips. It makes them feel like a part of their school day.

    "I also include requests for any items we might need for upcoming projects," says Staib. "These could be for things like toilet paper rolls or paper towels. I also include a birthday list and the student of the week."
- A Kansas teacher's newsletters feature the lunch menu for the week, upcoming activities, and any successes students have had during the week. "These are anything from getting a perfect score on a paper to helping out another student on the playground," he says.

"The plans are how we show parents that we take a well-thought-out approach to education—and aren't just monitoring kids all day," says one teacher at this Canadian school.

Speed Letters Save Time

For teachers at a Midwest school, sending notes to parents is a snap!

That's because they write the message on a Speed Letter that takes only three minutes to complete.

Although the form can communicate with parents about negative behavior, teachers are encouraged to use it to let parents know when their kids have done something praiseworthy.

Each form has three carbonless copies—one for the principal, teacher, and parents. This means that everybody knows that the student has been recognized.

The notes go out in the mail, and the school pays the postage. (See Speed Letter.)

Use Communication Folders

Teachers in a Texas school send folders home with students every Monday. The folders include the student's discipline chart from the previous week, samples of homework and class assignments, and a letter from the teacher.

The letter explains to parents what will be happening in the upcoming week of class.

It also describes any academic assignments or social activities and outings that are planned.

Parents sign or initial the folders, and their kids return them to school on Tuesday.

Teachers try hard to make sure this is the only communication they send home with the kids.

If you want to use the communication folder idea, here are some twists you can add:

- Write a positive note to parents in each folder. Teacher Pam Negovetich includes a sheet on which she writes a positive note to parents about the student's performance that week.

    Negovetich sends out the folders on Friday, and parents are asked to sign the attachment and return them with their children on Monday.

    "I try to write positive comments like, 'Sue is really trying to read with more expression. Great!' But if there are problems, I'll note them too.

    "The attachment is dated. Underneath the date, I write my comments. Parents sign next to them to acknowledge they've read them. There's also enough space for parents to write comments to me."
- Color code the important points. An Ohio teacher colorfully highlights the areas in the folder where students need improvement or where their behavior needs to change.

    It's a simple but effective way to drive home important points to parents.

    "I highlight the kids' academic work. While the folder reflects their efforts in class, it also focuses on their behavior during school hours.

    "To make a distinction between the two areas, I use a yellow marker to highlight students' academic work.

IDEA FOLDER LETS PARENTS HELP KIDS LEARN

Teachers know that if parents are more involved in their kids' education, their job will be easier. So an Ohio teacher created an Idea Folder for parents to help her teach their kids.

"I frequently send home a folder with students that contains an idea parents can work on with their kids," she says. "For example, one sheet asked parents to help with 'P' words.

"Parents explain the words to their children, and the kids draw pictures to represent words. It's a fun activity for parents and kids.

"The ideas reinforce the skills that I'm teaching in the classroom, but the important thing is that they encourage parents to do some teaching too. At conferences, parents tell me they look forward to seeing the Idea Folder."

"If a student has caused behavior problems in class, I highlight that information in pink. This is a good way to immediately draw parents' attention to problems their kids are having."

Happy-Grams Are Good Icebreakers

Teacher Charla Lear has been teaching in the same district for 15 years and knows most parents. But she still finds that a short positive note helps break the ice with parents at the start of the school year.

"I use Happy-Grams a lot to make initial positive contact with parents of my students," says Lear of Weaubleau, Missouri.

"Before you contact parents with a problem, I think that it's important to tell them something positive about their kids. On Happy-Grams, I'll write that their son or daughter wrote a great paper or helped hand out papers in class. It doesn't have to be anything major, just a short positive note. Generally, I write only a sentence or two."

Lear doesn't bother to put the Happy-Grams in envelopes. She wants her students to read the good news before they take it home to their parents.

Journals Increase Parent Involvement

Getting parents to take their share of the responsibility for their kids' learning isn't always easy. In fact, with some parents it's a major chore!

Teaching Principal Sharon Aucoin, however, has had great success in this area. As part of a Hooked on Books program, she has parents of her students keep a Dialogue Journal, in which she and parents exchange comments about kids' reading progress.

"The Dialogue Journals have been an exciting communication vehicle for myself and parents," says Aucoin. "Of 26 parents, 25 were faithful correspondents last year."

Here's how the Dialogue Journals work: Parents keep a journal from Tuesday through Wednesday that includes a record of student reading.

On Friday, kids return the journals to school for Aucoin's comments. On the following Tuesday, the process starts again.

As you can see, it's a simple way to communicate regularly with parents.

COMMUNICATE MORE THAN JUST GRADES ON REPORT CARDS

Teachers in a New Jersey school requested more space on report cards, so they can write comments to parents.

Most teachers now make at least one comment every marking period. This could be something like, "It's great to see you made the honor roll this time" or "Just a little more and you'll make the honor roll next time."

Comments could also be about behavior and cooperation or any exceptional work a child has completed.

"This not only involves parents in helping their kids at home, but it also opens up avenues of communication between myself and parents," says Aucoin of Terence Bay, Nova Scotia.

"Parents sometimes use the Dialogue Journals to ask questions about curriculum or to just find out what's happening in the classroom.

"It takes time to do this, but I've bought into it because I really believe in the effectiveness of the journals. They're my main vehicle for regular parent communication.

"Parents feel that they're involved in their kids' education, and I get comments like, 'I feel like I'm helping my child with her learning. This is a great habit.'"

Mark Statement Gives Feedback on Math

An Alberta teacher sends Mark Statements home with her students to update parents about their progress in math. She says they're also an excellent way to communicate with parents.

The statements let teachers show parents and students their exact math grades for the month and how students stack up against the class average.

Monitoring the monthly report actively involves parents in their kids' education.

"The statement is set up on the computer as a spreadsheet," says the teacher. "I enter students' marks into the computer as soon as I tally them."

Information on the Mark Statement includes the type of task graded, the student's score out of total points possible, the kid's percentage, the average student mark in the class, and the percentage weight of the assignment toward the final grade.

"The Mark Statement shows exactly how kids have performed on each math task in a month—homework, quizzes, and tests," she says. "On the bottom of the statement, I enter the class average for the month and the student's overall grade.

"There's also space for me to write comments and observations if necessary. Several teachers have found this to be an excellent and useful communication tool. (See Monthly Mark Statement.)

"Beginning with the first statement I send home, I ask kids to have their parents sign and return the Mark Statements—and for parents to include their own comments if they choose to add any.

"The statements have been a consistent way to report to parents. If there's a problem with a student's work, I find that parents pick up on it right away and get in touch with me.

"Students appreciate the feedback too. They expect the statements at the end of the month. If I'm late, they get on me right away!"

Keep Parents Updated on Homework Status

How do you let parents know when their kids aren't completing homework assignments or are doing poorly on tests? Or how do you let parents know students are doing homework assignments or scoring well on tests?

Here's how a Maryland teacher takes care of both sides of the homework issue:

- Good and bad homework notices. "Whenever students get to the point where they have two or more zeros (no credit given) on homework assignments, I send a 'bad homework note' to their parents," says the teacher. "This must be signed and returned to me. Parents aren't shy about writing comments on these notes, either. For instance, it's not unusual for me to receive a message that says, "Thank you for letting me know. You will see improvement!"

    "On the other hand, if a student has no zeros on homework for a quarter or was late with it only once, I send a letter of congratulations called a 'good homework note' to parents. Many students take a real sense of pride and accomplishment in these notes and keep them in the notebook they use to organize materials for school."

    One good reason to keep parents current on student progress is to avoid 'last-minute' questions about grades. "Because the notes keep parents updated, it's tough for them to say they were never aware of their kids' progress." (See Good Homework Notice; see Bad Homework Notice.)

- Test and Quiz slips. "After every test or quiz, I send home a slip that gives the student's grade and a note about the number of homework assignments missed so far in the quarter. The slip must be signed and returned." (See Test/Quiz Slip.)

    "Parents tell me they appreciate the feedback. They often attach a comment to the slip that says something like, 'Thanks so much for this information. I like to know how my son is doing on a regular basis. Eric loves math, and your teaching must have a lot to do with this!"

Connect with the Right "Parent"

Because of divorce and remarriage, blended families, single-parent families, and grandparents as guardians are common today. This can make it difficult to keep names straight when you try to contact the home.

Here are four ways to make sure your communications get to the right person:

1. **Ask students for the name of the parent you'd like to contact.** "I've become much more conscious of asking for parents' names," says an Indiana teacher. "Because of divorce and the blending of families, I never assume anything.

    "For instance, I always ask students, 'What is your mother's full name? Is she the parent I should call?' This eliminates a lot of problems."
2. **If the recordkeeping office can't assure you of a parent's name, telephone and ask to speak with a responsible adult.** "If I don't know a parent's name, I'll telephone and ask, 'Is this the home of (student) and are you an adult who's responsible for (student)?'" says a Colorado teacher. "If the people I call indicate they are, I give them my message."
3. **Ask students to provide you with personal information.** "I have all my students write on index cards their full names, their birthday, and their parents' full names and phone numbers—both home and work," says a Michigan teacher.

"I alphabetize the cards and keep them in a small file. Before I make any parent contact, I double-check my information."

4. **If you have access to a computer, keep family-contact information on a database.** "I have kids fill out a card that gives me the information about their address and telephone numbers of both mother and father," says an Iowa teacher.

"Then I type the information into a computer database. This makes it easy to access the information when I call students' parents."

Remember: If you keep index cards or a computer file, update the information periodically. Family breakups can happen any time during the year.

And if you're mailing materials home to parents, you might want to consider using unmarked envelopes to make sure they go directly to parents. An Indiana teacher simply addresses the envelopes to the parents and doesn't include a return address. You never know when a student will intercept a letter, especially when he or she knows it's bad news.

"In the past, students went through the mail and pulled out any official correspondence from school," the teacher says. "Now they can't 'screen and toss' because my letters are unmarked. They'd have no idea what they're throwing away.

"This technique has been great for parent communication! I've had parents comment to me, 'I didn't know my son was struggling. I'll make sure he gets with the program.'"

Thank Parents for Helping

Once you've developed a good relationship with parents and they're helping their child at home, be sure to thank them for their time and consideration.

An easy but effective way to show your gratitude is to send thank-you notes. For example, you can use them to tell parents that you appreciate their help in getting their kids to behave in the classroom.

"Our computer teacher designed several versions of a thank-you note that teachers can choose from," says an Eastern teacher. "When parents put in extra time working with their kids at home, it makes my job easier. I always make a point to send a note thanking them. It's a common courtesy, but it also significantly improves my relationship with these parents.

"They know that I'm not communicating with them only when there's a 'desperate' situation and I want their help."

Home Visits Develop Personal Relationships

Although they require a time commitment on your part, home visits are an opportunity to develop a stronger relationship with parents. With this as a foundation, parents and teachers can effectively work together to help kids succeed in school. Here are ways other schools approach home visits.

- **Focus on the benefits of home visits**

  Teachers in a Western school meet with parents in their homes early in the fall to introduce themselves.

  The visits open up communication that wouldn't exist otherwise between parents or guardians and the school, says a teacher. This helps prevent later problems.

"We have one kid who's given us fits for years. At the meeting, his grandmother explained why. She told us the boy's mother was in prison, and the father's gone.

"Now when the boy says he wants to see his mother, it takes on a whole new meaning."

Teachers at this school saw 480 of 500 parents by November—outside of classroom time. Some teachers scheduled meetings at 6 A.M. and others at 7 P.M. to accommodate parents. One teacher even met parents on weekends.

A Southern teacher agrees that meeting parents in their homes builds a good personal relationship. Here's her story.

"Meeting parents and seeing where my students lived was an eye-opener," she says. "I taught in an area of the Appalachian Mountains.

"Sometimes, I'd have to drive to the base of a mountain, hike to where the family lives, and visit a cinder-block house with a dirt floor. I appreciated the entirely different view of my students' lives.

"The visits really brought myself and parents closer together. It's one thing to have parents come to school for a conference night—if they bother to attend.

"But this doesn't compare to the personal nature of home visits. It's tough for parents not to cooperate with you after they've welcomed you into their home. Suddenly, you're both on common ground. A strong relationship is how you really get parents working with you to benefit students.

"Home visits aren't required where I now teach. I still make them as often as I can because they have such a positive effect on my parent relationships!"

- **Make home visitation a challenge**

A Southern school has set up a Home Visitation program, complete with incentives to encourage teachers to make home visits. This is something you might want to suggest at your school. Read how the program works . . . .

Three different 'clubs' were set up to recognize teachers incrementally, according to the percentage of their students' homes they visit during the first 100 days of the school year:

  –The 25/25 Club. If a teacher visits 25 percent of students' homes in the first 25 days of the new school year, he or she receives a parchment certificate acknowledging the fact.
  –The 50/50 Club. For visiting 50 percent of kids' homes in the first 50 days of school, a teacher receives another certificate.
  –The 100/100 Club. This certificate is awarded to teachers who visit each of their student's homes during the first 100 days of school.

The names of teachers who earn club membership are compiled and passed along to a secretary who enters them on the parchment certificate. Then the principal signs each certificate.

Teachers receive their certificates at a staff meeting—to the applause of their peers. They've also designed an attractive poster for each club, which is displayed in the faculty lounge. On the poster, they write the names of others who have earned membership in a club. To make the program work, it's kept strictly voluntary.

Since teachers have increased the number of home visits, several benefits have been noticed. First, the classroom discipline situation improved because home visits cement the relationship between a teacher and his or her students.

Second, teachers now have a better overall view of their students' home lives—which helps them improve their teaching methods.

For example, if a student comes from a home where there's not much support—for whatever reason—the teacher can make necessary instructional adjustments.

Teacher participation in the Home Visit program is also impressive—75 percent of the teachers made the 25/25 Club, 55 percent achieved the 50/50 Club, and several reached the 100/100 Club goal!

Teachers Answer Parents' Questions

An Iowa school makes a Homework Hotline available to kids and parents, so they won't have to sit around the kitchen table and scratch their heads over a homework problem.

The hotline coordinator says teachers who work the hotline receive about 100 calls a night from students and parents seeking help with homework.

"The Homework Hotline started because we feel it's important to provide support to students who need help with homework and who may not have the resources at home or who have parents who work nights," says the coordinator.

"We also wanted to let kids know that choosing to do homework after school is a good decision."

Teachers volunteer to staff the Homework Hotline and are paid $15 an hour. They refer to teachers' manuals to answer questions for students in all grades.

"Teachers appreciate having the Homework Hotline number available because they can refer kids to it. They encourage kids to use the number and ask them to write it in the front of their textbooks.

"Parents have called me to say they appreciate having the service also. They want to help the kids with homework but get frustrated because they don't have all the answers."

The Homework Hotline is publicized at the beginning of the school year through flyers sent home with kids. It's also printed on school lunch menus and on refrigerator magnets kids take home. Local media publicized the number after a news release was distributed.

Use Positive Communication Ideas

No matter what strategy or method you use to reach parents, a positive attitude always helps. Here are some general tips you can use to make your communication upbeat.

- Be enthusiastic. Students and parents want to hear what's good about school. When you make a comment, focus on the positives of the situation.

    "This is as important when you work with parents as it is with students," says a Texas teacher. "If someone gives you an idea that you're not too sure will go over well, don't shoot it down. Nothing kills good working relationships more effectively than negative attitudes."
- Listen and seek input. One of the great skills anyone can learn is to listen. Parents appreciate someone who takes time to hear what they have to say, without interruptions or defenses.

After you've listened, make sure you understand what parents are talking about. Briefly summarize what you've heard and ask if they have anything else to add. This lets them know you really are interested in their thoughts.

- Show an interest in the person's point of view. Leaning forward as the other person talks and making eye contact show you're interested in what he or she is saying. Be respectful, however, of personal space and don't stare.
- Use welcoming body language. The physical signals you make can tell others if you're open to conversation or not. Experienced teachers say a smile when you ask a question or while you're listening can enhance communication with parents. Don't put a physical block like a desk, table, or your arms between you and the other person's ideas.
- Treat everyone equally. You'll establish better relationships if you don't give some people preferential treatment. Sure, you're going to like some parents more than others. Your relationships will be better with everyone if you show the same interest, regardless of your personal preference.
- Don't put the student down. When you need to discuss a problem with a parent, you should never take the tone that his or her kid is a loser. Always say, "What can we do to help John be a better student and accomplish better grades?"

Strategies To Reach Difficult Parents

Although it's by no means exhaustive, here is a list of 10 difficult situations you're likely to face with parents—along with ways to resolve the problem. Add to the list as new situations arise, so you'll know how to deal with the problem if it happens again.

1. **Argumentative parents.**
   - Don't confront parents about their child's behavior or performance in front of others.
   - Don't tell parents how to work with their child. Instead, offer options.
   - Don't allow your emotions to overheat. Take time to think before you speak.
   - Try to discover and explore why these parents are upset and argumentative with you.
2. **Demanding parents who take up large amounts of your time.**
   - Answer their questions promptly and courteously.
   - Provide opportunities for them to volunteer at the school.
   - Set up a regular method of communication that you have control over.
   - Direct specific questions to another school employee who could better answer them.
3. **Parents who do their child's homework.**
   - Discuss the importance of having the child do the work to learn the lesson.
   - Explain that this behavior will not be acceptable and the child's grades will fall.
   - Provide guidelines for completing homework.
   - Offer ways the parent can help the student with homework, while still allowing the student to do the actual work.
4. **Parents who ignore homework assignments.**
   - Inform parents of your school's homework policy and what steps will be taken if homework is not finished.
   - Explain the importance of having the child do the work.

- Discuss the negative impact on the student's grades if homework isn't turned in on time.
5. **Lack of discipline at home.**
    - Accept that every home will have different sets of rules.
    - Tell parents the importance of consistency for the child's sake.
    - Try to work together in handling discipline problems.
    - Be consistent with discipline rules in the classroom.
    - Set up a regular time you can discuss classroom behavior with parents.
6. **Parents who really don't care about their child's education.**
    - Communicate as much as possible by telephone, newsletters, personal notes, and home visits.
    - Invite the parents into the school.
    - Show parents samples of the child's work.
    - Focus on the positives about their child.
7. **Parents who had a bad school experience themselves.**
    - Try to put them at ease with your school facilities.
    - Include them in as many positive school activities as possible.
    - Develop a personal relationship.
    - Always focus on the importance of a good education for their child.
8. **Two-career parents who see the school as a baby-sitter.**
    - Phone them at work to set up a meeting.
    - Accommodate their schedules when trying to meet with them.
    - Explain what steps they can take to help the child.
    - Offer suggestions for activities they can do at home with their child.
9. **Absent or divorced parents.**
    - Keep an up-to-date file on both parents and where the child is living.
    - Find out if one parent or both receives mailed information from the school.
    - If both parents wants to be involved, respect their choice.
    - Don't try to force a joint meeting if parents don't want one.
10. **Apathetic parents.**
    - Invite them to exciting school activities.
    - Show them samples of their child's best school work and emphasize the child's positive aspects.
    - Ask them to help with specific activities that are related to their personal hobbies or interests.

Case Conference Forms To Handle Angry Parents

If you're like most other principals, you don't have the time to contact the parents of every student who causes problems at school.

That's why savvy principals look for ways to encourage teachers to take the initiative in this area.

As important as the job is, though, no teacher likes to deal with hostile parents. And no principal likes catching an earful from parents unhappy after talking to their kid's teacher.

To help her teachers cope with parents and eliminate surprises for herself, a Canadian principal has them complete a Case Conference form whenever they talk to parents about a problem student.

The form has space for the teacher to identify what was said, whether recommendations were made, and to request some kind of follow-up by the principal. (See Case Conference Form.)

"The Case Conference form is especially useful if the teacher has had a meeting or a phone call with a parent that just didn't go over well," she says. "For example, if parents strongly believe that their son or daughter needs special assistance, and the teacher disagrees, the teacher can use the form to ask for my help in something like assessing the student's abilities."

The principal says that after she reviews the form, she gets back to the teacher. "I may be able to give advice on how to help parents understand the school's point of view. Sometimes, I call parents myself to talk about how they're feeling.

"The form means that teachers won't feel completely alone when dealing with parents," she says. "It also warns me that something may be coming my way. I like to think of it as my 'safety net' because it lets me know what the situation is before I have to defend myself to parents."

MATERIALS YOU CAN USE

Speed Letter

To the parent or guardian of: _____

From: _____

Date: _____

Reason

☐ Work proficiency
☐ Good attitude
☐ Tardy to school
☐ Excessive or unexplained absences
☐ Positive behavior
☐ Discipline
☐ Work deficiency
☐ Other _____

The educational progress of your child is dependent on home and school communication.

This notification is one method of keeping you informed about your child's activities.

Please share this notice with your child. If you wish to respond, please do so by using the back of this form or calling the school.

Please be advised that: _____

_____

_____

_____

_____

Thank you for your cooperation.

Monthly Mark Statement

Teacher
School

Thursday, Nov. 14, 1994
Report for Joseph Jones, #153

TASK	SCORE	OUT OF	%	CLASS AVERAGE	% OF GRADE
1. Assignment, Sept. 16	13.0	17.0	76.5	80.2	5.3
2. Quiz, Sept. 17	92.0	100.0	92.0	61.8	31.1
3. Project, Oct. 1	23.0	25.0	92.0	79.2	7.8
4. TEST, Oct. 1	7.0	7.0	100.0	90.2	2.2
5. Quiz, Oct. 15	12.0	13.0	92.3	56.3	4.0
6. Assignment, Oct. 18	15.0	15.0	100.0	66.5	4.7
7. Quiz, Oct. 21	9.0	13.0	69.2	69.2	4.0
8. TEST, Oct. 28	88.0	100.0	88.0	62.8	31.1
9. Quiz, Oct. 31	9.0	10.0	90.0	68.8	3.1
10. Notes, Oct. 31	9.0	10.0	90.0	87.3	5.0
Student's overall grade and class average:			89.5	67.3	

Student's mark
(A, B, C, D, F)

Class marks
L = Lowest   A = Average   H = Highest

Teacher/Parent Comments:

Monthly Mark Statement

Teacher
School

Date
Student name and ID number

TASK	SCORE	OUT OF	%	CLASS AVERAGE	% OF GRADE
1.					
2.					
3.					
4.					
5.					
6.					
7.					
8.					
9.					
10.					

Student's overall grade and class average:

Student's mark
(A, B, C, D, F)

0% |—|—|—|—|—|—|—|—|— 100%
                        L   A   H

Class marks
L = Lowest   A = Average   H = Highest

Teacher/Parent Comments:

Good Homework Notice

Dear Parent/Guardian of _____:

I'd like to take this opportunity to inform you that _____ has completed every math homework assignment for the _____ quarter. Your child should be commended for the continuous effort necessary for this accomplishment! I hope to see this pattern continue, and I'd like to thank you for the time you have spent working with your child.

Sincerely,

Teacher

Bad Homework Notice

Dear Parent/Guardian of _____:

This notification is to inform you that _____ is not keeping up with the math homework.

_____ Number of homework assignments not done at all

_____ Number of homework assignments turned in late or incomplete

I usually give homework assignments Monday through Thursday nights. These are not lengthy, and I do expect students to attempt them. I check homework daily. If the homework is completed on time, full credit is given. If the homework is incomplete in any way or late, 1/2 credit is given. If the homework is not done, no credit is given. The student is given one week to do any make-up assignments. The homework grade counts for 35% of the report card grade.

All students are aware of my policy. Any support that can be offered from home would be much appreciated!

_____   _____
Teacher Signature   Parent/Guardian Signature

Test/Quiz Slip

A (name of class) Update

Student Name: _____

Date: _____

Test/Quiz Grade: _____

Number of homework assignments missed so far this quarter: _____

Teacher Name: _____

Parent/Guardian Signature: _____

Date: _____

Additional Comments:

Case Conference Form

Date: _____

Teacher: _____   Student: _____

Individual with whom the conversation took place:

Names of those who also participated in the conversation:

Areas discussed:

Recommendations:

Follow-up action requested:

_____   _____
Teacher signature   Date

_____   _____
Principal signature   Date

Building a strong parent-teacher partnership

What makes the difference in how your child performs in school? The answer might surprise you. It's not your child's IQ, the teacher, the school, or your education level—although these play a part.

Study after study tells the same story. Children who do best in school have parents who are actively involved in their children's education. And one of the best ways to get involved is to build a strong parent-teacher partnership. Here are some ideas to help you.

WHERE DO I START?

First, get to know your child's teacher early. If possible, drop by to say hello before the school year even begins. If the school has an "Open House" for parents, take advantage of it.

Drop the teacher a note telling a little bit about your child—likes, dislikes, interests, and hobbies. Remember that teachers need your suggestions and support to be most effective. After all, who knows your child better than you? By working as a team, your child's education can take off like a shooting star!

KEEP IN TOUCH

Throughout the year, use these ideas to stay in touch:

- Try to attend parent-teacher conferences, parent organization meetings, workshops, and special presentations.
- Tell the teacher about any special situations that may affect your child's success at school—health problems or changes in the family.
- Remember how great you feel when you get a note of thanks? Teachers feel the same way. Send a note to the teacher to express your appreciation. *Example:* "Thanks for sparking Philip's interest in reptiles. He's so excited!"

LEND A HELPING HAND

Busy schedules often make it difficult for parents to help out. But volunteering does have a way of building the parent-teacher relationship.

If you hear of an upcoming activity that you'd like to be part of, ask how you can help. *Suggestions:* Volunteer to chaperone a field trip, read a favorite story to the class, talk about a hobby, or help do things from home, such as videotaping an educational program.

CONFERENCES THAT COUNT

Parent-teacher conferences can be wonderful times for all of you to focus on your child's needs. Here are some suggestions to help make your conferences more effective:

1. Before the conference, take a few minutes to review your child's assignments and tests. Notice strengths and areas that need improvement.

continues

Building a Strong Parent–Teacher Partnership continued

Building a strong parent-teacher partnership

CONFERENCES THAT COUNT continued

2. Make a list of questions you'd like to ask. *Examples:*
- What are my child's strengths? Weaknesses?
- How much time should she spend doing homework?
- Is he turning in assignments?
- Are there any subjects my child seems to struggle with?
- Does she follow directions?
- Are there any behavior problems?
- Does he work well independently? In a group?
- How can I help my child at home?

Tip: Find out if there's anything your child wants you to ask.

3. Be sure to ask questions if you don't understand something the teacher says.

4. Tell the teacher a little bit about your child's school experiences.

5. Once you get home, let your child know what you and the teacher discussed. Share something positive the teacher said—it helps build a good attitude toward school.

SOLVE PROBLEMS TOGETHER

When there's a problem, try to resolve it as soon as possible. A "How can I help?" approach works best. The goal is to focus on solutions.

First, get a clear understanding of the problem. Find out what's already been tried and ask what you can do to help at home. Together, come up with a plan to help your child improve—based upon the situation and your child's needs. Once you and the teacher have agreed on a plan, talk it over with your child.

At home, make expectations clear. Follow through with the plan and monitor improvements. When your child knows you and the teacher are behind her, she'll be encouraged to do her best!

✓ PARENT CHECKLIST

Do your actions show that you and the teacher are working together for your child's benefit? Take this little quiz to see what messages you're sending:

- ☐ I look over papers the teacher sends home.
- ☐ I keep the teacher informed about changes in my child's life.
- ☐ I attend conferences and school activities whenever possible.
- ☐ I try to volunteer my time.
- ☐ I talk about the teacher with respect.
- ☐ I contact the teacher if there is a problem.
- ☐ I provide a quiet time for homework and study.
- ☐ I have a good working relationship with my child's teacher. We're members of the same team.

LANGUAGE DIFFERENCES

Even if you're not comfortable speaking English, your child will benefit when you meet with the teacher. If necessary, take a friend to translate or ask the teacher to speak slowly. You can also ask for important information to be written down for you.

Perhaps you can share a part of your culture with the class—some folklore, a native costume, or even unusually shaped coins. The teacher will appreciate your offer.

LIVING APART

What if you only see your child a couple of times a week? You can still be involved in your child's education.

- Give the teacher some stamped, self-addressed envelopes. The school can mail progress reports, conference schedules, and notices about school activities.
- Attend parent-teacher conferences to show your child that both parents are behind him—acting as a team.
- Provide your child with a special folder to save school papers for you. That way, you'll see your child's finished work as well as the teacher's comments.

# Chapter 2–2

Work Together for Student Success

Successful Parent–Teacher Conferences	2–2:1
Prepare for Conferences	2–2:1
Parent-Teacher Conference Dos and Don'ts	2–2:2
Prepare Early	2–2:3
Improve Conference Attendance	2–2:5
Turn Conferences into "Solution Sessions"	2–2:5
Help Parents Prepare for the Conference	2–2:6
Have Students Participate in Conferences	2–2:7
Techniques To Use with Aggressive Parents	2–2:7
At-Home Learning Support	2–2:8
Parents as Partners	2–2:8
Research Findings	2–2:8
Strategies	2–2:9
Conclusion	2–2:11
Parent Study Skill Review Nights	2–2:12
Education Technology Training Center	2–2:13
Family Reading Tree	2–2:14
Materials You Can Use	2–2:16
Planning Worksheet	2–2:16
Conference Planner for Parents	2–2:17
Parent Invitation	2–2:18
Parent Questions	2–2:19
RIOT Program	2–2:20
RIOT Contract	2–2:21

RIOT Time Sheet	2–2:22
Homework Expectations	2–2:23
All Aboard the Reading Train!	2–2:24
"Way to Go" Certificates	2–2:26
How To Build School Success at Home	2–2:28
Parent Involvement: The Key to School Success	2–2:30
24 Learning Activities Your Child Will Love	2–2:32
Test-Taking Secrets	2–2:34
Read-Aloud Pitfalls	2–2:36
A Sample of Read-Aloud Favorites	2–2:38
For the Love of Writing	2–2:40
A Love for Reading	2–2:42
Learning Resources for Parents	2–2:43

Chapter 2–2

Work Together for Student Success

SUCCESSFUL PARENT–TEACHER CONFERENCES

PREPARE FOR CONFERENCES

Even though most schools require parents to attend parent–teacher conferences at least once a year, these conferences remain an underused method of school-to-home communication.

Among the factors that contribute to this situation is the lack of preparation for the event. Most conferences are well organized, and teachers are well prepared. Frequently, however, little is done to shrink the communication gap between parents and staff. Most parents, for instance, view teachers as "experts" and hesitate to ask questions of them. Other parents don't understand what questions they should be asking. On the other hand, teachers often speak over parents' heads and fail to solicit their opinions and cooperation on improving student achievement.

Education Consultants Joan S. Wolf, of the University of Utah, and Tom Stephens, executive director at the School Study Council of Ohio, say that for conference communication, teachers should be prepared in four areas:

1. *Building rapport with parents.* Teachers must remember first and foremost that they and parents share the same goal: a well-educated, well-adjusted child. They also must be sensitive to the fact that parents view children as an extension of themselves. Therefore, teachers should exercise caution when discussing students' strengths and weaknesses. Wolf and Stephens also recommend using small talk to break the ice at conference sessions and stress that, to avoid resurrecting uncomfortable memories of school, teachers should not ask parents to sit in small child-size furniture.

2. *Obtaining information from parents.* Unlike teachers, who tend to talk too much during conferences, parents vary in their willingness to speak, say Wolf and Stephens. Teacher are best served by asking open-ended questions that cannot be answered with a "yes" or "no." For example, ask, "Which activities has Felix mentioned lately?" Teachers should then focus on listening and guard against interrupting the parent or talking over the ends of the parent's sentences.
3. *Providing parents with information.* Teachers should offer information about a student's progress on the basis of the parent's reaction, say Wolf and Stephens. If conversation is difficult and nonproductive, teachers have three options.
    a. Close the conference and reschedule it for another time.
    b. Complete the conference, covering all areas planned, expecting little if any change as a result.
    c. Repeat the first two steps—building rapport and obtaining information—hoping that rapport will improve.

    When the conference flows smoothly, teachers can proceed with a review of the student's progress. For specific tips on how best to present this information, see Parent–Teacher Conference Dos and Don'ts, which is a simple checklist reminding teachers how to best interact with parents. The list can be used as a guide to preparation of materials for a conference and can be reviewed quickly before the actual meeting.
4. *Summarizing and follow-up.* Many teachers mistakenly end the conference without summarizing how the parent and teacher will cooperate to improve student achievement and/or behavior. Wolf and Stephens say that teachers should alert parents to time constraints when the conference begins.

PARENT–TEACHER CONFERENCE DOs AND DON'Ts

When giving parents information about student's progress, follow these rules for best results.

DO

- Organize information into broad categories. Have an agenda, and when appropriate, provide an outline for parents to follow.
- Begin with positive information.
- Cite specific examples related to the shared information.
- Encourage parents to discuss each point, and clarify it as needed.
- Have examples of the student's work, dated and noting progress.
- Emphasize how instruction is individualized.
- Encourage parents to ask questions.
- Listen to what parents have to say. Try to understand them before making yourself understood.

DON'T

- Overwhelm parents with information.
- Use educational jargon.
- Speculate on why there are difficulties.
- Be evasive. If you don't know the answer, admit it.
- Defend an archaic grading system.
- Predict life's successes from any test scores or other data.
- Describe problems to parents. They are not interested in why teachers are unable to help the student.

Prepare Early

Preparation for parent/teacher conferences should start early in the fall. Why? Because you need to lay the groundwork by developing relationships with parents, communicating with them, and informing them of any problems as they arise.

Even if you've started preparing early, a checklist can help with final preparations. Teachers at Principal Pam Stanfield's school use a checklist to make sure they haven't forgotten anything. (See Planning Worksheet.)

Education Consultants Joan S. Wolf of Salt Lake City, Utah, and Tom Stephens of Columbus, Ohio, have researched effective parent/teacher conferences and given presentations on the subject.

Wolf is a professor in the Department of Special Education at the University of Utah, Salt Lake City, Utah 84112. And Stephens is Executive Director of the School Study Council of Ohio, 665 East Dublin Granville Road, Columbus, Ohio 43229.

Both say that competencies needed by teachers for conducting effective conferences center around four points: Building rapport with parents; obtaining information from parents; providing parents with information about their child's progress; and making recommendations on how the parents can help the child.

Let's take a closer look at these four steps.

1. **Building rapport**

    Teachers must remember that both they and parents should have the best interests of the child at heart. According to Wolf and Stephens, teachers need to realize that parents often consider their children as extensions of themselves.

    Regardless of any relationship that has already been developed, teachers must be sensitive to parents when discussing their child's strengths and weaknesses at conferences.

    Wolf and Stephens offer these strategies to make parents feel more comfortable at the conference:
    - Make the parent feel welcome. This is basic but remember that conferences usually take place on the teacher's turf—the classroom. For some parents, just being in a school brings back memories of frustration and failure. You can make them feel comfortable by providing adult-sized chairs to sit in and offering them something to drink.
    - Begin with small talk. As simple as it may sound, discussing the weather or a recent school event can help break the ice. Once you've started a conversation, it is much easier to move on to other topics.

2. **Obtaining information from parents**

    After you've established rapport with parents, it's time to move on to seeking information about the child.

    The teacher must be a good listener. Don't take notes—instead, focus on listening carefully to what the parent is saying.

    According to Wolf and Stephens, parents vary in their willingness to talk. And the teacher should be prepared to elicit necessary information.

    If teachers need to ask questions, they should start with general ones that can't be answered by a simple "yes" or a "no." For example, ask: "Which activities in school has Felix mentioned lately?" Don't ask: "Has Felix mentioned what we are now doing in school?"

3. **Providing parents with information**

    At this point, you should explain how much progress has been made. If all is going well, start describing the student's progress and how parents can help him or her do even better in school.

    If things aren't going smoothly, several options are available:
    - Close the conference and reschedule it in hopes of being more successful next time.
    - Complete the conference covering all the areas planned, expecting very little, if any, change as a result of this session.
    - Repeat the first two steps, hoping that a second time around will help the rapport level.

    If you're ready to proceed, here are some dos and don'ts for informing parents about student progress.

    DO:
    - Organize information into broad categories. Have an agenda and, when appropriate, provide an outline for parents to follow.
    - Begin with positive information.
    - Cite specific examples related to the information you're sharing.
    - Encourage parents to discuss each point—clarify as needed.
    - Have examples of the student's work available. Be sure each is dated, noting the progress.
    - Emphasize how instruction is individualized.
    - Explain how student progress is evaluated.
    - Encourage parents to ask questions.

    DON'T
    - Overwhelm parents with information.
    - Use educational jargon.
    - Speculate why there are difficulties.
    - Be evasive—if you don't know the answer to questions, say so.
    - Defend an archaic grading system. If it's yours, change it!
    - Predict life's successes from any test scores or other data.
    - Describe your problems to the parents; they aren't interested in why you are unable to help their child.

4. **Summarizing and following up**

    A common mistake teachers make during conferences is neglecting to close on time. This step is important because it lets both the teacher and the parents know what needs to be done next to help the child.

    Wolf and Stephens suggest that when the conference begins, both you and the parents should be aware of any time limits. At the beginning of the conference, teachers must know much time has been reserved for the meeting.

    Before the conference ends, it's important for the teacher to summarize what has been discussed. This doesn't have to be formal. It can be as simple as the teacher saying, "Let me restate what we have discussed." or "We're almost out of time, so let me summarize."

    Be sure to include in the summary any activities that were discussed for either the parents or the teacher to work on. Remember to set up another conference time if necessary and then stand, thank the parents, and walk them to the door.

Improve Conference Attendance

Conference preparation means nothing if parents do not participate in the conferences. Many principals say that offering conference times other than during the school days improves the attendance rate, as does school-provided transportation to and from the conference site. Principal Jerry Fair says that about 65 percent of students at his Milwaukee, Wisconsin, school are bused from as far away as 13 miles, adding to the indifference many parents feel about attending conferences. "Many just won't make the trip," he says.

Fair now holds conferences for 1 day at the school, where parents in the school's immediate neighborhood can attend, and on the following day moves the conference location to a church in the neighborhood from which students are bused. The result has been a dramatic increase in attendance.

For other parents, the issue preventing them from attending conferences is not disinterest, but homemaking and child-care obligations. The Parent–Teacher Association at Assistant Principal Carol Chanter's school addresses these obligations by providing a low-cost meal and free baby-sitting service to parents who attend the evening sessions. Parents can eat in the cafeteria with their children before meeting with teachers, and the free baby sitters make it possible for more parents to attend.

Turn Conferences into "Solution Sessions"

There will be conferences where you have to tell parents something about their child they don't want to hear.

No matter how it's delivered, your basic message will be, "Your child won't keep quiet in class" or "He just doesn't want to listen" or "If only she would work harder."

These are hard judgments to communicate under any conditions—but even tougher when you know that parents have heard them before. They're frustrated and discouraged—and it's highly unlikely they have the magic "fix" for the problem.

But Teacher Kathy Detloff has found a way to turn this seemingly hopeless situation around.

Her solution not only helps students become better learners, but it also motivates parents to become enthusiastic supporters of their children's education.

Detloff's approach was inspired by a professional development course about individual learning styles. "The course taught that each individual learns differently," she explains.

She says she found out that some kids learn best by seeing, others by hearing, and still others by doing "hands-on" projects, for instance.

"I sometimes have lazy kids," says Detloff of Swanville, Minnesota. "But that doesn't hold true with all students who have problems. The majority of the kids who struggle in my class are kinesthetic/tactile learners, rather than kids who learn visually."

So instead of starting conferences by pointing out problems, Detloff questions parents about their kids' at-home interests and hobbies and draws correlations to how these clues help students learn better at school.

"If I find out that a student enjoys tearing apart and rebuilding toys, I'll point out that he or she may respond better to a situation where he or she can move around and do hands-on activities, rather than to lectures.

"And I let the parents know that I'll be glad to incorporate this into my teaching to help their kid.

"This approach really gets parents' support. They know I'm going to try to help their child, and there's a possibility for positive change. And once you get the parents believing there's hope, you get their support. And the change in teaching style can help kids too!"

Help Parents Prepare for the Conference

Just because you're prepared for conferences, it's no guarantee that things will go great.

Always consider the other half of the equation—parent preparation.

Many teachers send parents a list of questions a few weeks before the conference. These questions are points parents can talk to their children about that might be discussed during the conference. (See Conference Planner for Parents.)

Here are four other ideas Administrator Stephen Kleinsmith suggests to help parents prepare for the meeting. Consider requesting that parents do these activities before attending the conference.

This information can be sent home with students or mailed directly to parents if you want to add more importance to it.

1. **Jot down some notes about the student.** Parents should take some time and consider interests their child has and any hobbies he or she is involved in. They should also think about any school rule or policy that is affecting their child now or will be in the remainder of the year.
2. **Talk with the child before the conference.** Review your notes and ask the student if there is anything he or she would like the parents to ask at the conference. Parents could ask their child what subjects he or she thinks are going well and which ones are going poorly.
3. **Tell students not to worry about the meeting.** Children sometimes get anxious over parent/teacher conferences. Parents need to emphasize that the purpose of the meeting is to help them and the teacher work together to make school a better place—not to punish the child.
4. **Be prepared to ask good questions at the conference.** Here's a possible list of questions parents may want to ask at a conference. Parents should pick the ones that apply to them.
   - Is my child in a different group this year or taking different subjects in school?
   - Is my child in a different reading or math group than last year?
   - How are the social skills of my child at school, and how does this compare to social skills at home?
   - What subjects does my child enjoy more than others?
   - Is he or she working up to potential?
   - Does he or she get engaged and participate effectively in group settings?

- Any test scores to talk about?
- Any recent behavior problems at home or school to discuss?

Have Students Participate in Conferences

Here's an idea that's a bit different. Teacher Judy Teague says that when students run their own parent/teacher conferences, parents tend to take a more active role.

"These aren't the traditional conferences where I say, 'Here are the grades. This is what your son or daughter has to work on,'" says Teague of Trail, British Columbia.

"Instead, kids show their moms and dads around the classroom and review books, projects, and assignments. Then students report their progress to their parents."

Teague says she schedules conferences for two or three kids and their parents during an afternoon. "A few days before each one, I give parents a list of sample questions to help them prepare," she says.

"This has the effect of getting them involved in their kids' education by forcing them to ask about what's happening in the classroom," she adds. "I tell parents to make comments about their kids' performance or offer suggestions about how they can improve. I also try to encourage them to give lots of praise, instead of just criticism."

While each group is meeting, Teague is available to answer questions or to talk to parents in private. "If something unexpected happens, I'm there to fill in the gaps that the kids can't."

To make sure conferences come off smoothly, Teague allows plenty of time for the kids to practice before the big day. "They brainstorm questions and then interview each other to prepare for their parents," she says. "And I'll offer suggestions if I think something needs to be discussed."

The program is popular with both students and parents, she says. "I've had parents say, 'I've never learned so much from my kids because they never talk much to me.'"

TECHNIQUES TO USE WITH AGGRESSIVE PARENTS

Some parents are just more frustrating to deal with in conferences than others. Here are some tips you can use to salvage a conference that's on rocky ground.

DO:

- Listen
- Write down what is said
- When parents take a breath, ask what else is bothering them
- Exhaust the complaint list
- Ask for clarification of any generalized complaints
- Show the list and ask if it is complete
- Ask for their suggestions on the solutions to any of the problems
- Write them down
- If possible, mirror their body posture during this process
- If the parent gets loud . . . get softer!

DON'T:

- Argue
- Become defensive
- Promise anything you cannot do
- Claim ownership of problems that belong to others
- Raise your voice
- "Put down" their feelings or their concern for a problem

AT-HOME LEARNING SUPPORT

PARENTS AS PARTNERS

Schools are most effective when parents reinforce messages students receive from teachers, says Stephen Kleinsmith, assistant superintendent in Millard, Nebraska. "If we want children to have high expectations of learning, then parents must regularly send those sorts of signals. They need to be involved. They need to show children that learning is a lifelong activity, and that they're working with the school as a team. Students at all levels tend toward higher levels of commitment to their schooling when their parents are involved. Children get better grades and score higher on national standardized tests, and the number of behavior and discipline problems [goes] down when parents are involved," he says.

Research Findings

For more than 10 years, researchers have shown that parent involvement in school activities improves student attitudes and performance, enhances students' self-esteem, improves academic achievement, builds positive parent–child relationships, and helps parents to develop positive attitudes toward school and the educational process. A search of digest information compiled by U.S. Department of Education's Educational Resources Information Center shows that many published reports support these assertions.

Parent involvement can offset negative external influences on children, such as poverty. Chavkin and Gonzalez[1] write that one of the most promising ways to increase students' achievement is to involve their families.[2,3] Walberg[4] found that family participation in education was twice as predictive of academic learning as family socioeconomic status. Establishing partnerships with families has many benefits for schools and families, but Epstein[5(p.701)] says, "The main reason to create such partnerships is to help all youngsters succeed in school and in later life."

Involvement in school activities may improve parent self-image. Becher[6] summarizes research by Herman and Yeh,[7] indicating "that parents involved in child care and educational programs develop positive attitudes about themselves, increase self-confidence, and often enroll in programs to enhance their personal development. They also are more positive about school and school personnel than uninvolved parents."

Student achievement and attitudes, inside and outside school, improve with parent involvement. Both Becher and Peterson[8] state that students' overall attitudes toward school and participation rates improve when parents actively participate in activities. Becher writes, "Substantial evidence exists to show that children whose parents are involved in their schooling have significantly increased their academic achievement and cognitive development."[9] Peterson[10] says, "Children whose parents are involved in their formal education have many advantages. They have better grades, test scores, long-term academic achievement, attitudes, and behavior than those with disinterested mothers and fathers."[11]

Strategies

At-Home Learning and Coaching

One of the most efficient ways to involve parents and improve student performance is to recruit the help of parents in the home. At-home learning and coaching extend learning beyond the classroom and can maintain or improve overall levels of parent involvement at the middle and upper grade levels, where it typically drops.

According to Kleinsmith, involvement peaks at the early grade levels, then falls off rapidly as children mature. "It's common to see a drastic drop-off in parental involvement from the sixth through the twelfth grades. At the elementary level, children like having their parents stop in for lunch or for cookies and milk. But teenagers usually don't feel that it's 'cool' to have their parents in school with them anymore, so parents stop coming," he says.

Statistics show that parents of adolescents are interested in their children's education and that many do, indeed, talk about school with their children in the home. *Youth Indicators 1993* reports that 85–91 percent of eighth-grade students talk with their parents about school-related issues and 90 percent of parents check students' homework.[12] The report also indicates, however, that parent involvement drops off significantly as participation requirements are added. This is especially true when involvement requires direct contact between parent and school. Sixty percent of students surveyed reported that their parents had spoken with a teacher or counselor at their school; only 29 percent said that a parent had actually visited a school classroom.

Kleinsmith advocates rethinking the basic structure of parent involvement programs to counteract this trend. "Schools know that as children mature, their needs change. What schools don't realize is that parents' needs are changing, as well, but their opportunities to be involved at the school usually stay the same. As children change chronologically and emotionally, so should the way parents are involved in school," he says.

At-home parent help actually is the preferred method of parent involvement among older students. Kleinsmith says, "We looked at one study in particular that asked 1,300 students, 'What's the best way to have your parents involved in school?' The students' reply was that they liked it when parents could help them with homework—to check [whether] they'd solved their math problems correctly and give assistance when needed."

Ascher[13] notes Walberg's suggestions[14] that when parents have limited time, as is typical with single and working parents, one of the most efficient activities for parents is helping their children with home-based learning projects. At-home learning is also both a natural and a convenient extension of school, according to Rich.[15] Since students spend far more time with parents than with teachers, parents are presented with far more "teachable moments" that can be used to reinforce concepts learned in school.[16]

Epstein[17] has also proved the value of home-based learning. Her work suggests that one strategy is to send work packets home for students and parents to complete together. Seventh-grade students who were given an English achievement test at the beginning of the school year earned scores similar to those earned at the end of their sixth-grade year. But for students who had marginal skills, the summer study packets given to the test group were related to increased test scores.

Mercedes Fitzmaurice of Research for Better Schools, in Philadelphia, Pennsylvania, recommends at-home activities as well, but adds that they do not have to be strictly principle- or content-related. One of the activities her organization suggests is to give students an assignment to interview their parents or family members. Examples of questions are as follows: What was your most frightening moment? When and how did you learn to do your favorite activity? What is your earliest memory? Students can then share answers in small groups or write them in story form as part of a booklet, with pictures, about their family. This type of activity brings schools and families together in nontraditional ways and helps students to exercise a variety of skills—brainstorming questions, speaking, note taking, organizing, and writing.

Brown[18] writes that "some activities can be adapted to almost any home situation. These are activities that parents or children engage in on a day-to-day basis." She suggests activities such as preparing questions about television programs that students watch with their parents and including children in meal preparation and grocery shopping.

A slightly different strategy for involving parents in home learning is used in Monroe, North Carolina, where parents can earn the rank of "five-star parent" by living up to obligations outlined in the Five-Star Parent Program. The program, which began in 1994, is cosponsored by the city Chamber of Commerce and won a 1996 Magna Award for excellence.

According to a description supplied by the district's public information officer, Luan C. Ingram, parents who participate in the program sign a special report card, which serves as a contract requiring them to participate in their children's education in four areas: expecting academic achievement and progress, participating in school activities, performing at-home follow-up, and promoting social and emotional development. Among the activities specified are establishing a reward system for students when they do well in school, attending a Parent–Teacher Association or Parent–Teacher Organization meeting or open house, reading or reviewing homework with students at least twice a week, and attending a parenting workshop.

Parents who meet all requirements are recognized by the principal of the school their children attend. They also receive a vehicle window sticker that says, "Proud Kid of a Five-Star Parent." After the program's first year, 26 percent of all elementary and middle school parents became five-star parents. Thirty-three percent of all elementary school parents participated.

Communicating Parent Responsibility

To cultivate partnerships with parents, it is often necessary to remind them that they have an important at-home role to play in student learning. Kleinsmith recommends that faculty and staff initially stress the topic with parents by sharing the following list of involvement responsibilities and options:

- Call or visit the school staff on a regular basis, and talk with teachers before problems occur. Don't wait until trouble occurs to make the first contact.
- Attend special events at your child's school, such as open house, parent–teacher conferences, curriculum night, booster club meetings, and Parent–Teacher Organization meetings. Also make time to be involved in your child's cocurricular activities such as drama, music, and sports.
- Serve on school building and district advisory councils or committees.
- Volunteer your time as a tutor, classroom or recess aide, or secretarial aide or as a carpenter/repairman. Serve as a monitor during cocurricular activities such as dances, athletic events, and field trips, or serve as a judge for activities such as science fairs and art shows.

- Help proofread and edit the school newsletter.
- Give a guest lecture on career occupations and/or travel abroad.
- Become involved in the student's curriculum planning, and discuss academic options with your son or daughter.
- Encourage involvement in school activities of the student's choice.
- Ask your son or daughter, "What good questions did you ask today?" or "What did you learn in school today?" Then practice good listening, a key to effective communication.
- Encourage reading, using the library, and purchasing books at a young age.

Conclusion

Learning is a 24-hour activity, and research shows that schools should make greater efforts to educate families on this issue. Clearly, there are learning benefits from actively involving students in even such routine daily activities as grocery shopping or meal preparation. Administrators are wise to evaluate the ways in which their school can provide these types of opportunities and to suggest that faculty develop take-home activities requiring parent and/or family involvement.

References

1. N.F. Chavkin and D.L. Gonzalez, Forging Partnerships between Mexican–American Parents and Schools, *Educational Resources Information Center Digest*, ED388489 (Charleston, WV: ERIC Clearinghouse on Rural Education and Small Schools, 1995).

2. N.F. Chavkin, ed., *Families and Schools in a Pluralistic Society* (Albany, NY: State University of New York Press, 1993).

3. A.T. Henderson and N. Berla, eds., *A New Generation of Evidence: The Family Is Critical to Student Achievement* (Washington, DC: National Committee for Citizens in Education, 1994).

4. H.J. Walberg, Improving the Productivity of America's Schools, *Educational Leadership* 41, no. 8 (1984): 19–27.

5. J. Epstein, School/Family/Community Partnerships: Caring for the Children We Share, *Phi Delta Kappan* 76, no. 9 (1995): 701–712.

6. R. Becher, Parents and Schools, *Educational Resource Information Center Digest*, ED269137 (Urbana, IL: ERIC Clearinghouse on Elementary and Early Childhood Education, 1986).

7. J.L. Herman and J.P. Yeh, Some Effects of Parent Involvement in Schools, 1980.

8. D. Peterson, Parent Involvment in the Educational Process, *Educational Resource Information Center Digest*, ED312776 (Eugene, OR: ERIC Clearinghouse on Educational Management, 1989).

9. Becher, Parents and Schools.

10. Peterson, Parent Involvement in the Educational Process.

11. Peterson, Parent Involvement in the Educational Process.

12. *Youth Indicators 1993.* Trends in the Well-Being of American Youth. National Center for Education Statistics, Office of Educational Research and Improvement, Washington, DC.

13. C. Ascher, Improving the School–Home Connection for Low-Income Urban Parents, *Educational Resources Information Center Digest*, ED293973 (New York: ERIC Clearinghouse on Urban Education, 1988).

14. H.J. Walberg, Families as Partners in Educational Productivity, *Phi Delta Kappan* 65, no. 6 (1983): 397–400.

15. D. Rich, *The Forgotten Factor in School Success: The Family, A Policymaker's Guide* (Washington, DC: The Home and School Institute, 1985).

16. Peterson, Parent Involvement in the Educational Process.

17. J.L. Epstein and S.C. Herrick, Implementation and Effects of Summer Home Learning Packets in the Middle Grades. Two Reports, *Educational Resource Information Center Digest*, ED339544 (Baltimore, MD: Center for Research on Effective School for Disadvantaged Students, 1991).

18. P.C. Brown, Involving Parents in the Education of Their Children, *Educational Resources Information Center Digest*, ED308988 (Urbana, IL: ERIC Clearinghouse on Elementary and Early Childhood Education, 1989).

Parent Study Skill Review Nights

Program Description

Joanie Wilson, who teaches in the Millard Public Schools in Omaha, Nebraska, helps parents become more involved in their middle and high school students' activities by conducting Parent Study Skill Review Nights, a 4-week program that teaches parents basic mathematics concepts so they can provide help if students ask for it.

Wilson says that the sessions have helped parents to polish rusty mathematics skills and have opened parent communication with the school. "I had one parent call me about a scheduling problem that was completely beyond my control, but she called because she felt that we had established a relationship through review night. Without this, she probably wouldn't have asked the question at all," she says.

Structure and Goals

Because parents meet only once a week for two hours, the information presented isn't exhaustive. But sessions provide enough background that parents can think through problems with their students, says Wilson.

Each session focuses on a different topic, including geometry, algebra, calculators, and word problems. Wilson uses hands-on activities to give parents information and to teach problem-solving strategies. The geometry session, for example, features paper cut-outs and folding activities to review terms. On that evening Wilson also talks about the development of visual and spatial ability and how geometry is especially difficult for students in the middle grades. During the algebra session, Wilson reviews the "BS Principle." "That simply means that you can do anything you want to the equation, but to solve it you have to do the same things to both sides," she says.

In addition to teaching review nights, Wilson writes mathematics-related articles for the school newsletter. Topics have included how parents can help their students study, how parents can help students ask good questions, and the myth of the "math gene." "I don't want parents giving their students an excuse to do poorly by saying they 'were never good at math' themselves," she says. "The reinforcement provided in these articles is one thing that parents have said they enjoy and find helpful."

Positive feedback and growing interest indicate that the program works. Class size more than doubled from the first year to the second. "I've received comments like, 'I've never understood the concept of the area of a circle' and 'I remember a lot more about math than I thought I did,'" says Wilson.

Parent Study Skill Review Nights are publicized through the school newsletters, at a study skills night for incoming sixth grade parents, and at open house.

Wilson says that both students and parents benefit from parents' participation in the review nights. Students, of course, have an additional resource when stumped by mathematics problems, and parents reach new comfort levels with the school. "After they spend four weeks with me, they feel good about the school, and they have a better understanding of the curriculum," says Wilson.

Education Technology Training Center

Program Description and Goals

When parents are not familiar with computers and technology, it can be difficult for them to feel comfortable helping their children with assignments that incorporate computers. Superintendent James Connelly and the school board for Bridgeport Public Schools in Bridgeport, Connecticut, established a state-of-the-art computer training center for parents—the Education Technology Training Center.

Raymond Krish, the district's education technology coordinator, says the facility creates a place for parents to go to learn about what the students are learning on computers in school. "The local university donated an entire floor to house the ed tech center, while two computer corporations donated the software needed to supplement our network," says Krish. "The technology budget for the year, approximately $70,000, was dedicated toward the purchase of 23 computers, the file servers, and additional software and furniture for the center."

The goal of the program is to educate parents to become computer literate so they can learn with the students. Because many families do not own a home computer, this computer laboratory allows parents to attend minicourses on the basics of computers, word processors, and office programs that produce spreadsheets.

"After just 18 months of operation, 7,000 to 8,000 parents have completed courses," says Krish. "Many of the parents who attend these classes return to the center to be an instructor or volunteer to help in the classrooms."

Courses

Schedules are spread out during the day to make it convenient for most parents to attend the course. Some classes are offered during school hours, while many are conducted at night. "Because of the overwhelming response to the program, we've added a couple of Saturday courses to our curriculum. The courses are free to parents and typically last from 2–10 hours," says Krish.

A typical computer course at the center is a basic two-hour class that introduces parents to how personal computers can be used and provides an orientation to the functions a computer allows a person to do. A more advanced class might be courses dedicated to learning word processing, databases, and spreadsheets. "One popular course has been an elementary course that allows the [students] and parents to work side-by-side on a computer," says Krish.

The courses are led by teachers, parents who have completed the courses previously, and representatives from the business community. Krish explains that teachers who participate in weekend and evening classes receive a stipend, but all other instructors volunteer their time.

"When there are computers available in the tech center, parents are welcome to come in and practice their computer skills." However, sometimes when no courses are scheduled, the school plans for teacher training courses or after-school workshops.

Course listings are publicized in the superintendent's newsletter, the local newspaper, and regularly attended parent meetings. "The response has been outstanding, and the parents who have taken all the courses are enthused about volunteering [in] the classroom and aiding teachers on computer assignments," Krish says.

Keys to Success

Krish says the strength of the program lies in community support. "We were able to make this idea work [because of] the donations and volunteers from the community," he says. "When the ed tech center was started, we publicized it widely and introduced parents and community members to it.

"We sent home fliers with students to excite parents and urge them to participate in our programs to learn how technology is being integrated into the school curriculum. Two computer companies supplied us with software, a number of corporations donated office furniture, and the university provided the space to house the ed tech center," he says.

Krish says they are considering making the center accessible to more parents by offering a busing service. This service would allow parents without cars to attend the courses, increasing participation.

"My best advice is to be flexible in terms of what you offer," says Krish. "Find out what the parents want and need by way of computer education. Try to create courses that parents will enjoy and still support what the [students] are learning in school, but stay away from courses that other adult education programs offer."

Family Reading Tree

A New York school has created a family reading program to motivate parents and children to read together at home.

"We ask that parents read to their children 15 minutes a night. Every time parents read for 15 minutes, they document it and send a note in with their child," explains a teacher.

"In school, we have a beautiful wooden carved tree our custodian made. This is what we add our 'reading' leaves on."

When the students bring in their notes saying they have read with their parents, teachers issue leaf-shaped certificates to the students.

"We put the tree near the front entrance, and it looks great—especially when we hang certificate 'leaves' on it.

"We start this in the spring, so there are leaves outside the same time as we put leaves on our reading tree."

Another Southern school has set up a reading program called RIOT (Reading Instead of TV).

"Students and their parents sign a contract to spend at least two 30-minute sessions a week in a reading activity instead of watching TV," says a teacher.

"For every minute spent reading alone, kids earn one point. To encourage family participation, we award double points for reading with a parent.

"After points are tabulated each month, we hold an awards ceremony in the media center. Pictures are taken of kids who receive awards and are posted on the RIOT bulletin board in the media center."

The teacher says class totals are also posted on the bulletin board. The class with the most points at the end of the year is treated to a pizza party. Individual RIOT awards are:

- More than 30 points—"Turn it Off!" bookmark
- More than 300 points—"Reading is the Key" pin
- More than 500 points—"Reading is Magic" pin
- More than 750 points—poster and a paperback book

"We give parents a form to record reading time and encourage them to post it on the refrigerator. Each month, we ask them to turn the form in to their kids' teachers, who then give them a new one."

The teacher tells me that the secret to the program's success is parent participation and aggressive teacher follow-up.

"Teachers have to be dedicated to RIOT," she says.

"If teachers don't get RIOT contracts back from parents, they call right away to ask why."

MATERIALS YOU CAN USE

Planning Worksheet

Remember the 3 C's: Competence, Confidence, and Compassion. And don't forget the fourth C—your student is somebody's child!

Competence

- ☐ Are you well-prepared?
- ☐ Do you have student work ready to share with parents?
- ☐ Are you well-organized?
- ☐ Can parents see that you're knowledgeable about child development, students' differing needs, subject matter content, teaching skills, and strategies?
- ☐ Are you staying on schedule with conferences?
- ☐ Do you have helpful materials available for parents' use in assisting their children?

Confidence

- ☐ Do you feel comfortable conducting the conferences?
- ☐ Are you relaxed, and do you put the parents at ease too?
- ☐ Are you a willing, active listener?
- ☐ Are you in a positive, problem-solving, "let's work as a team" frame of mind?
- ☐ Did you leave defensive words and responses at home?

Compassion

- ☐ Do you show parents how much you genuinely care for their child?
- ☐ Are you warm and welcoming?
- ☐ Do you smile?
- ☐ Are you friendly?
- ☐ Is your room arranged so that parents feel comfortable during the conference (privacy, comfortable chairs and table)?

Conference Planner for Parents

Review the questions on this sheet and discuss them with your child before the parent/teacher conference. Bring this sheet along to discuss concerns with your child's teacher.

1. What do you want to know about your child's performance and academic achievement?

2. What does your child find most rewarding about school?

3. What are your child's biggest concerns or frustrations with school?

4. Do you have any concerns about the school or this class that we should know about? What are they? What can be done to alleviate your concerns?

5. What can your child do to improve in this class? What can you do? What can the teacher or school do?

Parent Invitation

Dear Parent or Guardian:

Your child's success in school is very important to all of us. By sharing our observations and insights, we can understand your child's strengths and how to best help him or her learn.

Will you please take the time to meet with me in your child's classroom? Please tell me what times and dates would be most convenient for you. (Please indicate in the space provided below the dates and times you prefer.)

Below are some questions that I may be asking you to talk about so I can better understand your child and his or her style of learning. Attached to this sheet are some ideas for questions that you, as a parent or guardian, might want to ask me, your child's teacher.

Please read this sheet and return the top portion to me by _____ or feel free to call me at school _____ with the times you'll be available. I look forward to making this a happy and productive year for your child!

Sincerely,

_____

- -

Questions Teachers May Ask Parents or Guardians

1. What does your child like most about school?
2. What does your child think he or she is "good at doing"? Describe your child's hobbies or interests.
3. What types of things are difficult for your child to do?
4. What activities do you and your child enjoy doing together?
5. How does your child do homework? Where is it done?
6. Describe your child's friends. Are you satisfied with your child's choice of friends and activities?
7. Are there any attitudes or behaviors your child has toward school that you would like to see changed?
8. What can I do to support you at home in academic, social, or developmental areas in which you would like to see your child improve?
9. Are there any areas in which you would like more information about what your child is learning or how students are graded?
10. What do you hope your child learns this year? What are your dreams for his or her future?

Source: Reprinted from *Getting Ready for a Conference*, with permission of the Wisconsin Department of Public Instruction, John T. Benson, Superintendent.

Parent Questions

1. What is my child's class schedule?
2. What will my child be learning this year in reading? Math? Science? Social Studies?
3. Are children grouped in reading, math, or other subjects? What group is my child in, and how are children selected for each group?
4. Do you think my child is working up to his or her ability?
5. In what areas do you think my child is doing well?
6. In what subjects do you think my child needs improvement?
7. What are the most important things you think children in your classroom should learn? How can I help encourage this learning at home?
8. How is my child's work evaluated?
9. Can you show me examples of my child's work—classroom projects, tests, special assignments?
10. How much time should my child spend on homework? How can I help with homework?
11. What can you tell me about how my child seems to learn best? Is he or she a "hands-on" learner? Does he or she need to move around? Does he or she enjoy learning in a cooperative group or prefer working alone in a quiet environment?
12. How do your classroom strategies complement my child's style of learning?
13. How do you discipline students in your classroom?
14. Does my child get along with other children? With you?
15. In what other ways can I reinforce classroom learning at home or be informed about my child's progress in school? Are there opportunities for parents to be involved in classroom activities?
16. What special interest activities are available to encourage my child to learn?

Source: Reprinted from *Getting Ready for a Conference*, with permission of the Wisconsin Department of Public Instruction, John T. Benson, Superintendent.

RIOT Program

What's RIOT? RIOT stands for Reading Instead of Television, and it is a family reading program. We have been so successful with RIOT in the past and would like to begin this reading incentive program again on March 1 and continue through March, April, and May.

The goal of this program is to increase interest in reading as a whole. As families read together, parents will appreciate the time spent with their children. This program will also be invaluable to young children just entering school who have older siblings in the program. They will enjoy being read to by their big brother or sister. It is also thrilling for these older children to be rewarded for their reading!

Description of the RIOT Program

You and your child will sign a contract agreeing to spend at least two 30-minute sessions (60 minutes a week) in a reading activity each week—instead of television. We encourage you, though, to go beyond the minimum of two sessions. For every minute they spend reading alone, students will be awarded a point. Double points will be given for reading done with a parent. The sky's the limit. At the end of each month, we will have an awards ceremony in the media center. Pictures will be taken of students who have received an award and posted on the RIOT bulletin board.

The RIOT bulletin board will be located in the media center. It will have a place for classes to post their progress throughout the program. The class with the most points/minutes at the end of May will receive a pizza party. In addition to posting class progress, we will use the bulletin board for pictures of individual students who have received awards at the monthly awards ceremony.

Awards

Students who have earned:

- More than 30 points will receive a "Turn It Off!" bookmark
- More than 300 points will receive a "Reading Is The Key" pin
- More than 500 points will receive a "Reading Is Magic" pin
- More than 750 points will receive a paperback book of their choice and a poster

You will be provided with a form to record your reading time. We suggest you post it on the refrigerator or in some other familiar place. This form should be turned in to the teacher at the end of each month. You will be given a new form for recording each month's reading. Please complete the attached contract and return it to your child's teacher. Your child may stop by the media center to see the award pins and bookmark.

RIOT Contract

We, the _____ family, do hereby agree to spend at least two 30-minute sessions in a reading activity each week. We understand and agree to the following:

- This is to be time spent together.

- The television must be turned off.

- Our child will earn a point for every minute he or she reads alone or double points for reading with a parent.

- We will be responsible for recording time on a monthly sheet provided by the school. This form will be turned in to the teacher at the end of the month.

- My child will receive awards based on the number of minutes read.

- This is to be an enjoyable and relaxing time for every member of the family.

_____   _____
Parent/Guardian Signature   Date

_____   _____
Child's Signature   Date

RIOT Time Sheet

Time sheet for the month of: _____

Student's name: _____ Teacher: _____

On the chart below, record the minutes you spend reading at home, instead of watching TV. Have a parent sign beside each line. You should put your time sheet somewhere you can easily find it—like the refrigerator. At the end of the month, you will turn in your time sheet to your teacher. The teacher will keep up with your points and will post class points on the RIOT bulletin board in the media center.

Date	Minutes read by myself	Minutes read with a parent	Parent's signature
Total Minutes			

Points: _____

Minutes read alone: _____

Minutes read with a parent: _____ × 2 = _____

Total points: _____

Homework Expectations

This information briefly explains my homework program and your child's responsibilities for all homework assignments. Please read and discuss this with your child. Keep this information for reference.

What are a parent's homework responsibilities?

Parents are the key to making homework a positive experience for their children. Therefore, I ask that parents make homework a top priority at home, provide necessary supplies and a quiet homework environment, set aside a time every day when homework should be done, provide praise and support, not allow children to avoid doing their homework, and contact me if they notice a problem. Please read and discuss this homework policy with your child. We can do this—together!

Thank you,

_____   _____
Teacher signature   Phone number

Homework Habits

- **Why do I assign homework?**
  I believe homework is important because it helps reinforce what has been learned in class, prepares students for upcoming lessons, teaches responsibility, and helps students develop positive study habits.

- **When will homework be assigned?**
  I will assign homework Monday through Thursday. I will give two days' notice before tests. Assignments should take no more than 30 minutes each night.

- **What are the student's homework responsibilities?**
  I expect my students to do their best job on each homework assignment. I expect homework to be neat—not sloppy. All written work should be done in pencil. I expect homework to be completely finished by class time the following morning.

- **What will happen if students do not complete their homework assignments?**
  If students choose not to do their homework, I will ask that parents begin checking and signing completed homework each night. If students still choose not to complete homework, they also choose to lose certain privileges. When three homework assignments have not been turned in, or are turned in incomplete, parents will be contacted.

- **What about legitimate reasons for a student not completing a homework assignment?**
  If there is a legitimate reason a student is unable to finish the assignment, please send a note to me on the date the homework is due stating the reason it was not completed. The note must be signed by the parent.

All Aboard the Reading Train!

Work Together for Student Success   2–2:25

All Aboard the Reading Train continued

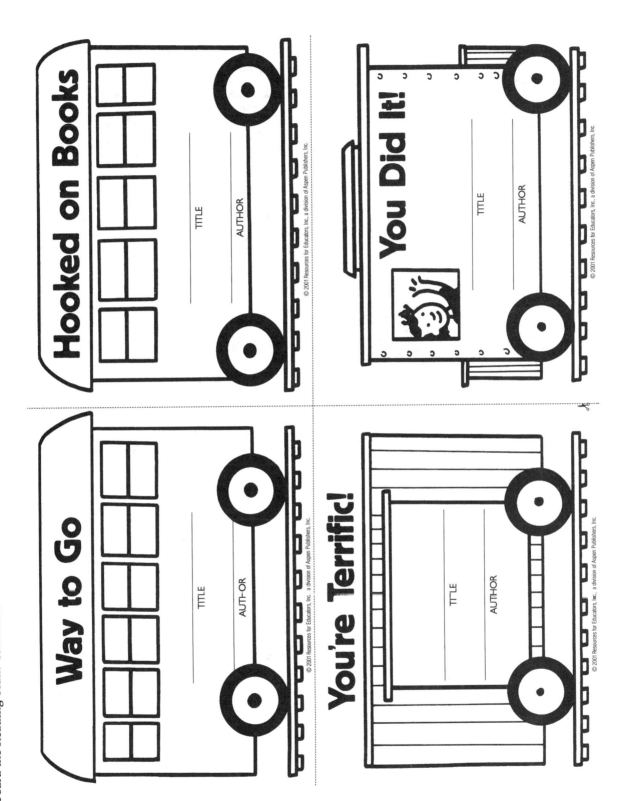

"Way To Go!" Certificates

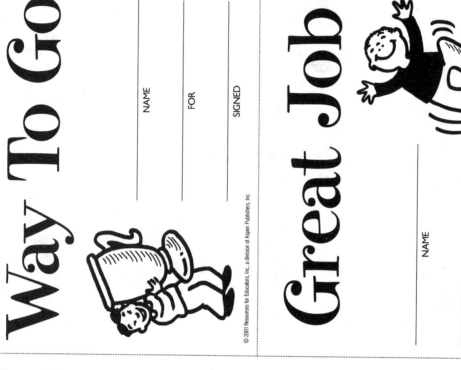

Way To Go

NAME

FOR

SIGNED

Great Job

NAME

FOR

SIGNED

"Way To Go!" Certificates

Dear Parents,

Here's a simple way to help your children develop can-do attitudes.

The next time you catch them putting forth extra effort, simply fill out one of these "Way to Go!" certificates. Be as specific as possible—for example, "You studied math every night this week."

Then, watch your children beam and your relationship grow!

P.S. They're great for coloring, too!

"Way To Go!" Certificates continued

How to build school success at home

Whether it's after school, on weekends, or during the summer, you can help your child become more successful in school.

Right in your own home and neighborhood are hundreds of things to do that will get your child excited about learning. They take very little time — and they're fun.

Many of them can be done as you go about your normal routines — buying groceries, preparing meals, and putting your kids to bed.

The fact is, children do a much better job in school when parents get involved and show an interest in learning.

This special report is full of practical ideas and activities that you can use to encourage success in reading, writing, math, science, and social studies.

Choose several activities that you and your child would enjoy.

GET INVOLVED
Research shows that children who take part in learning activities at home do not fall behind during their time away from school. No other type of parent involvement does more to increase school achievement.

READING
- Place a chalkboard or message center in your kitchen. Write messages to your children as they begin to read. When they get older, tack on cartoons, and interesting newspaper articles.
- Several excellent games that will help your child's reading skills and provide family fun are *Spill & Spell, Scrabble, Scrabble Sentence Game for Juniors,* and *Boggle.*
- One of the easiest ways to build reading success is to read aloud to your children. It only takes a few minutes and will become one of the best parts of your day. Set aside a regular time and begin building pleasant reading memories. They'll be "hooked on books."
- Leave "irresistible books" around the house about their favorite subjects like dinosaurs, snakes, sports, and horses. Also, make sure they see *you* reading for pleasure.
- Books aren't the only way to get reading practice. Encourage your kids to read traffic signs, cereal boxes, cartoons, billboards, menus, and interesting newspaper articles.

MATH
- When your child is young, put her counting ability to work. Let her count out forks, napkins, and the number of people having dinner.
- Give kindergarten children practice in sorting things like silverware, blocks, laundry, and money (into stacks of quarters, dimes, nickels and pennies).
- Many children's games involve counting and problem solving. Some good choices are *Monopoly, Checkers, Battleship, Yahtzee, Parcheesi, Uno, Chinese Checkers,* and card games.
- The kitchen is a great place to get math practice, especially when you measure ingredients: "I need half a cup of raisins and one cup of flour." Dividing food into equal portions is a good way to teach fractions.

continues

How To Build School Success at Home continued

SCIENCE

- Plant seeds, bulbs, or cuttings to open up the world of plant growth. All you need is a small amount of space and some light.
- Learning to observe the world carefully is an important part of science. Magnifying glasses, microscopes, binoculars, and telescopes are fascinating to children and help strengthen their powers of observation.
- Pets are a great way to learn about animal life first-hand. If you can't have a dog or cat, try a gerbil, a lizard, or goldfish. Learning to take care of pets also teaches responsibility.
- Trips to natural history museums, science museums, planetariums, and aquariums are excellent ways to stimulate interest in a subject. Follow up these trips with a visit to the library.
- Most libraries have several books packed with science experiments that you can do at home with common household materials. You'll also find field guides for identifying insects, trees, seashells, rocks, and minerals.

SOCIAL STUDIES

- Encourage your child's interest in his family history. Have him talk to older relatives, collect family stories, or make a family tree. It's important for him to feel connected with the past. So, get out those old photo albums, and start talking.
- As you ride through your community, point out places of interest. Take your child for a visit to an airport, museum, local farm, historical site, or a tour of the local newspaper.
- Talk about current events with your child. Point out places mentioned in the news on a map or globe.
- Show your child a map of his community. Find your home, the school, shopping areas, and other familiar places.

WRITING

- The best way to build writing skills is to find good reasons to write. Don't be too concerned about spelling and grammar in the early years.
- If your child is too young to write, copy down stories or jokes that he makes up. These make great gifts for friends and relatives.
- Maybe it's time for your child to begin a journal or diary. All you need is a notebook. Allow him to dictate the entries to you. Then let him take over the job.
- Writing letters will be much more fun if your child creates his own stationery. Have him decorate the borders of a sheet of paper, adding his name and address on the top. You may want to put lines on the paper. Make a dozen copies or so. Once he receives a reply, he'll be so excited there'll be no stopping his writing.
- Since children learn by example, let them see you write checks, shopping lists, notes, and letters. Explain what it is you're writing.

Dear Editor,

My kids used to complain that car trips were boring. And when they got bored, that's when the trouble began — arguing, tears, and tantrums. What a headache that was!

After my third child was born, I was determined to find a way to make trips more enjoyable. I had to find a way to keep them occupied. I asked all my friends how they handled car trips and got a lot of great ideas.

I ended up putting together a whole collection of activities in a travel bag used just for trips. Here's what I've found works best, and makes the time pass more quickly:

We take two decks of playing cards, a cassette player and tapes, pads and pencils for drawing, writing, and playing games like tic-tac-toe. We also take magnetic traveling games like Checkers or Parcheesi, books and children's magazines, crossword puzzles, or word finders.

Sometimes we play "I spy." For example, "I spy something yellow," or "I spy something that starts with the sound 'ssss'."

Something else that worked for me is traveling with another adult. We share the driving and laugh when the kids ask for the tenth time, "How many more minutes until we get there?"

The Happy Traveler

Parent Involvement
The Key to School Success

"Research confirms that regardless of the economic, racial, or cultural background of the family—when parents are partners in their children's education, the results are improved student achievement, better school attendance, reduced dropout rates, and decreased delinquency."

Richard W. Riley, Secretary of Education of the United States

When you get involved with your children's education, everyone benefits. For one thing, getting involved sends an important message to your children: Education is important!

You're probably already doing more than you realize. After all, it's the little things you do each day that make the most difference.

We are pleased to offer you the following suggestions. We hope they will help you get even more involved with your children's education.

FAMILY LIFE

Parent involvement begins at home. Here are some ways to strengthen family life *and* help your children be more successful in school.

♥ Eat together as a family whenever possible. A *Reader's Digest* survey showed that children whose families eat together at least four times a week scored higher on academic tests than students whose families eat together less often.

♥ Play board games that build learning skills and are fun as well. For example, *Spill & Spell, Scrabble for Juniors,* and *Monopoly* improve vocabulary, concentration, math, and strategy skills. These are skills children need for school.

♥ Read to your children regularly—even for just five minutes—to strengthen reading, writing, and speaking skills. Whether you read aloud or listen while they take turns, it's a fact that reading improves achievement.

♥ Limit the amount of time your children watch TV and monitor what they watch. Select quality programs to watch together and talk about them afterward.

♥ Talk with your children about everything under the sun. They'll appreciate the attention, and your conversations will do more to strengthen their language skills than anything else.

♥ Listening is also important. Try to answer your children's questions and encourage them to share their ideas and feelings.

♥ Set reasonable limits at home. Your children will deal more successfully with the limits set at school.

♥ Spend an hour or two each week enjoying a family outing. Nature walks are fun; so are trips to the zoo, museums, or library. Here's another idea: Pick up cans and bottles along the road and visit the recycling center.

♥ Good school attendance is as important for children as showing up for work is for adults. Allow your children to stay home only if they are genuinely sick. Pick up assignments if they are absent more than a couple of days.

♥ Most teachers believe that showing an interest in what children do at school is the most important thing parents can do to motivate their children.

continues

Parent Involvement: The Key to School Success continued

HELPING WITH HOMEWORK

"Research tells us that the time spent doing homework directly affects a child's achievement ... by doing assigned homework, children will increase skills and do better in school."

Lee Canter, *Homework Without Tears*

Try some of these suggestions to reduce homework headaches.

◆ Let your children know homework is a top priority. If you think it's important, they'll be likely to think so, too.

◆ Set up a specific time for homework and keep distractions to a minimum—including TV, stereo, and other family members.

◆ Pick a quiet study area. Keep supplies, such as paper, pencils, and erasers, nearby.

◆ Review homework directions with your children, if necessary. They can do one or two examples while you watch to make sure they're on the right track.

◆ Be available for questions, but allow your children to be responsible for their own work.

◆ Look over finished assignments to see that the work has been completed.

◆ If forgetting assignments is a problem for your children, require them to show you each day's homework.

◆ Discuss what your children are studying and how it relates to life in the "real world."

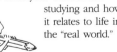

PARTNERSHIP WITH THE TEACHER

A survey by the National Education Association showed that 90 percent of teachers *want* parents to be involved. Here are some ways to keep the lines of communication open and build a better relationship with your children's teachers.

● Try to attend parent-teacher conferences and "Open House" nights.

● If there's a problem at school, talk it over with your children's teachers. They will appreciate your interest and concern.

● Let teachers know if there have been any changes in your family that might affect behavior at school.

● Read notes, newsletters, and announcements that teachers send home. Keep track of upcoming school-related events by marking them on your calendar.

● If you're divorced or separated and your former spouse receives school information, give teachers a handful of self-addressed, stamped envelopes so you can stay informed, too.

● "Thank you" notes are a nice way to tell teachers you appreciate what they're doing.

● Set a good example by saying something positive about a teacher in front of your children.

HELPING THE SCHOOL

Whether you spend time in a classroom or help from home, your efforts benefit your children *and* their classmates. Here are some ways you can help out.

■ When possible, take part in PTA or PTO meetings and activities. Without the help of these organizations, most schools couldn't provide the services they offer.

■ Serve on a school advisory committee.

■ Write a note to a teacher or principal asking how you can help the school.

■ Rearranging your work schedule (going in early or staying late) is another way to free up some time for helping your children's school.

■ Check with other family members, such as grandparents, to see if they'd be willing to volunteer in some way.

■ If you want to help at school but work full-time, see if a co-worker would be willing to set up a job-sharing arrangement. Or, volunteer during your lunch hour from time to time.

Ways to help in the school
- Read a children's story.
- Tutor children who need extra help.
- Prepare an ethnic food.
- Share a hobby or collection.
- Discuss your job.
- Share your professional skills.
- Assist in the school office or computer lab.
- Volunteer in the library or lunch room.
- Supervise the playground.
- Share stories about your cultural heritage.

Ways to help outside school
- Call other parents when needed.
- Help with after-school events.
- Cut out materials for bulletin boards and projects.
- Buy supplies and deliver them to the classroom.
- Bake goods for a special event.
- Ask local businesses to donate needed items.
- Help make the school grounds more attractive.
- Go with the class on a field trip.
- Help with school projects at home (nights or weekends).

24 learning activities your child will love

You've probably heard how important it is to "get involved" with your children's education. But what type of parent involvement increases school achievement more than any other?

Surprisingly, simple learning activities done at home are the most effective way to help kids do better in school. That's why we've collected 24 activities that help with language, math, science, writing, thinking skills, and more. Enjoy them with your children.

These activities require a minimum of time, effort, and supplies, but the rewards are great. They'll give academic skills a boost and show your kids that learning is enjoyable. Keep in mind that not all activities are appropriate for all ages—you may need to change them a bit for your kids. Although some activities will require your help, others may be done by your children alone.

Instructions: Help your child cut out the 24 activity squares. You can fold each square in half and put them in a box or jar. Every few days, ask your child to pick an activity. Then let the joy of learning begin!

1. Read a good story out loud to your child—and stop at an exciting part. Turn to your child and say, "What do you think will happen next?"

2. Think of a number—15, for example. How many ways can you "say" that number? *Examples:* 10 + 5, 3 x 5, 30 ÷ 2, 19 - 4. Continue with other numbers.

3. Write a secret message using invisible ink. How? Use a toothpick dipped into lemon juice and milk. When the paper is dry, hold it up to the light. Can you see it in the dark?

4. Think of answers to "what if" questions to develop creative thinking. *Examples:* "What if you could see into the future?" "What if there were no TV?" "What if we had no electricity?"

5. Give each letter of the alphabet a numerical code, such as A=10, B=15, C=20. In this case, the word *cab* would be written 20-10-15. Write a note in code and see if a parent can figure it out.

6. Name all the animals you would keep if you owned a zoo. Can you think of an animal for each letter of the alphabet? Can't think of an animal that starts with *x*? Make up your own and tell what it looks like.

7. Think of a number from 1 to 100. How quickly can your child figure out your number through clues? All you can answer is "higher" or "lower." For example, if your number is 24 and your child guesses 15, say, "higher." Continue until she guesses correctly.

8. Write down all the words you can think of, using the letters in the word *relationship*. How many can you think of in one minute? Try to make your words at least three letters long. *Examples:* ship, tip, ten, late.

9. Make paper airplanes and have a flying contest. Let each person launch a plane several times from the same spot. Then use a tape measure to see which plane flew the greatest distance. How is the winning plane different from the others?

continues

24 Learning Activities Your Child Will Love continued

24 learning activities your child will love

10 Make up a story together. Begin telling some of the story yourself. Ask your child to add a part. Then you add a new twist, and so on. If it's a winner, perhaps you can write it down.

11 Plan an indoor family picnic. Together make a list of the things you'll need. Then gather the items and enjoy your picnic. Don't worry if you've forgotten something—you'll plan better next time!

12 Design a family tree. On a sheet of paper, put your name in a box. Draw lines from your name to boxes containing your parents' names. Then add lines to their parents' names, and so on. Share something interesting about each person on your "tree."

13 What's your favorite book? Write a letter to the author in care of the publisher. If necessary, ask a parent for help. You can tell the author his or her book is your favorite, or ask for an autographed picture.

14 Think of several words that begin with the same first letter. Try to put them together in a logical sentence. *Example:* "Hungry Harriet holds horse hair high over her head."

15 Write down five things you did today in the order they happened—one item per line. Cut them into strips, cut each strip in two pieces, and mix them up. Can you put them back in order?

16 Check the newspaper or the weather report on TV to find the warmest spot in the country. How about the coolest? Can you find these places on a map? Talk about why you think they have such temperatures.

17 Put together a family joke book. Write one or two jokes per page and staple the pages together. Ask friends or family members for ideas or borrow a joke book from the library.

18 Serve a dinner made up of foods having the same color. For example, list every yellow food you can think of and write out a menu. Try to include a variety of food for a well-balanced meal.

19 Make rhythm instruments. Put beans in a plastic jar for "maracas" or glue sandpaper to two blocks of wood. Can you think of other ideas? Now turn on some music and keep time.

20 Together go for a short walk in your neighborhood. When you get home, write down all the things you both remember hearing or seeing. Would your experiences change depending upon the time of day?

21 Extend your arms out by your sides. Let your child measure from fingertip to fingertip. Then ask him to measure your height. Is it the same? Is this true of people younger than you?

22 Make a list of possible uses for a paper cup, toothpick, or rubber band. See if you and a parent can also "brainstorm" ways to make mornings easier.

23 Can you write the directions for making a peanut butter and jelly sandwich? Let a parent read the instructions back to you as you try to make the sandwich. Congratulations if you included all the steps. If not, rewrite them and try again.

24 Make a batch of play dough together. Mix 1 cup flour, ⅓ cup salt, a few drops of oil, and enough water to make it easy to handle. Take a handful and add a drop or two of food coloring for variety.

Test-Taking Secrets:
Improving Your Child's Success

Why do children of equal ability often score so differently on tests? Is it because one child studies more than the other? Maybe—but this is not always the case.

In fact, good test-taking skills can be as important as knowing the material. Without these skills, your child's scores are not likely to reflect what he or she knows.

 Test scores are not a perfect measure of what your child can do—but they *are* important. They may affect your child's yearly grade or placement in school. Besides, the ability to do well on tests can help throughout life—whether it's getting a driver's license or getting a job.

So, how can you help improve your child's test scores? Whether it's a teacher-made test or a standardized test, here are some test-taking secrets that get results.

Develop a healthy attitude toward tests

First, help your child understand why tests are necessary. Explain that a test is like a yardstick. Schools use them to measure how much students are learning—and how well schools are teaching. They let teachers know if your child needs extra help, and they also show areas of strength.

It's best not to make too big a deal about test results—especially on a single test. Many things can affect your child's score on any given day. If he does poorly on a test, he may need reassurance. Point out some of his successes.

Prepare for tests—one day at a time

Some students get so worried about tests that they don't do well on test day. The best way to avoid "test anxiety" is to space studying over several days or weeks. Begin by marking major test dates on the family calendar.

Next, help your child schedule regular times to review. She can talk about the subject, read about it, or "teach" the material to someone in the family.

Finally, encourage your child to pay attention to the teacher's review. She needs to know what kinds of questions will be on the test and what material will be covered.

The night before a big test

"Cramming" the night before a test usually makes things worse and interferes with clear thinking. If your child has kept up with daily assignments and has been reviewing all along, cramming shouldn't be necessary. When possible, try to spend a relaxing evening at home. It's also important for your child to get a good night's sleep.

continues

Test-Taking Secrets continued

Start the day off right

Getting up early on test day helps prevent the morning rush and allows time for a complete, unhurried breakfast. Avoid topics or arguments that may be upsetting. By starting the day on a pleasant note, you're more likely to send your child off to school with good feelings.

Stay cool on test day

Remind your child to have extra paper, two sharpened pencils, and a good eraser. Suggest that she get a drink of water, use the rest room, and take a few deep, relaxing breaths just before the test. To avoid nervous "jitters" as the test is passed out, it may help if she silently repeats a comforting thought. Example: "I've studied hard, and I'm going to do my best!"

Follow the directions

Reading or listening carefully to the directions is probably the most important thing your child can do. If the instructions are unclear, he should ask the teacher to explain them. And tell him to be sure to put his name on the test paper before he begins.

Develop a test-taking strategy

To build your child's confidence, suggest that she have a clear test-taking strategy. For example, many teachers recommend the following: Look over the entire test before starting; answer the easiest questions first; don't spend too much time on one question; and, if there's time, check your work and go back to the ones you skipped.

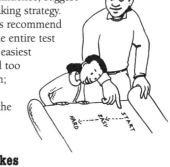

Learn from your mistakes

When your child receives her test back, it's important for her to understand what she did wrong. A test can be an opportunity to see where more work is needed.

SPECIAL TIPS FOR STANDARDIZED TESTS

Standardized tests measure the performance of one group of students against the performance of other groups of students. They help schools see how well their programs are succeeding.

Here are some ways to help your child do his best:

1. Get your child used to multiple-choice questions by making up a few at home.

2. Explain that some test questions may be unfamiliar to him. This is normal and he shouldn't worry about it.

3. Standardized tests are usually timed. Tell your child to see how many questions are on each section and how much time he has. This way, he can pace himself.

4. Remind your child to relax and do his best—without worrying. After all, his work throughout the year is a better measure of his achievement than any single test score.

TEST-TAKING TIPS

Multiple Choice

1. Read the whole question before making a choice.

2. Eliminate the choices that you know are wrong. Try the rest to see which one makes the most sense.

3. Check to make sure each answer is next to the right number or letter.

True-False

1. Read each sentence carefully.

2. If you don't know the answer, guess. Hint: There are usually more true answers than false answers.

3. On a true-false test, your first answer is often correct, so it's best not to change it.

Matching

1. Do the easiest matches first, and then tackle the tougher ones

2. Ask the teacher if all or only some of the matching choices will be used.

3. If a choice can be used only once, lightly cross it out after you use it.

Fill In the Blank

1. Read the entire sentence twice to make sure you understand it.

2. Look at each sentence carefully for possible clues.

3. If you're not sure, take a guess. An empty blank will never be correct.

Read-Aloud Pitfalls

What's one of the best ways you can help your children become good readers? Reading books aloud to them.

You don't need to be an excellent reader or to have a great voice. All it takes is a pleasant, relaxed attitude. You want your kids to get the message that "Reading is fun. Let's do it again soon."

Some parents try so hard to make the most of reading time that the enjoyment gets lost. Here's a look at common read-aloud pitfalls, how they can affect kids, and simple ways to avoid them.

The Briber

Pitfall: You want your child to love reading, so you offer her a reward for every book you read to her.

Result: Your child *was* interested in reading. Now all she seems to care about is how many prizes she has collected.

Better: Let the motivation be the pleasure of reading and the time you spend together. If not, the joy of reading will be lost in favor of the prize.

The Chooser

Pitfall: You've picked out a book *you* want to read aloud. It's all about birds.

Result: The trouble is, your child's not interested. He doesn't like birds. He wants you to read the dump truck book, or the one about the tigers.

Better: Most children want to choose the books you read aloud. When they do, they're more likely to pay attention. If you have a book you'd like to read, try reading it *after* you read a book your child has chosen.

The Limit Setter

Pitfall: Your child keeps asking questions. You feel frustrated by constantly being interrupted to answer them. So, you decide to limit them.

Result: Your child may not understand the story. Sometimes he needs to ask questions and hear your explanation to get the meaning.

Better: Research shows it's valuable to stop along the way to answer your child's questions. The benefits of reading aloud are greatest when children can actively take part in the process.

The Marathon Runner

Pitfall: You're determined to read several books to your child in one sitting—no matter how long it takes.

Result: Your child isn't interested in hearing more than one, and she's not paying attention. All she wants to do is go play with her friends.

Better: Let your child's interest guide the amount of reading you do. If she's following a story, by all means, keep reading. But if you're losing her, bring read-aloud time to an end until tomorrow.

continues

Read-Aloud Pitfalls continued

Read-Aloud Pitfalls

Page 2

The One-Timer

Pitfall: Your child wants to hear the same book for the millionth time. You don't think you can stand to read it again.

Result: Your child misses a chance to hear her favorite book. She loves knowing what's going to happen and never tires of hearing the same thing over and over again.

Better: Before you begin reading a favorite book, explain that you'll only read it once per session. It's natural for young children to want to hear the same book repeatedly. And natural for you to get weary of it. *Note:* Research shows that repeated readings help your child learn to recognize new words—a very valuable part of building "sight" vocabulary.

The Postponer

Pitfall: You keep planning to read aloud day after day, but it never seems to happen.

Result: Your child thinks that you don't care about reading. After a while, he doesn't seem interested in reading.

Better: Set aside a time each day when you and your child can cozy up together and read. Many parents choose to read books at bedtime. After a while, it'll become a habit you'll both enjoy.

The Professor

Pitfall: You want to challenge your child. You steer away from books that are short and easy.

Result: Your child seems interested at first but soon gets bored. Why? Because she can't understand what you are reading. The book may be too complicated or long.

Better: Look for a variety of reading material—some easy, some hard, some short, some long. Glance at your child now and then to make sure she's still paying attention.

The Questioner

Pitfall: You want your child to develop thinking skills. While you're reading, you stop every page or two to ask questions.

Result: The only thing your child can focus on is what's going to happen next in the story. He wishes you'd just keep reading without asking questions.

Better: Let the story flow naturally. If you interrupt to ask too many questions of your own, your child may become confused. It's always a good idea to talk about a book or ask questions, but save most until the end. *Examples:* "Who was your favorite character?" "Why?" "Did you ever have anything like that happen to you?"

The Sprinter

Pitfall: You're in a hurry. You have to leave in 10 minutes, but you promised your child you'd read a book.

Result: She just got comfy on your lap, but knows you're in a rush. Instead of listening, she starts wriggling and giving you a hard time for leaving.

Better: One of the most common reading mistakes is reading too quickly. Your child needs lots of time to form mental images in her head. It's better to read a few pages slowly than to rush through a book. ♥

A Sample of Read-Aloud Favorites

Why do some children love to read whereas others almost never read for pleasure? Often, someone helped these young readers get *excited* about reading.

They have seen others enjoying books and have listened to wonderful stories. In short, these children have experienced the pleasure that reading can bring. Your child can, too!

In this special report on "read-aloud" books, we are pleased to present a small sample of the books children love most. But first, we'll answer a few of the most common questions parents ask about reading.

Q *How can I help my child get excited about reading?*

A The easiest way to improve your child's reading, writing, and speaking skills is by reading good books aloud. Studies have shown that reading aloud is probably the most important activity in building reading success and enjoyment. It's also a good idea to keep a wide variety of reading materials around the house and to make sure your child sees *you* reading for pleasure.

Q *Where do I find the books that are best for my child?*

A There are thousands of wonderful children's books to choose from. If you need help finding good books, check with the school librarian or drop by your public library for advice. Several guides have been published that describe hundreds of excellent books for young readers. Some of the best resources include:

♥ *The New Read-Aloud Handbook* by Jim Trelease (Penguin)
♥ *Choosing Books for Kids* by Oppenheim, Brenner, and Boegehold (Ballatine)
♥ *New York Times Parent's Guide to the Best Books for Children* by Eden Lipson (Random)
♥ *The RIF Guide to Encouraging Young Readers* by Ruth Graves (Doubleday)

Q *What suggestions can you give to make read-aloud time a success?*

A Build read-aloud time into your daily routine. A regular time—even just 15 minutes—can help create a lifelong reader. And it's never too late to show your child reading is fun. Choose books on topics your child is interested in—he will be more likely to read and enjoy them.

Q *Can you name a few of the best read-aloud books for elementary children?*

A The list below will get you started. Most of these books are highly recommended on popular "read-aloud" book lists, including *The New Read-Aloud Handbook* by Jim Trelease and the Reading is Fundamental *Children's Bookshelf*. Some of these books are available in Spanish, but check with a librarian to be sure.

We urge you to review books personally to see if they're appropriate for your child.

Amelia Bedelia by Peggy Parish (K–4): Amelia is a lovable girl who is a walking disaster. She creates a giant mess because she takes directions literally. Many sequels.

Bedtime for Frances by Russell Hoban (K–2): Frances is a badger who can't get to sleep. Many of the bedtime excuses children give are humorously contained here.

Charlotte's Web by E.B. White (K–4): Wilbur, a barnyard pig, is supposed to be butchered in the fall. The animals—especially a spider named Charlotte—and the farmer's daughter work to save his life.

continues

A Sample of Read-Aloud Favorites continued

A Sample of Read-Aloud Favorites

Cricket in Times Square by George Seldon (3–6): A classic story of a cat and mouse who live in Times Square and discover Chester, a musical cricket. A wonderful tale of friendship and sacrifice.

Crow Boy by Taro Yashima (K–4): A shy little schoolboy is ignored and taunted by his classmates. Finally, a special teacher brings out the boy's silent gifts. Everyone sees that differences in people make life exciting. A wonderful message!

If I Ran the Zoo by Dr. Seuss (K–4): Gerald McGrew populates the zoo of his imagination with wonderful, funny, and exotic creatures. Only Dr. Seuss could describe these rare species!

If I Were in Charge of the World by Judith Viorst (3–6): A collection of 41 humorous poems about children's hopes, fears, and feelings.

Ira Sleeps Over by Bernard Waber (K–6): Ira wonders if he should take his teddy bear when he spends the night at his friend's house. Can lead to interesting family discussions.

Island of the Blue Dolphins by Scott O'Dell (4–6): An inspiring story based on the experiences of Karana, an island girl, who is marooned on an island off the coast of California.

James and the Giant Peach by Roald Dahl (3–6): The story of James, a young orphan, who leaves his miserable life with mean relatives to live inside a giant peach. Inside the peach, James meets a marvelous group of characters.

Little Bear by Else Holelund Minarik (K–1): A series of books about Little Bear and his family. Covers things that are important to children, such as birthdays, playing, and wishing.

Make Way for Ducklings by Robert McClosky (K–2): This modern classic follows Mrs. Mallard and her eight ducklings as they search for a new home.

Mike Mulligan and His Steam Shovel by Virginia Lee Burton (K–2): The heartwarming story of Mary Anne, the old-fashioned steam shovel, who proves she and her owner can still be useful to the town of Popperville.

Miss Nelson is Missing by Harry Allard (K–4): After they're faced with an unpleasant substitute, the children in Miss Nelson's class come to realize what a wonderful teacher they have.

My Side of the Mountain by Jean George (3–8): Sam Gribley is a modern-day Robinson Crusoe. He describes his year of surviving as a runaway in the mountains.

Storm Boy by Colin Thiele (3–6): An Australian hermit and his son live by the sea. They adopt and train a little pelican that is lost to thoughtless hunters.

Tales of a Fourth Grade Nothing by Judy Blume (3–5). This book is about Fudge, who is two-and-a-half and usually the center of attention in his family; and Peter, who feels like a "fourth grade nothing."

Tar Beach by Faith Ringgold (K–3): Story of a young girl living in Harlem in the 1930s who dreams she can be free, flying anywhere she wants to go.

The Hole in the Dike, retold by Norma Green (K–2): The inspiring legend of a brave little Dutch boy who discovers the hole in the dike and plugs it with his finger until help arrives.

The Island of the Skog by Steven Kellogg (K–2): A boatload of mice find the island of their dreams, but are frightened by a scary monster already living there. They learned that talking about problems can sometimes overcome obstacles.

The People Could Fly, retold by Virginia Hamilton (K–up): This Newbery Medal winner contains 24 African-American folktales selected for children.

The Reluctant Dragon by Kenneth Grahame (3–5): This is a charming book about a reluctant dragon who wants nothing to do with violence. Wonderful introduction to a legendary time and place.

The Sign of the Beaver by Elizabeth G. Speare (3–up): The story of two boys — one white, the other Native American — who come of age in the Maine wilderness before the Revolutionary War. A sensitive study of their developing relationship.

Tikki Tikki Tembo by Arlene Mosel (K–2): An amusing legend of how the Chinese people changed from giving their firstborn sons very long names to giving them shorter ones.

Where the Red Fern Grows by Wilson Rawls (3–7): A 10-year-old boy grows up in the Ozark Mountains and works to buy a pair of hounds. A wonderful book of perseverance, courage, work, and life and death.

Where the Sidewalk Ends by Shel Silverstein (K–8): A hilarious collection of 130 poems. Full of surprise endings and exciting rhythms — sure to tickle your child's funny bone.

For the Love of Writing

Your child may not become a famous author, but he or she will be writing in every school subject—and throughout life. In fact, future job success may depend on the ability to write effectively.

How will writing skills be learned? By practicing them—just like other skills. Yet few kids will practice on their own—they need reasons to write. Here are 10 ways you can promote the writing habit and help your child enjoy writing.

1. Use interests to encourage writing.

Does your child have a favorite TV star? Does she scramble to watch a certain sports team or player? Has she been asking you about a birthday party? If the answer to any of these questions is yes, then your child has many opportunities to write. Grab her interests, and soon she might be creating one of these:

A letter to a favorite TV or sports personality. A trip to the library information desk will help you find addresses for TV networks and sports teams. What a thrill it will be when your child gets a response in the mail—and maybe an autographed photo!

A scrapbook about a favorite sports team or player. Your child can read articles from the sports section and clip them for a scrapbook. Encourage her to make notes about the game. Who was her favorite player? What was the best play of the game? How could the team have played better?

An invitation to a birthday party. Help your child create her own invitations by hand or on the computer. Or buy prepared, fill-in-the-blank cards. When the party is over, help her write thank-you notes to her friends who brought gifts.

2. Include your child in your family's daily writing.

Let your child see you writing letters, checks, grocery lists, and memos. He will realize that writing is a natural and important part of everyday life—not just something he has to do at school. Here are some ideas:

- When you write a letter to family or friends, read it aloud. See if your child wants to add a sentence or two.

- As you look through the refrigerator before a shopping trip, call out the grocery items you need. Ask your child to add them to the list.

- Time to pay bills? Have your child address the envelopes or enter items in your check register.

- Consider a family message center—complete with paper, pen, and bulletin board—where family members can post notes. For example, leave reminders about appointments, activities, or birthdays. Write a note of congratulations or good luck to someone in the family.

3. Keep writing supplies handy.

Select a drawer or choose a sturdy box as a place to keep writing supplies. These might include stationery, lined paper, pens, pencils, felt-tip markers, stamps, envelopes, erasers, crayons, and small notebooks. Add a dictionary and a collection of sample letters that your child can use as a guide.

continues

For the Love of Writing continued

4. Make writing portable.

When you're on the go, carry a small notebook and pen in your pocket, purse, or glove compartment.

- When your child says something that you want to treasure, say, "That's so interesting, I want to write it down so I won't forget."

- If you're driving down the road and see a sign that captures your imagination or tickles your funny bone, say, "Please get the notebook out and write that down."

- Encourage your child to keep his eyes and ears open. When he sees something interesting, have him jot it down. He may want to write about it when he gets home.

5. Enjoy a family writing night.

Ask family members to join in a writing night once or twice a month. You can write letters to family and friends, or write thank-you notes to helpful people in your community. Each person can contribute a section to the family letter or write his own letter. The payoff is more than improving writing skills — it's receiving a reply in the mail!

6. Start a family journal.

Keep a family journal in which everyone writes entries. They can be as simple as one sentence: "We went to the zoo today." Or, they can tell all about the trip to the zoo — including everyone's favorite animals. To get things going, take the journal out often and write something about the day. Ask if your child would like to add an idea. Then, keep the journal in a central location so she can get it out whenever she'd like.

7. Read aloud to your child.

When you read aloud to your child, you give him lots of new ideas to write about — as well as new words to use. Read stories, newspaper articles, and letters. Pause in your reading to ask questions: "What do you think will happen next?" "What shall we write about in our letter to Aunt Juanita?"

8. Talk and listen.

If you want your child to use new words in her writing, talk with her regularly about a variety of topics. When you listen to your child's ideas, she gets the message that her thoughts are worthwhile — and she'll be more inclined to write.

9. Build your child's confidence.

After reading something your child has written, give honest praise telling what you think. Say, for example, "I enjoyed the way you described the cat."

Also, post your child's work where it can be seen. Or, keep an album of stories and poems she writes. If you have a computer, enter them in her directory.

10. Be patient — improvement takes time.

Writing takes practice, just like any skill. Help your child write small amounts at first so he doesn't become overwhelmed. When you talk about his writing, tell him the things you like. According to some writing experts, pointing out all your child's mistakes can be discouraging for younger writers. Regardless of your child's age, it's a good idea to be gentle with criticism.

A Love for Reading

Reading enjoyment begins at home

Why do some children love to read, while others never read for pleasure? It's usually because someone helped them get excited about reading.

In most cases, they have seen others enjoying books. They have sat and listened to wonderful stories. In short, these kids have experienced the pleasure that reading can bring.

Since reading enjoyment begins at home, there's a great deal you can do to encourage your children's love for reading. The checklist below may give you some ideas. Or use it to see how many things you're doing now.

❑ I regularly read good books aloud to my children — even if it's just a few minutes at a time.

❑ I try to get my children excited about books. Example: I read the first part of an exciting story so that my children get hooked and want to continue.

❑ My children have their own library cards, and we visit the library often.

❑ I expose my children to a wide variety of printed material, such as books, magazines, newspapers, encyclopedias, advertisements, and signs.

❑ Whenever possible, I encourage my children to read. Example: If we cook together, they read the recipe directions.

❑ If my children are struggling to read a difficult book, we take turns reading. That way, they are less likely to get discouraged.

❑ I look for books that relate to my children's interests. I know they'll be more motivated to read about topics they enjoy.

❑ We play games that build reading skills, such as *Spill and Spell, Scrabble Sentence Game for Juniors,* and *Boggle.*

"Reading aloud to your children is the single most important activity in building reading success and enjoyment."

❑ I limit TV viewing and video games so that my children will have plenty of time for pleasure reading.

❑ My children know how important reading is to me. They often see me reading, and I tell them about interesting things I've read.

❑ We have a family silent-reading time. I read my favorite magazine, newspaper, or novel, while my children read their own books or children's magazines.

❑ When we visit the library, I point out interesting children's magazines. Examples: *Ranger Rick, In Your Own Backyard, 3-2-1 Contact, World, Highlights for Children, Cricket.*

If you're already doing most of the above, that's great! If not, try adding a few as your schedule permits. When you stimulate the joy of reading in your children, you'll have hungry readers on your hands...and in the library...and at school...and in the car...

Editor's Note: If your children have access to a computer, there are many software titles that provide an excellent blend of reading practice and motivation. For more details on recommended programs, see *Kidware: The Parent's Guide to Software for Children* by Michael Perkins and Celia Nunez (Prima Publishing, 1995).

Learning Resources
for Parents

Does your child have a math question? Like experimenting with science? Need a list of great books to read? Want to learn more about United States history?

Here's some good news—there are plenty of books and Web sites designed to spark your youngster's interest in learning. Here are several resources we recommend for your and your child.

Language Arts

Why is reading aloud to your child the number one suggestion from reading experts across the country? Because it builds your child's desire to read in just a few minutes each day. For a terrific source of read-aloud stories, check out this book, edited by Jim Trelease. It's a collection of 50 fairy tales and famous stories from around the world. **Hey! Listen to This: Stories to Read Aloud**

Need some good book ideas for your child? BookHive has them! This Web site has thousands of great books to recommend. Just like a librarian, BookHive tailors its suggestions to your child's age and interests. **www.bookhive.org/bookhive.htm**

Poetry is fun! Don't believe it? Then log on to KidzPage. Read the poems aloud with your youngster for guaranteed giggles. (Try the Ogden Nash poem about the hippopotamus!) Click on the "Verse and Worse!" button for fun limericks and other silly stuff. **www.veeceet.com**

Mathematics

When you tell your youngster that math is fun, does he just roll his eyes? You might be able to convince him with a copy of this terrific book by Janice VanCleave. It teaches basic math skills in an easy, step-by-step method that doesn't talk down to kids. Each lesson comes with a nifty hands-on project or activity. Designed for ages 8–12, but so easy to read that some younger kids will like it, too. **Math for Every Kid: Easy Activities That Make Learning Math Fun**

Does your child have questions about math that leave you both stumped? Can't figure out how a word problem works? Find the answers at Ask Dr. Math, a forum designed specifically for elementary school math questions. An archive lists answers for most questions, but a real "Dr. Math" will e-mail answers to any new puzzlers you present. **http://mathforum.com/dr.math/drmath.elem.html**

At A+ Math, your child can play interactive math games like "Matho," a cross between math and Bingo. The site also provides math worksheets and flashcards for use offline, concentration games, and a "Homework Helper" where children can check their math homework online. **www.aplusmath.com**

Learning Resources for Parents continued

Learning Resources *for Parents* Page 2

Science

📖 Who knew that polymers were fun to play with? Or that they're easy for kids to whip up at home? Get ready to turn your kitchen inside-out in the name of science with this book of activities, by Jill Frankel Hauser. Your youngster will have a blast making these safe, simple, inexpensive projects (with your supervision) using common kitchen ingredients. **Super Science Concoctions: 50 Mysterious Mixtures for Fabulous Fun**

💻 How can a rock float? It's a mystery...a Geo-Mystery, to be exact! Kids can learn some cool geology facts by teaming up with Rex the Dino Detective. Rex will lead your child through some fancy detective work, from the case of the floating rocks to the mystery of the golden cube. This interactive site includes answers to common questions about rocks and fossils. **www.childrensmuseum.org/geomysteries/index2.html**

💻 Science fairs don't have to be a headache—just visit the Internet Public Library. This online library's science fair resource site can guide your child through the whole process. Your youngster can learn about the scientific method or choose a topic and read about sample projects. The site's links offer lots of good ideas and encouragement. **www.ipl.org/youth/projectguide**

RESOURCES FOR PARENTS

You want to be involved in your child's education. But how can you help? And where do you start? One of the best places to start is the Internet! There you can find a huge variety of sites to help you with your child's education.

• You might begin with ERIC, the Education Resources Information Center, which has brochures for parents on everything from keeping children drug-free to learning a second language.
www.eric.ed.gov/resources/parent/parent.html

• The U.S. Department of Education's Web site offers parents a guide to using the Internet as an educational tool, with links to hundreds of family-friendly sites. **www.ed.gov/pubs/parents/internet**

• You might also visit the national Parent-Teacher Association (PTA) Web site and learn how to get involved at your child's school. The PTA site has great resources for parents. Go to the site and click on "Parent Involvement."
www.pta.org

History

📖 Where can you find fun facts and interesting information about history? This Scholastic Homework Reference Series book, by Anne Zeman and Kate Kelly, includes maps, timelines, charts, and graphs to make history homework easier. **Everything You Need to Know About World History Homework**

💻 Did you know that it used to be illegal to sing out of tune in North Carolina? Or that Alaska's official state sport is dog-mushing? Your youngster can find nuggets of information about each state, as well as short biographies of United States presidents. **http://tqjunior.thinkquest.org/5744**

💻 Did anything historic happen on your child's birthday? Visit "America's Story" together and find out. Click on the "Jump Back in Time" button, type in a birth date, and see

what happened on that day. Your youngster can read about famous Americans and explore a timeline of United States history. She can also learn about the games and songs that children enjoyed long ago. **www.americaslibrary.gov/cgi-bin/page.cgi**

Note: Remember, the Web is changing at the speed of light. Although these sites were current at the time of publication, all are subject to change without notice.

Chapter 2–3

Improve Parenting Skills

Meeting Parent Needs 2–3:1

Parenting Skills 2–3:1
   Issues and Strategies 2–3:1
   Elements of Effective Programs 2–3:4
   Conclusion 2–3:6
   Parent Center 2–3:7
   Project Healthy Start 2–3:7

Partnering on Discipline 2–3:9

Enlist Parent Support 2–3:9
   Share Policies Up Front 2–3:9
   Weekly Notes Home 2–3:9
   Discipline Form Letters Save Time 2–3:10

Materials You Can Use 2–3:11

Classroom Discipline Plan 2–3:11
Weekly, Daily Report Forms 2–3:12
Tardiness Report 2–3:13
Bus Behavior Report 2–3:14
Disruptive Behavior Report 2–3:15
Secrets of Effective Discipline 2–3:16
12 Ways To Build Responsibility 2–3:18
Building Your Child's Character 2–3:20

Chapter 2–3

Improve Parenting Skills

MEETING PARENT NEEDS

PARENTING SKILLS

A key component of effective involvement is helping families to meet their basic obligations: to provide a safe, nurturing home environment for children; to support their children's educational endeavors; and to establish appropriate expectations of behavior. Many parents fall short of these goals—some for lack of resources such as time and money, others for lack of knowledge about basic parenting skills. They may be unsure of how to deal with misbehavior, how to set limits, even how to provide for basic nutrition.

Schools can play a significant role in counteracting these problems and helping parents become more effective coaches, disciplinarians, and when appropriate, providers. In turn, children can become more attentive, higher-achieving students because they are better prepared to learn and because they receive consistent messages at home and at school.

Issues and Strategies

Changing Family Structure

Despite strong political emphasis on family values, few American families fit the classic mold of *Leave It to Beaver*—a two-parent household led by a bread-winning father and a stay-at-home mother. The U.S. Census Bureau reports that the number of single-parent families grew from 3.8 million in 1970 to 11.4 million in 1994, an increase of 200 percent. Increasingly, students live with relatives who are not their biological parents.

Socioeconomic factors affect students' home life, as well. *Youth Indicators 1993*, a publication by the National Center for Education Statistics, reports that, in 1993, one of five children younger than 18 years old lived in a household in which the income was below the poverty level.[1]

These demographic factors are important, say school leaders, because they influence the amount of time and energy that parents and guardians have to commit to school activities and parenting. As a result, many students lack quality, day-to-day parental supervision and don't arrive at school ready to learn.

Problems Requiring Help with Parenting Skills

Many factors contribute to parents' need for assistance with parenting skills. The following discussion addresses these problems and strategies that can be used in schools to overcome them.

Lack of Time

Parents lack adequate time to refine parenting skills. Most parents, especially single parents, work long hours to support their families. This frequently leaves little time for them to spend with their children and saps their enthusiasm for attending school events and parent workshops.

Gretna R. Willis, coordinator of special instructional programs at the Wicomico County Schools in Salisbury, Maryland, says that conducting parent-related events when and where they are most convenient for parents engages many parents who can't or won't forfeit their personal time to participate in events held at school. "So often we ask them to come to us," she says. "But many of them just don't feel comfortable at school because it dredges up negative memories." Her district's Parents Can Make the Difference program reverses this traditional flow of information by delivering information at the workplace, where parents spend much of their time. The arrangement eliminates many problems that school-based sessions create, including the need for additional child care.

This program focuses on many parenting skills needed to create a home environment conducive to learning. It is unique because it takes into account parents' time limitations and provides them with information without asking them to make an additional commitment during nonbusiness hours.

Parent sessions can also be organized at community centers and churches, says Principal Jerry Fair, of Milwaukee, Wisconsin. He plans mobile parent–teacher conferences in neighborhoods from which many of his students are bused. More parents participate in teacher conferences when they don't have to travel to the school, he says.

Lack of Parenting Resources

Few parents receive formal training on how to raise a child. Some consult books or magazines for guidance, but for a majority of parents, effective parenting skills are learned by trial and error.

Educators, through training and experience, understand how best to cope with and solve difficult behavioral problems, such as students who defy authority. Consequently, teachers and school staff are in an excellent position to share their collective expertise with parents. Many schools foster this sharing by organizing a variety of parenting publications in parent resource centers. These areas in the school give parents access to books, magazines, journals, and videotapes about both general and specific parenting techniques.

Tom Wailand, a principal in Bradenton, Florida, reserves a portion of the school media center as a parent resource library, where he offers materials on general child development, setting limits, when to be firm and when to give in, and specific education-related topics such as attention deficit disorder. He says many parents, especially first-time parents, often are unsure about how to help their sons and daughters when trouble arises. "I've never talked to a parent who didn't want to help reinforce school discipline at home, but I have talked to many who didn't know how. The resource center is a way to give them the information they need," he says. Assistant Principal Carol Chanter of Casselberry, Florida, says that she tracks use of her parent resource center to determine when it should be open and to learn what specific subjects most interest parents.

Many parent resource centers make materials available for checkout so parents can read at their convenience. But schools are not the only location at which this service can or should be made available. According to Marie Warecek, an elementary guidance counselor and alcohol and drug abuse prevention coordinator in Black River Falls, Wisconsin, parents prefer that checkout materials be available at locations other than the school. "We asked parents where they would be most likely to read and check out materials on parenting, and they chose the public library as opposed to the school," she says.

The El Paso Independent School District in Texas takes a slightly different tack in educating parents. According to materials supplied by Gary Napier, a publication specialist with the district, the Read to Your Babies program aims to promote literacy among preschool-age children and their parents by raising parents' awareness of age-appropriate book titles. Brochures and fliers that identify specific publications are distributed in both English and Spanish and are available by age (e.g., infants to 24 months and toddlers). To complement the publicity campaign, elementary schools hold parent workshops to teach parents techniques for reading to children.

In addition to written materials, many schools offer seminars or minicourses on parenting skills, as well as courses designed to improve parents' personal knowledge and/or job skills. Assistant Principal David Jordan of Henderson, Kentucky, does this through a school-based Parent University program. A variety of sessions are available, including graduation equivalency courses, which are offered in cooperation with the community college. Other examples of minicourses that have been offered through the Parent University: Diffusing Anger; Shared Parenting in Joint Custody; Preparing for College; Everything You've Always Wanted To Know about Your School Board and School Councils; Creative Thinking Skills; and Parenting Preschoolers with Less Stress and More Success.

The Parent Center at the Murrieta Valley Unified School District in Murrieta, California, provides a wide range of services to promote type 1 involvement and related information for parents. In addition to regularly scheduled workshops and classes in parenting, the center also offers adult activities such as area trips, resources and referral services, access to technology, and child care while parents use the center. The adult-activity element is a feature not commonly seen in parent programs, but it is an important part of helping parents feel at ease and at peace with themselves, a factor that is reflected in how they deal with their children.

Marecek's Black River Falls School District shares resources with various state and local organizations to offer parent programs through an initiative called Building Collaborative School–Family–Community Involvement. The parenting component of the program trains school staff and community members to facilitate small group sessions about parenting skills. Sessions include a review with parents of how they themselves were parented, how that influences relationships with their own children, and how those relationships can be improved. The sessions help parents understand techniques to improve children's self-esteem, which, in turn, improves their attitude and performance at school.

Lack of Basic Needs

For some families, securing basic necessities such as food, shelter, and medical services occupies so much time that parenting becomes a secondary priority. Organizing a system to help families cope with these unfortunate situations puts students in a better position to learn, and it enables families to devote more attention to education and appropriate parenting techniques, says Principal Fred Ortman. "Children can't learn if they're hungry, tired, or sick."

Many students at Ortman's school in the Los Angeles area come from poverty-stricken or homeless families. Project Healthy Start helps those families meet basic needs by offering nutrition and cooking classes, and laundry and shower facilities. Basic medical services, including immunization and well-child checkups, are also available. Even though these measures don't address parenting skills per se, they do address basic parenting obligations, which must be met if parents are to have time and opportunity to concentrate on issues such as discipline and academic expectations.

Like Ortman, Principal Elaine Newton of Sierra Vista, Arizona, tends to the needs of severely disadvantaged families through a school wellness center that offers parenting classes featuring physicians and dentists as presenters. Wellness coordinators also administer a clothing exchange that Newton organized with more affluent surrounding districts. Coordinators solicit and clean donations and leave them in the clothing exchange room for parents to pick up as needed. The center is paid for with federal grant money, a portion of which was also used to hire two Hispanic women to provide assistance to that segment of the school's population.

Elements of Effective Programs

Labor-intensive, parent-outreach programs can improve both student achievement and, to some degree, a child's general well-being. Powell writes that studies of parent education programs show promising results.

> Evaluations of intensive parent- or family-oriented early-childhood programs serving low-income populations have found positive short-term effects on child competence and maternal behaviors and long-term effects on such family characteristics as level of education, family size, and financial self-support.[2] Others[3] suggest that the magnitude of program effects is associated with the number of program contacts with a family and the range of services offered to the family.[4]

What makes parent education programs effective? Powell[5] cites four essential elements.

1. **Content must be determined by parent needs.** Effective programs use school staff as facilitators who approach parents as equals, rather than as experts. Cochran says that open-ended discussion of parent-initiated topics is preferred to the one-way flow of information provided by traditional lecture sessions, because it ensures that program content does, indeed, meet parents' needs.[6]
2. **Attention to parent and student needs must be balanced.** Although programs may inform parents of ideal ways to address their children's needs, these programs should not focus solely on students. The best outreach programs contain elements that address parents' own social concerns, including interpersonal relationships. Parents who are better able to cope with their own problems can, in turn, give more attention to their children.
3. **Programs must fit the target audience.** Specific programs will not work with all parent groups. Like classroom lesson plans, parent education programs must be tailored to a specific group of parents. Special attention should be given to cultural and socioeconomic characteristics.
4. **Discussion must be parent centered.** Effective adult education takes advantage of participants' experience through discussion of problems and concerns. This process provides parents the opportunity to comprehend information in the context of their own families, as well as to hear new ideas from others in the same situation.[7]

The dynamics of the Parent Can Make the Difference program are an excellent example of this strategy.

Relating to Single and Working Parents

In addition to the program elements identified here, Rich[8] recommends that schools use the following guidelines to generate quality relationships with single and working parents.[9]

- Be sensitive to parents' scheduling difficulties, and announce meetings and other events far enough in advance for parents to arrange for leave from work.
- Create a more accepting environment for working and single parents; those undergoing separation, divorce, or remarriage; and those acting as custodial parents.
- Schedule teacher–parent–counselor meetings in the evening, with child care provided.
- Allow open enrollment so children can attend schools near parents' workplaces.
- Provide before- and after-school child care.
- Be careful about canceling school at the last minute due to weather conditions, leaving working parents with no resources for the care of their children.
- Facilitate formation and meeting of peer support groups for teen, single, working, and custodial parents.

- Provide both legal and custodial parents with regular information on their child's classroom activities and any assistance they may need to become involved with the child's learning.

Conclusion

Many factors contribute to parents' inability to fully support their children as students. But schools can take steps to help them, through parent education workshops, by collecting and providing resources, and by meeting families halfway—not only by giving parents the information that they ask for, but by taking it to them, rather than expecting them to come to the school.

The experience represented by the resources in this chapter shows that helping parents to become involved in their children's education goes beyond teaching them parenting skills. It also involves helping them to meet basic parenting obligations, such as providing food and shelter. Without these basic necessities, students are ill-prepared to learn. Schools that help families with these problems give them an opportunity to focus time and energy on other issues, such as discipline and expectations. The net result: students are better equipped physically, emotionally, and mentally for the classroom and their achievement is higher.

References

1. *Youth Indicators 1993.* Trends in the Well-Being of American Youth. National Center for Education Statistics, Office of Educational Research and Improvement, Washington, DC.

2. D.R. Powell, *Families and Early Childhood Programs* (Washington, DC: National Association for the Education of Young Children, 1989).

3. C.M. Heinicke et al., Early Intervention in the Family System: A Framework and Review, *Infant Mental Health Journal 9* (1988): 111–141.

4. D.R. Powell, Parent Education and Support Programs, *Educational Resources Information Center Digest,* ED320661 (Urbana, IL: ERIC Clearinghouse on Elementary and Early Childhood Education, 1990).

5. Powell, Parent Education and Support Programs.

6. M. Cochran, "Parental Empowerment in Family Matters: Lessons Learned from a Research Program," in *Parent Education as Early Childhood Intervention,* ed. D.R. Powell (Norwood, NJ: Ablex, 1988), 25–30.

7. Powell, Parent Education and Support Programs.

8. D. Rich, *The Forgotten Factor in School Success: The Family. A Policymaker's Guide* (Washington, DC: The Home and School Institute, 1985).

9. C. Ascher, Improving the School–Home Connection for Low-Income Urban Parents, *Educational Resources Information Center Digest,* ED293973 (New York: ERIC Clearinghouse on Urban Education, 1988).

PARENT CENTER

The Murrieta Valley Parent Center, California, occupies four rooms at Sivela Middle School, two of which are classrooms. One room is a resource library with books, videotapes, and audiotapes; the other room is a child-care center. The manager of the parent center is Kate Van Horn. The program, which began in 1994, won a 1996 Magna Award for excellence in education.

Parenting classes and resources are the center's main attraction, with 24 courses offered during the 1995–1996 school year and more than 900 titles in the center library, which are available for checkout. The center also offers single evening workshops covering topics that range from homework completion strategies to cardiopulmonary resuscitation. For parents looking for peer support, support groups have been organized. Support groups include parents of autistic children and parents of children with attention deficit disorder. Other services available to parents include education in English as a second language; instruction in arts and crafts for family and home projects; access to computers, fax machines, and photocopiers; job preparation workshops; and low-cost child care.

For more information about the parent center, contact manager Kate Van Horn, 24515 Lincoln Avenue, Murrieta, CA 92562; telephone (909) 696-1588.

Project Healthy Start

Program Description

To ease the burden of poverty and homelessness on students, an elementary school in the Los Angeles area annually offers medical and dental care, laundry facilities, nutrition classes, and emergency food to 50–100 families, according to Principal Fred Ortman. The resources are available thanks to Project Healthy Start, a collaborative effort of the city, county, police department, Los Angeles Department of Child and Protective Services, local hospitals, and area drug and alcohol rehabilitation centers.

A blue-ribbon committee of community and school representatives used state grant money to develop the program, which includes a health clinic constructed especially for the program. The clinic at Oleander Elementary School was converted from an unfinished classroom in the school's recent addition and is one of three in the district.

"The facility includes a bathroom facility with a shower, an exam room, a full kitchen with a washer and dryer, and a room equipped for education, training, and [in-house] services [for] parents," says Ortman. "It also includes an office for the child protective services worker, a nurse, and a community aide."

Services

To identify specific services that should be provided by the program, the committee surveyed parents about their needs. "The survey validated our assertion that the basic necessities of life were missing for many children," says Ortman.

Survey findings included the following:

- Forty-three percent of parents lacked adequate access to medical and dental care for their children.
- Only 10 percent of parents said their families received three balanced meals a day.
- Seventy-five percent of parents cited student behavior problems, including the wearing of gang attire and emulation of gang members.
- Eighty-two percent of parents identified the problems of poverty (e.g., lack of utilities, transportation, and sleeping space) as affecting their families.

As a result, the committee planned for three distinct services:

- *A full kitchen and laundry facilities.* Nutrition programs in both English and Spanish are open to parents who don't know how to cook or who know very little about nutrition and meal preparation, says Ortman. "On a regular basis, parents come in and teach other parents how to prepare nutritious meals. This service is provided through a partnership of the county, school, and community." The kitchen is adjacent to a classroom area, making this an easy, convenient activity. Ortman adds that laundry facilities are also available, so students can have their clothes washed.
- *A food distribution program.* For families in need, Project Healthy Start provides food in return for volunteer service. "Participants in the program pay $14 each month and receive $35 worth of groceries in return for two hours of work," says Ortman. Parents are placed according to their interests and abilities, which have included working in a classroom or cleaning the school grounds.
- *A medical examining room.* The school nurse and volunteer physicians perform routine medical services and tests for students in need. Specifically, the school offers well-child checkups, immunizations, and referrals when children need more comprehensive care. Health checkups for students' siblings and dental checkups also are provided.

Center Operation

With the exception of the County Health Department nurse who is a full-time staff member, the clinic is staffed by volunteers from a local health maintenance organization and the medical school at nearby Loma Linda University.

"The head of the nursing service helps us find doctors willing to donate their time to help people in need in the community," says Ortman. "Many of them are private practitioners who want to give something back to the community. We also get people from the county. Some local dentists donate their time as well."

Students are referred by school staff to Project Healthy Start through a case management study team. If a teacher notices that a child is consistently coming to school dirty, for example, that teacher will fill out a criterion paper that identifies for Healthy Start staff what he or she has observed.

Referrals are forwarded to a case study team that determines how to address the student's area of need. The team then routes the referral to the appropriate agency; for example, abuse cases are turned over to child and protective services.

Results

Although conditions for many students and neighborhood residents are better now than in the past, Ortman says there is still "a long way to go." He continues to believe that schools are obligated to help severely disadvantaged students cope with their living situations to improve achievement and learning.

"Just because our students come from the low socioeconomic strata doesn't mean they don't deserve the cleanest and best facilities we can give them," says Ortman. "The child doesn't have control over his or her environment and home life, so our focus was to take care of those children so they can learn. This is a big step in the right direction, for children and families and for us as agencies in the community."

PARTNERING ON DISCIPLINE

ENLIST PARENT SUPPORT

When students are a persistent discipline problem, parent involvement is essential. Easier said than done? Up to a point, yes.

The reality is that many parents don't get involved because they aren't aware of what you're doing and how they can help reinforce your classroom rules.

Here are some ways other teachers get parents to back their discipline efforts.

Share Policies Up Front

At the beginning of the school year, it's a good idea to send a list of your classroom rules and penalties home to parents. Then everyone will know exactly what's expected.

Worried that this might not have any impact on parents? Try what this Minnesota teacher does.

"I send home a list of my expectations and ask parents to sign and return it to me," she says. "I do this to avoid the 'You never told me about the rules excuse.'

"Of course, some parents don't return the form. When this is the case, though, I've still covered myself. I can call a parent for help with student discipline and say, 'Your son or daughter is at the third consequence stage—this is why I'm calling.'

"If the parent says, 'What are you talking about? I know nothing about your discipline system,' I remind him or her about the form I sent home, and I'll point out that it wasn't returned to me.

"Then I'll give a quick rundown on my system before we start talking about the student's problem again."

Weekly Notes Home

Discipline problems often have their roots in poor academic performance, which is related to students not doing their homework. A Florida school uses a no-surprises approach by keeping parents informed of their kids' performance in this area on a weekly basis.

"I send a report home with kids every Friday," says a teacher. "It's a very simple form, which includes questions like, 'Has your son or daughter done his or her homework?' Beside each question is a happy face, sad face, and an in-between face. I simply check one of them, so parents know how the student is doing in that area. Then they sign and return the forms.

"This system doesn't require a lot of my time, and it's an excellent way to let parents know about a problem early on—and to increase their involvement."

When kids show no improvement in problems areas, this teacher arranges a conference with their parents. During the meeting, they make arrangements for the next step: a daily note home and behavior contract.

"The note is tailored to the individual child," says the teacher. "For example, if the student hasn't been turning in homework, the note might say, 'I turned in my homework,' and have a big happy face on it. When the student finishes his or her assignment, the teacher signs and dates the note and sends it home with the student.

"Parents are told that if they don't get a note, they should assume it's a bad one and take the appropriate steps at home. These would be punishments that we talked about at the teacher/parent meeting."

For example, parents may agree that if the student receives a good slip, he or she can stay up a little later. If it's a bad one, however, the consequence might be no television, going to bed early, or no 'game time' with parents later in the evening.

To develop the most effective consequences, the teacher has parents ask themselves, "What does my child like?" and "What will my child work for?"

"I've been pleased with how the approach has worked so far," she says.

"I've stressed the importance of completing homework this year, and there's been a marked improvement in that area."

Discipline Form Letters Save Time

Classroom teachers at a New York school can choose from one of three form letters to notify parents when their kids break school rules.

The form letter idea is a major time-saver for teachers. They no longer have to call or write parents after each incident.

The letters notify parents about bus behavior, tardiness, or disruptive actions on the school grounds. Each one contains a short, standardized description of the problem behavior, a rationale for why it is forbidden and a request for parent cooperation.

All the teacher has to do is fill in the time, date, class, disciplinary action taken, and if a conference with parents is required.

The bus and disruptive behavior at school letters also include a checklist of offenses under the type of misconduct, so teachers can quickly indicate the specific problem by marking the appropriate box.

For example, the disruptive behavior letter lists things like running in the hallway, tampering with school property and rude, discourteous, or annoying conduct.

It also provides space for the teacher to write additional comments if he or she feels they are needed.

Parents must sign and return the letter. Once it comes back to the school, the classroom teacher receives the original, and a copy goes to the guidance counselor who helps track repeat offenders.

If the problem isn't solved after the third letter home, a meeting is scheduled with the counselor to work on the student's behavior.

The form letters aren't meant to replace individual contact with parents. But they have reduced the paperwork load on teachers and cut down on the time it takes for them to inform parents about disciplinary matters involving their children.

MATERIALS YOU CAN USE

Classroom Discipline Plan

Dear Parent(s):

I will be your child's teacher this year. In order to guarantee your child and all students in my classroom the excellent educational climate they deserve, I have developed a Discipline Plan that will be in effect at all times.

When in my classroom, students must comply with the following rules:
- ☐ Follow directions the first time I give them.
- ☐ Keep hands, feet, and objects to themselves.
- ☐ Be in assigned seat ready to work when the bell rings.
- ☐ Come to class with all required materials.
- ☐ Raise hand and wait to be recognized before speaking.

If a student chooses to break a rule, the following consequences will occur:
- ☐ First time student breaks rule: Warning.
- ☐ Second time student breaks rule: 15 minutes detention.
- ☐ Third time student breaks rule: 30 minutes detention, call parents.
- ☐ Fourth time student breaks rule: 30 minutes detention, call parents, send to principal.

If a student is severely disruptive, he or she will be sent immediately to the principal.

Included in my Discipline Plan are ways to positively reinforce students who behave appropriately. In addition to frequent praise and positive notes sent home, I will reward students with free class time and special class activities.

In order for the plan to have its greatest effect, I need your support. Please discuss this letter with your child, then sign and return it to me. Thank you for your cooperation.

Sincerely,

Teacher Name

_____
Parent/Guardian Signature   Date

_____
Student's Name   Date

Comments:

Weekly Report Form

Student: Week Of:

Has your son or daughter done his or her homework?

Does your son or daughter sit quietly and attentively in class?

Does your son or daughter show respect for classmates?

Does your son or daughter obey playground rules?

Daily Report Form

I turned in my homework!

Teacher Signature: _____   Date: _____

Improve Parenting Skills 2–3:13

Tardiness Report

Student's Name _____   Date: _____
Student's Address: _____   Student's Class: _____
Home Phone: _____   Parent(s) Name: _____

▪▪

Dear Parent(s):

Your son/daughter reported late to school as follows:

Day _____   Date _____   Time _____
Day _____   Date _____   Time _____
Day _____   Date _____   Time _____
Day _____   Date _____   Time _____

Punctuality is necessary for satisfactory performance in school. Tardiness takes valuable time away from instruction and disturbs the class.

Please talk to your son/daughter about the importance of punctuality. If the tardiness has occurred following the lunch period, it might be necessary to prohibit him/her from going home for lunch.

If you have sent an explanatory note, please understand that this letter is sent to you as a matter of routine.

Please note: The fact that you or another parent drives the student to school is not a legitimate excuse for tardiness. Your cooperation is appreciated.

☐ First notice   ☐ Second notice   ☐ Third notice   ☐ Fourth notice

Disciplinary action taken: _____
_____

Previous warnings/disciplinary actions: _____
_____

_____   _____
Parent's Signature   Date   Individual Submitting Report

Bus Behavior Report

Student's Name _____   Date: _____
Student's Address: _____   Student's Class: _____
Home Phone: _____   Parent(s) Name: _____

■ ■

Dear Parent(s):

Your student was reported for disruptive/disorderly/unsafe behavior while riding the school bus on the following date(s): _____, on bus # _____, route # _____.

Safety for all students requires that everyone obeys bus rules. By not obeying the bus rules, your son/daughter may have jeopardized the safety and well-being of all students riding the bus. Your son/daughter was reported by the bus driver.

A second reported offense by the bus driver will result in the suspension of your son/daughter from riding the bus to and from school for one week. A third reported offense will result in his/her suspension from riding the bus. In that instance, it will be your responsibility to provide transportation for the pupil.

Please speak to your son/daughter about this situation so there is no repeat of such incidents.

Infraction:
- ☐ Improper boarding/departing
- ☐ Bringing articles aboard of an injurious or objectionable nature
- ☐ Failure to remain seated
- ☐ Refusing to obey driver
- ☐ Fighting/pushing/tripping
- ☐ Tampering with bus equipment
- ☐ Destruction of property
- ☐ Failure to keep on seat belt
- ☐ Other (specify): _____
- ☐ Hanging out the window
- ☐ Creating difficulties with pupils from other schools riding the bus
- ☐ Lighting matches/smoking
- ☐ Spitting/littering
- ☐ Unnecessary noise/shouting
- ☐ Using obscenities
- ☐ Rude/discourteous/annoying conduct
- ☐ Throwing objects out of bus

Supporting details: _____

Disciplinary action to be taken: _____

☐ Reported first offense   ☐ Reported second offense   ☐ Reported third offense

_____   _____
Parent's Signature   Date   Individual Submitting Report

Disruptive Behavior Report

Student's Name _____ Date: _____
Student's Address: _____ Student's Class: _____
Home Phone: _____ Parent(s) Name: _____

■■■

Dear Parent(s):

Your son/daughter was reported for disruptive and/or disorderly behavior at school on _____.

As you know, this type of behavior deprives students of learning and creates a potentially dangerous classroom situation. I know that you share our concern for providing a proper and safe learning environment for all students. It is essential that students follow all school regulations. Please discuss this infraction with your son or daughter so that there will be no repetition of this behavior.

Infraction:
- ☐ Fighting/pushing/tripping
- ☐ Tampering with school property
- ☐ Destruction of school property
- ☐ Destruction of another's property
- ☐ Rude/discourteous/annoying conduct
- ☐ Running in corridor/stairs/lunchroom
- ☐ Misbehaving in school yard
- ☐ Calling out without permission
- ☐ Making jokes/wisecracking
- ☐ Unnecessary noise/shouting
- ☐ Using obscenities
- ☐ Disruptive during fire/shelter drill
- ☐ Making a mess in the lunchroom
- ☐ Other (specify): _____

Location:
- ☐ Classroom
- ☐ Lunchroom
- ☐ Auditorium
- ☐ Gymnasium
- ☐ Stairwell
- ☐ School yard

Supporting details: _____

Disciplinary action to be taken: _____

☐ Reported first offense   ☐ Reported second offense   ☐ Reported third offense

Previous warnings/disciplinary actions: _____

Comments:

_____   _____
Parent's Signature   Date   Individual Submitting Report

Secrets of Effective Discipline

Time after time, parents, teachers, and principals rank discipline as one of the top problems they face. But what is discipline? Some people think it means punishing kids and making them obey.

Actually, effective discipline has more to do with teaching children to make good decisions—and to be responsible for their behavior. Plus, effective discipline is a key to school success.

What's the secret to discipline that works? Start with the seven ideas below.

DISCIPLINE AT SCHOOL

1. Talk with your child about school rules and regulations—and their importance.
2. Show interest in your child's activities.
3. Talk to teachers about your child's behavior and ask for suggestions.
4. If there's a problem at school, talk to your child and get his viewpoint.
5. If a problem continues, contact the teacher.
6. Team up with the teacher to come up with appropriate consequences.

Set limits—fair but firm

Since no two families are alike, only you can decide what rules work for you. But all children need rules that are fair and easy to follow.

It's best to sit down with your children and explain each rule. If your kids see them as fair, they'll find them much easier to accept—and obey. Once the rules are in place, firmly enforce them. The fewer the rules, the better.

Finally, state rules in a positive way that tell children what you *do* want—not what you don't want.

Tip: Some areas in which families choose to make rules: Peacefulness—settle disagreements without violence. Respectfulness—speak politely. Routines—follow a set bedtime on weekdays. Permission—ask before going out.

Use the power of consequences

This might be one of the most effective discipline techniques you can use. It teaches children that their actions have results—and shows them that they are responsible for what they do.

There are two types of consequences. Some happen naturally. *Examples:* Bike left out in the rain? It rusts. Homework missed? You get a zero.

Sometimes a consequence to misbehavior isn't automatic—you have to pick it. The trick is finding consequences that relate to the misbehavior. Fighting over TV? It's turned off. Toy misused? It's put away for a while. Curfew missed? Stay home next time.

It can be difficult to stand by and watch your children learn a hard lesson. But if you try to shield them from mistakes, they will lose an opportunity to learn.

Tell your children—in advance—what consequences you plan to use. Then you won't be in the hot seat trying to figure out what to do when you're upset. Some families write down consequences along with the rules.

Be consistent but flexible

When your children break a rule, try to deal with it the same way each time—even if they plead, beg, and whine. Giving in tells them the rule isn't firm and that you'll change it if they keep nagging.

Being consistent is challenging. Why? Because children know their parents' "soft" spots and often push them every chance they get. "Oh, come on, Mom. Don't be *mean*. You let Joey do his homework later!"

Tip: Being consistent doesn't mean you can't be flexible. If you have a visitor, for example, it's fine to extend bedtime. The important thing is to explain why the rule isn't being followed. "You can stay up later tonight so you'll have more time to be with Gramps."

continues

Secrets of Effective Discipline continued

Secrets of effective discipline

Give encouragement and praise

Children often repeat behavior that gets your attention. When they do something you like, notice it! Whether it's making the team or getting a good grade in school, children need their successes recognized.

Comment on efforts and improvements, too, such as waking up on time in the morning or tackling homework without prodding. Praise works best when it is specific to behavior. *Example:* "I see you cleared your place after dinner. I appreciate your help." Praise is least effective when it describes the child, not the job ("What a good boy you are!").

Tip: Here's a secret that will have a big impact on behavior. Try adding privileges when kids do well. It encourages them to try even harder. Find privileges your children will really appreciate, such as a special outing or staying up later.

Set up routines

Tired of all the hassles surrounding mornings, chores, and bedtime? Try using simple routines.

Children thrive on routines. Once they're in place, they know what to do without needing constant directions. Doing the right thing becomes automatic and family life is less chaotic.

For example, a typical bedtime routine may start at 8:15 p.m. and include: book bag ready to go, bath taken, pajamas on, teeth brushed, and bathroom picked up—all by 8:45 p.m.

Don't sweat the small stuff

Whenever possible, try to ignore little things. In other words, pick and choose your battles. It will make life a lot more pleasant. Let's say your child is being annoying. Consider ignoring the behavior that's not destructive or dangerous. Your lack of attention takes away your child's audience and spoils the fun!

When possible, keep a sense of humor. Laughter helps keep communication alive. For example, your child's room is so messy that you feel like blowing up. Try saying, "Looks like a tornado hit. As soon as you clean up the debris, we'll make some cookies together!"

Love works magic

All the best discipline theories in the world won't work without love. Children respond best when they understand the rules are there because you care. Your relationship is the basis upon which everything else rests.

You can cement your relationship by talking, listening, and spending time with each of your children—even when life gets hectic. Some parents actually write in parent/child dates on their calendars.

When your children's behavior gets out of hand, sometimes it's hard to see the positive. It helps to look beyond the behavior and focus on their strengths.

Children don't learn right from wrong overnight. But, with time and patience, most children eventually learn to do the right thing—even when you're not around.

Tip: Kids need to know you love them—and hear it often—no matter how old they are.

DISCIPLINE CHECKLIST

- ☑ I involve my children in making family rules and decisions.
- ☑ My children know what will happen when they break rules.
- ☑ I provide consequences that are fair and relate to the rule broken.
- ☑ I try to be consistent in the way I respond to misbehavior.
- ☑ I notice my children's efforts and accomplishments.
- ☑ My children know and follow routines at home.
- ☑ I try to ignore nondestructive, attention-getting behavior.
- ☑ I don't expect perfection in myself or my children.

Editor's Note: If behavior problems are severe and nothing seems to work, it may be valuable to look for help. Check with the school counselor or your family doctor.

12 WAYS TO BUILD Responsibility

And help your child succeed

Years ago, children shared the workload of the family—everyone helped out. These days, many kids have almost no responsibilities.

When these same children are faced with tough decisions—such as whether to use drugs—they are less likely to make responsible choices.

What can you do to help your children become responsible and be more successful? Give them lots of practice. There's no better place to start than at home. This special report shows you 12 ways to strengthen the all-important quality of responsibility in your children. Choose an area each of your children need help with, or work on a separate area each month.

1 Doing chores

Work together as a team. Write down on small slips of paper what must be done each week: cleaning the bathroom, vacuuming, or dusting the furniture. Fold the slips in half and put them in a jar or box.

Once a week, have the kids pick slips to see what their weekly jobs are. At first, work alongside them so they'll know just what to do. They might not do the job as well as you, but praise their efforts. When their jobs are completed, they're free to play.

2 Putting things away

Talk with your children and decide together where their books, toys, clothes, and other things belong.

Some parents choose a time each day—others once a week—when all possessions must be put away. If belongings are still scattered around the house at that time, say nothing, collect the items, and store them in a closet. Your children can have their "missing" items the following week, or sooner if they do an extra job.

3 Helping ease the morning rush

Good planning is the key. Have your children set the breakfast table, make lunches, take baths, and lay out clothes the night before. If getting the kids out of bed is a problem, try an alarm clock. If that doesn't work, have them go to bed earlier the next night.

Keep breakfast simple so your children can help prepare it. Find a regular place for all school-related items. Use this spot for homework assignments, notes, and school forms.

4 Getting homework done

Sit down with your children and decide *when* and *where* homework will be done. Make it clear that keeping track of assignments and completing homework is *their* responsibility—not yours. For most children, a daily assignment sheet works well.

If they have trouble with an assignment, make sure they understand the directions, and work on a couple of problems or questions together. Then have them work alone.

If your children aren't completing their homework, insist that it be done *before* other activities.

continues

12 Ways To Build Responsibility continued

5 Taking part in your community

Communities, large and small, work better when everyone takes some responsibility. Let your children see how *you* are involved with the community. Take them along when you vote, recycle, or donate clothing. Tell them why you attend PTA or PTO meetings or volunteer your time.

Now show your kids how they can contribute, for example, by collecting food for those in need.

6 Learning to make smart decisions

As your children gain practice making decisions, they'll make smarter decisions. When they're young, offer simple choices: "What kind of toothpaste would you like?"

As your children get older, give them more difficult choices. Let them experience the consequences of their poor decisions—as long as they're not in danger. Share a few important decisions you've made and what you've learned from your mistakes.

7 Caring for living things

Learning to care for a pet or a plant can also help develop responsibility. Some pets, such as dogs and cats, require far more time and attention than others, so choose carefully.

A small garden plot offers many opportunities for "growth." First, the soil must be prepared. Then comes planting, watering the soil, pulling the weeds, and gathering the harvest.

8 Becoming more independent

If your children are capable of doing something themselves, let them. This includes making the bed, fixing sandwiches, and putting dirty clothes in the hamper.

To make responsibilities clear, create a "job chart" for each of your children. Place the items they are responsible for on the left side of the chart and the days of the week across the top. As they complete their tasks, have them put check marks under the correct day.

9 Following family rules

Imagine playing a game where the rules are constantly being changed by someone else. Pretty frustrating, isn't it?

What about the family rules in your home? Write them down and discuss each one at a family meeting. Make the rules short, clear, easy to check, and reasonable. Talk about what happens when someone ignores the rules.

Example: If no fighting is allowed, kids who fight should go to a "cooling off" area. When they're ready to talk things out and come up with a peaceful solution, they may return.

10 Managing money wisely

Giving your children an allowance when they're young makes sense. There's no right amount, but it's better to start small and increase it as they grow older.

Most experts suggest that children be allowed to decide how their allowances should be spent—within reason. If they run out of money before the week is out, resist the temptation to give more. Over time, your children will learn the value of money and the consequences of poor money management.

If they insist on designer clothes and shoes that cost a fortune, tell them how much you're willing to spend. They can use their allowances to pay the difference.

11 Responsibility through stories

Lecturing your children on responsibility is usually not effective. It's much easier for them to learn about responsibility through story characters or the lives of great men and women. With a little effort, you can find a story that brings out some aspect of responsibility you'd like your child to learn. For example, *Tikki Tikki Tembo*, by Arlene Mosel, involves a young boy's sense of responsibility for his brother.

You can make up your own stories, or tell about a time when a member of your family was especially responsible.

12 Setting a good example

It's a good idea to ask yourself a few questions from time to time. For example, do you get involved in your community? Do your share around the house? Put your things away? If you do, your kids will probably learn to do the same. It may take awhile, but it's well worth the effort!

Building your child's character
BOOK BY BOOK

As parents, you want your children to have the positive character traits you value. How can you pass on these traits to your kids? One way is through reading books. Whether they're reading on their own or you're reading aloud, your children will learn from the characters' courage, tolerance, and perseverance.

There are many books that highlight positive character traits. Here are some of our favorites to get you started.

COURAGE

Chrysanthemum by Kevin Henkes. Your children will enjoy reading this story about a mouse named Chrysanthemum. She courageously endures teasing from classmates who make fun of her name. (ages 4–8)

Robinson Crusoe retold by Edward W. Dolch, Marguerite P. Dolch, and Beulah Jackson. Part of the Scholastic Junior Classics series, this timeless story is about a man who is shipwrecked on a deserted island. (ages 9–12)

Young Martin Luther King, Jr.: "I Have a Dream" by Joanne Mattern. Introduce your children to the life of the civil rights hero and the courage he displayed. (ages 4–8)

FRIENDSHIP

Crash by Jerry Spinelli. Crash Coogan enjoys making fun of a new classmate. But Crash soon learns a life lesson when his grandfather gets sick: How to show compassion and be a friend. (ages 9–12)

Frog and Toad Are Friends by Arnold Lobel. Day after day, the lovable characters Frog and Toad demonstrate the qualities that make good friends. (ages 4–8)

The Wind in the Willows by Kenneth Grahame. Who can resist the charms of Ratty, Mole, Toad, and Badger? These lovable characters teach children and parents that friends stick together. (ages 6 and up)

HONESTY

The Emperor's New Clothes by Hans Christian Andersen. By reading how the emperor's lies make him a fool, your children can learn the importance of honesty. (ages 4–8)

A Bargain for Frances by Russell Hoban. Thelma wants to buy a new tea set, so she tricks Frances into buying her old one. How will these friends work out their differences? (ages 4–8)

Lincoln: A Photobiography by Russell Freedman. Most every child knows President Lincoln's reputation as "Honest Abe." In this book, filled with text and photos, your youngster can learn about Lincoln's life and presidency. (ages 9–12)

continues

Building Your Child's Character continued

Building your child's character BOOK BY BOOK

KINDNESS

Charlotte's Web by E.B. White. This classic tale of a girl, a pig, a spider, and their friends in the barn teaches about kindness to others and true friendship. (ages 9–12)

The Meanest Thing to Say by Bill Cosby. Little Bill and his friends learn a lesson in kindness. A new boy comes into their class and challenges the kids to say the meanest thing they can to someone else. (ages 6–10)

Tale of the Mandarin Ducks by Katherine Paterson. Set in Japan, the story is about a captured mandarin duck set free by a kitchen maid. Children will learn about thoughtful behavior as the bird tries to return the maid's kindness. (ages 4–8)

PERSEVERANCE

Holes by Louis Sachar. This book weaves mystery into a story of friendship, survival, and endurance. A boy is wrongfully convicted of theft and sentenced to time in a juvenile detention camp. (ages 9–12)

The Incredible Journey by Sheila Burnford. Three runaway pets make their way home through the Canadian wilderness. On the way, they face starvation, exposure to the elements, and attacks by wild animals. (ages 6–12)

Little House on the Prairie by Laura Ingalls Wilder. This beloved series of books chronicles the story of Laura Ingalls Wilder's family. They endured hard work and hard times in the pioneer days with love and strong family values. (ages 9–12)

RESPONSIBILITY

Arthur's Pet Business by Marc Brown. Arthur is determined to prove that he's responsible enough to have his own puppy, so he starts his own pet business. Perky, Arthur's first customer, has a surprise for him. (ages 4–8)

Bloomability by Sharon Creech. Dinnie, a 12-year-old girl, has to adapt to her new life when she is sent away to a school in Switzerland. Can she make new friends—and act responsibly when they get in trouble? (ages 8–12)

The Wump World by Bill Peet. In this book, the world of the "wumps" is invaded by aliens who overbuild and pollute their land. The story teaches children important lessons about taking responsibility for the world around them. (ages 4–8)

Talking about character

Discussing these books can get your children thinking about how to use the character traits in their own lives. As you read together, occasionally stop and ask a question. Here are some ideas to get your conversations rolling:

- ❏ Does this book remind you of anything that's happened to you in real life? How did you handle it?
- ❏ I admired the son for being kind. How did you feel about him?
- ❏ In this book the girl was scared, but she showed courage. Can you think of things you have done that showed courage?
- ❏ The mouse kept trying and trying, and his hard work paid off in the end. I feel that way when I work hard at something. Do you?
- ❏ How do you think the character felt when the other kids were mean to her?
- ❏ This reminds me of when I was in elementary school. Did this ever happen to you?
- ❏ Which character in the book is most like you? Why?

TOLERANCE

Beethoven Lives Upstairs by Barbara Nichol. This entertaining book is made up of a series of letters between a young boy and his uncle. The boy is upset about the "madman" who is making a racket on the piano upstairs. (ages 4–8)

How Smudge Came by Nan Gregory. This is the story of a young woman with Down syndrome. Having a dog is against the rules of the home where she lives. What will Cindy do with the puppy she found? (ages 4–8)

The Secret Garden by Frances Hodgson Burnett. A spoiled girl finds happiness and friendship in her new home, while learning tolerance toward a sour and difficult boy. (ages 9–12)

Editor's Note: Consider reading aloud books that are above your children's reading level. Also, parents should review the appropriateness of each book for their children before sharing it.

Index

A

Absent parents, 2–1:13
Academic fairs, 1–1:21
Administrative accessibility, 1–1:9
Aggressive parents, 2–2:7
Angry parents, 2–1:13—2–1:14
Apathetic parents, 2–1:13
Argumentative parents, 2–1:12
At-home learning
  opportunities, 1–3:5
  parental involvement, 2–2:8
  strategies, 2–2:9—2–2:11
  success building, 2–2:28—2–2:29
Atmosphere, 1–1:7
Attendance, 1–4:6
  policy, 1–4:7
  sticker, 1–4:7
Auction, 1–1:21
Audience, 1–2:11

B

Back-to-school nights, 1–3:3
Breadmaking, 1–1:20—1–1:21
Breakfast program, 1–1:19—1–1:20
British primary school system, 1–1:16
Broadcasting, 1–2:3—1–2:4
Bus behavior report, 2–3:14

C

Case conference, 2–1:13—2–1:14
  form, 2–1:20
Character building, 2–3:20—2–3:21
Chocolate night, 1–1:21
Clasp envelopes, 1–2:20—1–2:21
Classroom assistants, 1–3:2

Clothing exchange, 1–1:15
Coaching. *See* At-home learning
Commitment assessment, 1–1:5
Committee development, 1–1:27
Communication
  difficult parents, 1–4:1—1–4:3
  folders, 2–1:5—2–1:6
  improving, 1–2:1
  involvement and, 1–2:2—1–2:5
  material, 1–2:25, 1–2:26
  positive, 2–1:11—2–1:12
  written, 2–1:3
Community school information councils, 1–1:26
Crisis communications, 1–2:22
Culture differences, 1–1:3–1–1:4
Custody battles, 1–4:8
Customer service, 1–1:9

D

Decision making table, 1–1:41—1–1:43
Difficult parents
  communication, 1–4:1—1–4:3
  custody battles, 1–4:8
  dealing with, 1–4:16—1–4:17
  discipline issues and, 1–4:3—1–4:5
  parent development, 1–4:3
  rules for, 1–4:5—1–4:6
  strategies for, 2–1:12—2–1:13
  student attendance and, 1–4:6—1–4:7
  working with, 1–4:8—1–4:9
Discipline, 2–1:13
  brochure, 1–4:14—1–4:15
  classroom plan, 2–3:11
  difficult parents and, 1–4:1—1–4:9
  form letters, 2–3:10
  partnership, 2–3:9—2–3:10

plan letter, 1–4:13
tips, 2–3:16—2–3:17
Disruptive behavior report, 2–3:15
Divorced parents, 2–1:13

E

Education
  quotes, 1–2:9
  technology training center, 2–2:13—2–2:14
Educational philosophy, 1–2:9
Educational plan, communication, 2–1:4—2–1:5
E-mail communications, 1–2:16
Emergency assistance, 1–1:15
Evening office hours, 1–1:9
Extracurricular activity boosters, 1–3:2

F

Faculty credentials, 1–2:9
Family
  approach, 1–1:15—1–1:16
  contacts, 2–1:8—2–1:9
  education center, 1–1:16—1–1:17
  involvement, v–vi. *See also* Parent involvement
  night, 1–1:19
  reading tree, 2–2:14—2–2:15
  structure, 2–3:1—2–3:2
  style meals, 1–1:16
Family-community partnership checklist, 1–1:38—1–1:40
Family-friendly schools, 1–1:7—1–1:8
Father recruitment, 1–3:4—1–3:5
Fliers, 1–3:3

I:1

Follow up, 2–2:2, 2–2:4
Fundraisers, 1–3:2

H

Handbook
   ideas, 1–2:9—1–2:10
   impression, 1–2:7—1–2:8
   information, 1–2:6—1–2:7
Happy-Grams, 2–1:6
Health services, 1–1:14—1–1:15
Homebound messages, 1–2:20—1–2:21
Home visits, 1–1:11—1–1:12; 2–1:9—2–1:11
Homework
   assignments, 2–1:12—2–1:13
   club, 1–1:17—1–1:18
   expectations, 2–2:23
   hotline, 2–1:11
   notices, 2–1:18
   status, 2–1:8

I

Idea cards, 1–2:17
Implementation planning, 1–1:5
Individual contact, 1–2:21—1–2:22
Informed parents
   communication folders, 2–1:5—2–1:6
   educational plan, 2–1:4—2–1:5
   Happy-Grams, 2–1:6
   homework status, 2–1:8
   journals, 2–1:6—2–1:7
   mark statements, 2–1:7
   newsletter communication, 2–1:3—2–1:4
   speed letters, 2–1:5
   telephone effectiveness, 2–1:2—2–1:3
   telephone schedules, 2–1:1—2–1:2
   written communication, 2–1:3
Invitation, 1–1:8, 1–1:24

J

Journals, 2–1:6—2–1:7

L

Language differences, 1–1:3—1–1:4, 1–1:10
Leadership assessment, 1–1:5
Learning
   activities, 2–2:32—2–2:33
   resources, 2–2:43—2–2:44
Literacy night, 1–1:20
Lunch with principal program, 1–2:14

M

Mark statement, 2–1:7, 2–1:16, 2–1:17
Media relations, 1–2:23—1–2:24
Meeting size, 1–1:24

N

Necessities, 2–3:4
Neighborhood meetings, 1–2:18—1–2:19
Newborn welcoming, 1–1:13
New Mom packets, 1–1:13
New school year letter, 1–2:30
Newsletter, 1–2:2—1–2:3, 1–2:10—1–2:12, 1–2:13
   column, volunteer opportunities, 1–3:3
   communication, 2–1:3—2–1:4
News releases, 1–2:21
Notes home, 2–3:9—2–3:10

O

Office helpers, 1–3:2
Open houses, 1–3:3
Orientation video, 1–2:19—1–2:20

P

Parent advisory group, 1–1:25—1–1:26
Parent advisory link, 1–2:15
Parent
   center, 2–3:7
   communication room, 1–2:5
   conference, 1–4:3—1–4:4
   connecting with right, 2–1:8—2–1:9
   development, 1–4:3
   difficult. *See* Difficult parents
   information exchange, 2–2:2, 2–2:3—2–2:4
   interest survey, 1–1:37
   lounge, 1–1:13—1–1:14
   notification form, 1–4:12
   outreach programs, 2–3:4—2–3:5
   participation policies, 1–1:4—1–1:5
   programs, 1–3:3
   report to, 1–2:27
   resource center, 1–1:12—1–1:13, 1–1:15
   resources, 2–3:2—2–3:4
   satisfaction survey, 1–1:49
   school attendance by, 1–4:4—1–4:5
   services, 1–1:14—1–1:15
   skills, 2–3:1—2–3:6
   socials, 1–1:19
   study skill review, 2–2:12—2–2:13
   support for discipline plan, 1–4:5
   survey, 1–1:24—1–1:25
   work calls and, 1–4:4
Parental involvement, 1–1:17; 1–2:12—1–2:15; 2–2:30—2–2:31
   at-home learning, 2–2:9
   attendance at functions, 1–1:54—1–1:55
   communication and, 1–2:2—1–2:5
   decision making, 1–1:24—1–1:27
   discipline, 2–3:9—2–3:10
   organizations and, 1–1:22—1–1:24
   parent-teacher conference planner, 2–2:17
   school report card, 1–1:47—1–1:48
   school teams, 1–1:28—1–1:29
   successful programs, 1–1:56—1–1:57
   survey, 1–1:2, 1–1:30—1–1:35, 1–1:36
   ways to increase, 1–1:50—1–1:51, 1–1:52—1–1:53
Parent-hosted meetings, 1–2:15
Parent-school cooperative checklist, 1–1:46
Parent-teacher conference
   attendance, 2–2:5
   dos and don'ts, 2–2:2, 2–2:4
   invitation, 2–2:18
   parent preparation, 2–2:6—2–2:7
   parent questions, 2–2:19
   planning worksheet, 2–2:16
   preparation, 2–2:1—2–2:4
   as solution session, 2–2:5—2–2:6
   student participation, 2–2:7
Parent-teacher partnership, 2–1:21—2–1:22
Partnership agreement, 1–1:44—1–1:45
Patriotic night, 1–1:21—1–1:22
Personal contact, 1–3:4
Phone call report, 1–2:28
Photographs, 1–2:9
Principal coffees, 1–2:14—1–2:15
Printed materials, 1–2:2—1–2:3
Program assessment, 1–1:1
   external, 1–1:2
   internal, 1–1:1—1–1:2
   lack of involvement reasons, 1–1:3—1–1:4
Progress report, midterm, 1–4:10
Project Healthy Start, 2–3:7—2–3:8

Q

Quiz slip, 2–1:19

R

Raffles, 1–1:23
Rapport, 2–2:1, 2–2:3
Read-aloud
   favorites, 2–2:38—2–2:39
   pitfalls, 2–2:36—2–2:37
Reading, 2–2:42
Reading program, 2–2:20
   contract, 2–2:21
   time sheet, 2–2:22
Reading train, 2–2:24—2–2:25
Recruitment, 1–1:23—1–1:24
Registration, volunteer information at, 1–3:4
Report
   cards, 2–1:7
   form, 2–3:12
   to parents, 1–2:27
Responsibility, 2–3:18—2–3:19
RIOT contract, 2–2:21
   program, 2–2:20
   time sheet, 2–2:22

S

School assemblies, 1–1:16
School improvement teams, 1–1:26—1–1:27
School logo, 1–2:12
School report card, 1–1:47—1–1:48
School teams, 1–1:28—1–1:29
Science night, 1–1:20
Self-assessment, 1–1:5
Sign in, 1–1:8
Single parents, 2–3:5—2–3:6
Social services, 1–1:14—1–1:15

Spanish material, 1–2:11
Special events, 1–1:18—1–1:21
Special project supervisors, 1–3:2
Speed letter, 2–1:5, 2–1:15
Sponsorships, 1–3:1
Staff members, 1–3:2
Staff relationships, 1–1:3
Star study, 1–1:21
Student performances, 1–3:3
Student status report, 1–4:11
Summary, 2–2:2, 2–2:4
Support group, 1–1:23
Surveys, 1–3:5—1–3:6

T

Tardiness report, 2–3:13
Teacher involvement, school teams, 1–1:29
Teacher-parent communication, 2–1:11
Telephone
    calling, 1–2:4—1–2:5, 1–2:13—1–2:14, 1–2:15—1–2:16
    effectiveness, informing parents, 2–1:2—2–1:3
    schedules, informing parents, 2–1:1—2–1:2
Testimonials, 1–3:4
Test slip, 2–1:19
Test taking, 2–2:34—2–2:35
Textbook selection committees, 1–1:27
Thank you, 2–1:9
Thanks Bank checks, 1–2:29
Time constraints, 2–3:2
Town meetings, 1–1:12
Tuesday drop-in night, 1–1:22
Two-career parents, 2–1:13

V

Volunteer
    application form, 1–3:12—1–3:13, 1–3:14—1–3:15
    assignments, 1–1:4; 1–3:6
    availability form, 1–3:11
    benefits, 1–3:6—1–3:7
    flier, 1–3:9, 1–3:10
    guidelines, 1–3:19
    interest survey, 1–3:16
    opportunities, 1–3:1—1–3:2
    reaching, 1–3:2—1–3:8
    recognition, 1–3:7—1–3:8
    recruitment letter, 1–3:17
    want ads, 1–3:18
    ways to help, 1–3:20

W

Way to go certificates, 2–2:26—2–2:27
Web sites, 1–2:16—1–2:17, 1–2:18
Welcome, 1–1:7—1–1:8, 1–1:10
Welcome wagon, 1–1:14
Wellness centers, 1–1:14—1–1:15
Working parents, 2–3:5—2–3:6
Writing, 2–2:40—2–2:41